A PASSION TO KNOW

20 PROFILES IN SCIENCE

A PASSION TO KNOW

20 PROFILES IN SCIENCE

Allen L. Hammond, Editor

CHARLES SCRIBNER'S SONS · NEW YORK

Permission to use the following selections has been kindly granted by:
Tracy Kidder, for "A Love of the Fray," from "Science as a Contact
Sport," Science 83, September 1983, copyright © 1983 by Tracy Kidder;
Simon & Schuster, Inc., for "Molecular Mission," from Scientific
Temperaments as adapted in Science 82, December 1982, copyright ©
1982 by Philip J. Hilts.
    All other selections copyright © 1984 by the American Association for
the Advancement of Science.
    All profiles in this book appeared, in slightly different form, in Science 80,
Science 81, Science 82, Science 83, and Science 84 magazine.

CONTENTS

ACKNOWLEDGMENTS

This book would not have been possible without the contributions of my colleagues at *Science 84* magazine, where these profiles were first published. Particular thanks are due Diana Morgan for her untiring efforts in rechecking and updating these materials and Margo Crabtree for collecting the photographs.

INTRODUCTION

STEREOTYPES OF SCIENCE

by Allen L. Hammond

You've met them before, in movies and television, in the funny pages of the newspaper. There is the stock figure in the white laboratory coat, mixing chemicals and muttering formulas; most likely he (it's always a he) will have thick glasses and unkempt hair. There is the mad scientist, a sinister figure notable for his glazed eyes and foreign accent, putting the final touches on some device that will destroy the world. There is the human calculating machine, an ascetic figure who speaks in chains of logic but is incapable of understanding human emotion. The scientists of our popular imagination, even when they look like ordinary people, lack an emotional core or a moral sense or some other essence of humanity: Star Trek's Mr. Spock, perhaps, or Stanley Kubrick's Dr. Strangelove.

The Spocks and Strangeloves are not isolated instances. Consider the award-winning PBS children's program "Sesame Street," seen by millions of preschoolers every week and known for its sensitive, nonstereotyped treatment of minorities. Yet even in this most enlightened of children's programs, the dominant scientific figure is a caricature called Dr. Nobel Price, a laughable figure who regularly reinvents galoshes or makes some other equally stunning nondiscovery.

According to historian of science George Basalla, most people get their first and often lasting impressions of science and of scientists from the comics, movies, and television. In a study of the popular media done about ten years ago, he found two dominant images—the absentminded professor and the mad scientist. And the images are persistent. A recent nationwide study of eight- to twelve-year-old children conducted for Children's Television Workshop found that they visualized scientists as middle-aged white males in lab coats, working in isolation with dangerous chemicals. Virtually the same image emerged from a study of children done by anthropologist Margaret Mead nearly twenty years ago.

These images tell us a lot about our culture's underlying attitude toward science. As humorist Russell Baker, an astute observer of human nature, has commented, "Obviously a lot of us fear and dislike science but don't dare admit it. The movies know it, however; they give us the mad scientist whom we can fear and despise without feeling bigoted and anti-intellectual." Science is viewed as abstract, cerebral, dangerous, difficult, an amoral pursuit—or sometimes as silly, impractical, out of touch with reality. It is not something ordinary people do.

The contrast between the stereotypes of science and the real thing has always been especially sharp to me. I grew up surrounded by scientists, in a fenced and guarded scientist town that came into existence to build the atomic bomb. Of some 12,000 souls who lived there when I did, a third had Ph.D.s. For me, scientists were quite literally the people next door, my friends' parents and mine. It was the doctors, the security guards, the man who ran the drugstore— now those were exotic lines of work! I never knew anyone whose father or mother was a lawyer. It was not until I went off to college that I realized this was unusual or that the people I grew up with were viewed by others as atypical, even bizarre.

The scientists I knew as a child were as remarkable in what they did for a living—building bombs—as they were unremarkable as individuals. But so pervasive and strongly held were the stereotypes, particularly of nuclear weapons scientists, among my college contemporaries that I quickly learned to view myself as having grown up in a kind of scientific ghetto. I found I had a lot in common with kids who had spent their childhood years on army bases; socially, it proved far more useful to talk about something else.

Later, looking back, I realized that perhaps the main characteristic these scientists had in common was absorption in their work, so much so as to be indifferent parents and spouses, although there were exceptions. In these matters they were very much like the too-busy lawyers, doctors, and other professionals that I have come to know since.

Just what is it that sets science and scientists apart in our minds? It may well be simply ignorance. The fact is, we do not know very much about the enterprise of science, about the life-styles of scientists, about what motivates and inspires them, about either the drama or the humdrum in their lives. Unlike doctors and lawyers, they are not frequent subjects in our literature or our sitcoms: no Perry Masons or Marcus Welbys. Our universities teach music appreciation courses but rarely science appreciation.

Just how thin our acquaintance is with even the superficial culture of science—the names of the subfields of science and of the most prominent practitioners—can be shown by a little experiment: ask a half-dozen friends who are devotees neither of music nor science to name two or three of the greatest composers of the past few centuries and what kind of music they wrote; then ask the same question regarding mathematics. Most of us can come up with Bach, Beethoven, Mozart, or half a dozen others; but in my experience you are likely to get an embarrassed silence in answer to your second question or else a mention of Einstein (a wrong answer—Einstein was an indifferent mathematician). Few people will mention Gauss (perhaps the greatest mathematician who ever lived) or Riemann or Gödel, and still fewer can tell you what kind of mathematics they did. You will fare little better if you try chemists. Our experience of the culture of science, let alone of its content, is simply very limited.

It need not be so. Science, as Sloan Foundation president Albert Rees has written, "is an enterprise with its own rules and customs, but an understanding of that enterprise is accessible to any of us, for it is quintessentially human. And an understanding of the enterprise inevitably brings with it some insight into the nature of its products." Perhaps the best way to get a grasp of this activity called science is through a closer approach to scientists themselves: who they are, how they live, how they think about the things that they do. That is the purpose of this book.

The collection of scientists profiled here is not typical in any exact sociological sense; these are not ordinary scientists. What makes them extraordinary is not specifically that they possess genius but that they are all driven to an unusual degree by the passion to know —in the same way that great artists are driven to create. And yet the ways in which that passion is expressed could not be more different: compare the self-effacing discipline of a Chandrasekhar with the loud persistence of a Wasserburg or the exuberance of a Glashow; contrast the isolation of a Gödel or a Heinrich to the sociability of a Wheeler or a Mead. Look at the eccentricity of a Gajdusek and at the straightforwardness of a Simon or a Zipser; at how a McElroy or a Ptashne thrives on controversy, while a Darwin shrinks from confrontation. The range of personalities and styles of doing science span the entire human spectrum; no stereotype does it justice.

Of course the profiles in this collection, abbreviated as they are, do not fully capture the complexity of these individuals or of their science. But I hope they do convey something of the rich culture of science—of its energy, its fascination, its human character—and whet the appetite for more.

Allen L. Hammond
Washington, D.C.

A PASSION TO KNOW

20 PROFILES IN SCIENCE

1
SUBRAMANYAN CHANDRASEKHAR

QUEST FOR ORDER

by John Tierney

Subramanyan Chandrasekhar is not sure what comes next. He survived a heart attack and open heart surgery during his latest project,
an eight-year study of black holes. When he finished it in the spring
of 1982 he was seventy-one, twice the age of practically everyone else
in the field, a time of life when most scientists are either retired or
enjoying an emeritus title—serving on committees, reminiscing at
award dinners, directing graduate students, toying with a few left-
over problems. That kind of scholarship would be impossible for
Chandrasekhar. It would be the moral equivalent of going to the
office without a plain dark suit, dark tie, and white shirt, the clothes
that he has worn every working day for nearly half a century at the
University of Chicago.

No, when he decides to work, he sits at a relentlessly neat desk
searching for mathematical order for at least twelve hours a day,
usually seven days a week, until after about a decade he has attained
what he calls "a certain perspective"—which is to say, until some
aspect of the universe has been completely reduced to a set of equations. Then, having written the definitive book on the subject, he puts
all his files in the attic and looks for a totally different area of astrophysics to teach himself. Just talking about "Chandra's style" makes
other astronomers tired. They can't understand how he regularly
forces himself to abandon a subject and start over—how, in a
discipline where a forty-year-old theoretician is considered way past
his peak, a man of sixty-three could profitably *begin* analyzing what
happens when things disappear down a black hole.

"He just batters his way through problems no one else could do,"
says his closest friend, Martin Schwarzschild, an astrophysicist at
Princeton University. "Chandra's concentration is unbelievable—a

1

mixture of sheer mathematical intelligence and phenomenal persistence. There is not one field that he's worked in where we are not now daily using some of his results."

Chandrasekhar, who is a great one for philosophizing about creativity and the aging scientific mind, turns uncomfortable when asked to explain his own professional longevity. But he allows that it probably has something to do with the meeting of the Royal Astronomical Society on January 11, 1935.

He arrived in London that Friday with great expectations for himself and mild suspicions concerning Sir Arthur Eddington. For months he and Eddington had been getting together, about twice a week after dinner, to discuss Chandrasekhar's latest calculations about the behavior of dying stars. They made an odd couple: the famed Eddington, eloquent, prepossessing, at fifty-two generally acknowledged as the world's finest astronomer, listening eagerly to a shy twenty-four-year-old from India who felt himself something of an outcast at Cambridge University. Chandrasekhar had been studying stellar structure for just a few years, ever since he won Eddington's classic book on the subject as a prize in a physics contest at Madras University in India. Now he was convinced that he had made a significant and startling discovery. That Friday afternoon he was to announce it.

But the day before, when a copy of the program for the meeting had arrived in Cambridge, Chandrasekhar had been amazed to discover that Eddington would also be speaking at the meeting. On the same subject. During all their discussions, while Chandrasekhar had been spewing out his figures, Eddington had never mentioned any work of his own in this area. It seemed an incredible breach of faith, yet Eddington offered no apology or explanation when the two men saw each other in the dining hall Thursday evening. His only remark was that he had used his influence to get Chandrasekhar extra time at the meeting—"so that you can present your work properly," as Chandrasekhar remembers him saying solicitously. Chandrasekhar was too deferential to mention Eddington's own paper, but the next day in London, at the tea before the meeting, another astronomer asked Eddington what he planned to say. Eddington wouldn't answer. He just turned to Chandrasekhar and smiled.

"That is a surprise for you," Eddington said.

Chandrasekhar's paper dealt with a fundamental question: what happens after a star has burned up all its fuel? According to the prevailing theory of the day, the cooling star would collapse under the force of its own gravity into a dense ball called a white dwarf. A star with the mass of the sun, for instance, would shrink to the size of the earth, at which point it would reach equilibrium. Chandrasekhar studied this collapse by considering what happens when a star's gas becomes so compressed that electrons move at nearly the speed of light—a state called relativistic degeneracy. He concluded that the enormous gravitational forces at work in a large star —any star more than 1.4 times as massive as the sun—would cause the star to go on collapsing beyond the white dwarf stage. The star would simply keep getting smaller and smaller and denser and denser until . . . well, that was an interesting question. Chandrasekhar delicately avoided it.

"A star of large mass cannot pass into the white dwarf stage," he concluded, "and one is left speculating on other possibilities."

Then it was Eddington's turn.

"I do not know whether I shall escape from this meeting alive, but the point of my paper is that there is no such thing as relativistic degeneracy," said Eddington, and proceeded to tear apart Chandrasekhar's paper. The speech was frequently interrupted by laughter. Eddington couldn't quarrel with Chandrasekhar's logic or calculations. But he claimed that the whole theory had to be wrong simply because it led to an inevitable and outlandish conclusion: "The star has to go on radiating and radiating and contracting and contracting until, I suppose, it gets down to a few kilometers radius, when gravity becomes strong enough to hold in the radiation, and the star can at last find peace."

Today, of course, such an object is called a black hole. That afternoon Eddington said it couldn't possibly exist.

"A *reductio ad absurdum*," he called it. "I think there should be a law of nature to prevent a star from behaving in this absurd way."

And there the matter rested, at least for the next few decades. Eventually, the theory would be vindicated, black holes would be accepted, and the dividing line mentioned in the paper (a stellar mass 1.4 times that of the sun) would go down in the textbooks as the Chandrasekhar Limit. But not for a long time after Eddington's speech.

"At the end of the meeting," recalls Chandrasekhar, "everybody came up to me and said, 'Too bad, Chandra, too bad.' I had gone to the meeting thinking that I would be proclaimed as having found something very important. Instead, Eddington effectively made a fool of me. I was distraught. I didn't know whether to continue my career. I returned to Cambridge late that night, probably around one o'clock. I remember going into the common room, the place where the fellows would meet. Of course nobody was there. There was a fire still burning, and I remember standing there in front of it and repeating to myself, 'This is how the world ends, not with a bang but with a whimper.'"

Today he has a different perspective on that afternoon.

The argument with Eddington dragged on for years, ruined any chance of his getting a tenured position in England, and finally persuaded him to give up the subject altogether (although the two men, remarkably enough, remained friends throughout). He believed in his theory, but others didn't. So, shortly after arriving at the University of Chicago in 1937, he put the theory in a book and stopped worrying about it. He instead began studying the probability distributions of stars in galaxies and discovered the curious property called dynamical friction—the fact that any star hurtling through a galaxy tends to slow down because of the gravity of the stars surrounding it. Then he switched again and considered why the sky is blue. The simple answer to this problem—that the atmosphere's molecules scatter the short-wavelength blue light while allowing other colors to pass through—had been found last century by Britain's Lord Rayleigh. But Rayleigh and a succession of physicists had all failed to unravel the exact mathematics of how light is scattered. By the middle of the 1940s, Chandrasekhar had worked it all out. And he enjoyed it so much, this switching fields, that he decided to made a career of it. He went on to more topics: the behavior of hot fluids in magnetic fields, the stability of rotating objects, the general theory of relativity, and finally back to black holes (but from a completely different approach). He now thinks he was lucky to be driven out of his original specialty.

"Suppose Eddington had decided that there were black holes in nature," he says, pausing to consider this proposition as precisely as possible. He is impeccably formal, true to his Brahmin roots, determined to keep his conversation as structured as everything else in his life. He actually speaks in complete sentences and logical paragraphs. He does this with a soft-spoken, gentle charm, digressing occasionally with jokes and allusions to everything from Picasso to Mother Goose to Keats, but always sternly bringing himself back to the original question.

"It's very difficult to speculate. Eddington would have made the whole area a very spectacular one to investigate, and many of the properties of black holes might have been discovered twenty or thirty years ahead of time. I can easily imagine that theoretical astronomy would have been very different. It's not for me to judge whether that difference—well, the difference would have been salutary for astronomy, I think I would say that.

"But I do not think it would have been salutary for me. My position in science would have been radically altered as of that moment. Eddington's praise could make one very famous in astronomy. But I really do not know how I would have reacted to the temptation, to the glamour.

"How many young men after being successful and famous have survived for long periods of time? Not many. Even the very great men of the 1920s who made quantum mechanics—I mean Dirac, Heisenberg, Fowler—they never equaled themselves. Look at Maxwell. Look at Einstein."

Chandrasekhar hastily interrupts himself to say that he is not comparing himself to these scientists or trying to criticize them. "You must not confuse things large and small. Who am I to criticize Einstein?" It is the problem in the abstract, he insists, that interests him. He is struck by the fact that, at age forty-seven, Beethoven told a friend, "*Now* I know how to compose." Chandrasekhar doesn't think there has ever been a forty-seven-year-old scientist who announced, "*Now* I know how to do research."

"When you discuss the works of a great artist or writer, the assumption always is that there is a growth from the early period to the middle period to the mature work and the end. The artist's ability is refined. Clearly he's able to tackle difficult problems. It obviously required an enormous effort, an enormous emotional control, to be able to write a play like *King Lear*. Look at the contrast between that and an earlier play, *Romeo and Juliet*.

"Now why is a scientist *unable* to refine his mind? Einstein was one of the great scientific minds. He discovered special relativity and a number of things in 1905. He worked terribly hard and did the general theory of relativity in 1916, and then he did some fairly important work until the early 1920s. From that point on he detached himself from the progress of science, became a critic of quantum theory, and effectively did not add to science or to his own enlargement. There is nothing in Einstein's work after the age of forty which shows that he attained a greater intellectual perception than what he had before. Why?

"For lack of a better word, there seems to be a certain arrogance toward nature which people develop. These people have had great insights and made profound discoveries. They imagine afterwards that the fact that they succeeded so triumphantly in one area means they have a special way of looking at science which must therefore be right. But science doesn't permit that. Nature has shown over and over again that the kinds of truth which underlie nature transcend the most powerful minds.

"Take Eddington. He was a great man. He said that there must be a law of nature to prevent a star from becoming a black hole. Why should he say that? Just because he thought is was bad? Why does he assume that he has a way of deciding what the laws of nature should be? Similarly, this oft-quoted statement of Einstein's disapproving of the quantum theory: 'God does not play dice.' How does he know?"

The exception that Chandrasekhar likes to talk about is Lord Rayleigh, the nineteenth-century physicist who did the original study on the color of the sky. He remained steadily productive in a variety of fields for fifty years and turned out some of his best-known work (such as the discovery of argon gas) in the latter part of his career.

"You know, when Rayleigh was sixty-seven, his son asked him what he thought about the famous remark by Thomas Huxley—that a man of sixty in science does more harm than good. Rayleigh thought about it a great deal and said, 'Well, I don't see why that should be so, provided you do what you understand and do not contradict young people.' I don't think Einstein could have said that, or Dirac, or Heisenberg. Eddington wouldn't have said that. There is a certain modesty in that remark. Now on the other hand you could say, as Churchill said when somebody told him that Clement Attlee was a very modest man, 'He has much to be modest about.' The really great discoveries have been made by people who have had the arrogance to make judgments about nature. Certainly Rayleigh did not add any really great fundamental insights like Einstein or Maxwell. But his influence on science was enormous because he added to the great body of knowledge, constantly inventing many things that were not spectacular but were always important. I think one could say that a certain modesty toward understanding nature is a precondition to the continued pursuit of science."

He again insists that he is speaking in the abstract, not about himself. But he could just as easily have been describing his own career. Plunging into a new field every decade is guaranteed to produce modesty: how can you contradict young men when they've been in the field longer than you have? And like Rayleigh, he concerns himself with important but unspectacular work, with rigorous studies that enlarge a body of knowledge rather than overturn it. He doesn't go for quick hits, for the single blinding insight or the revolutionary discovery that wins a Nobel Prize. He has always insisted on a long and complete analysis of a whole field, no matter how useless it may seem to others.

In the 1960s, for instance, he wrote a book on tangerine-shaped geometric figures called ellipsoids, which at the time were guaranteed not to win anyone fame or fortune. His reason for writing this book, he said in the Introduction, was that all the previous research had left the subject "with many gaps and omissions and some plain errors and misconceptions. It seemed a pity that it should be allowed to remain in this destitute state." So he tidied it up by systematically analyzing the forces acting on a rotating ellipsoid—the gravity holding it together, the centrifugal force pulling it apart, and the point at which it becomes unstable. Other scientists thought he was wasting his time studying these idealized objects. Why study an abstraction that doesn't exist in the universe? Yet today, twenty years later, the book is being applied in ways that couldn't have been anticipated. It turns out, for example, that the properties of these imaginary objects are shared by many real galaxies, and scientists are using the book to understand what holds the Milky Way together as it spins.

"I think my motivations are different from many scientists'," he says. "James Watson wrote that when he was a young man, he wanted to solve a problem that would win him the Nobel Prize. So he went ahead and discovered DNA. Clearly that approach justified itself in his case. But my motive has not been to solve a single problem but instead to acquire a perspective of an entire area.

"I started studying black holes eight years ago, particularly the theory of how a rotating black hole reacts to external perturbations such as gravitational and electromagnetic waves. If you know that, you can determine what happens to a black hole when an object such as a star falls into it. Well, there are individual pieces of this work that have attracted attention, but to me what is important is the final point of view I have of the subject. That is why I wrote the book. I see it as a whole with a perspective. Obviously there are a number of problems in the area that I can still work on, but I don't feel inclined. If you make a sculpture, you finish it—you don't want to go on chipping it here and there."

In 1983 Chandrasekhar received the Nobel Prize in physics, in part for his work on black holes. So what next? This is a problem for a man in his seventies. The chief drawback to his style of research is that it requires enormous amounts of time and energy. It has meant starting work every day at 6:00 A.M. and continuing as late as midnight. One of his collaborators, a graduate student who had the misfortune of living in an apartment visible from Chandrasekhar's office, used to be surprised by late-night calls at home when Chandrasekhar needed help with a problem. This went on until Chandrasekhar happened to mention to the student's wife that he felt free to call when he could see a light in the couple's window. From then on the window was heavily shielded with a curtain.

"He hasn't really had time for other things, for travel and friends.

He's always had an intense discipline about his work, an insistence that everything be neat and perfect," says Chandrasekhar's wife, Lalitha, who met him when they were both physics students at Madras University. She speaks uncomplainingly about his career and the sacrifices required of her—the long hours spent by herself, the abandoning of her career to follow him to the United States, the many years between visits to their families in India. But she also thinks that by now he has earned the right to relax, and so do his colleagues.

"Chandra's had to pay an enormous price, and it's steadily increased as he's gotten older," says Schwarzschild. "This last book was a *tour de force*—an example of willpower conquering exhaustion. I don't really know what he can do after that. His contributions have all come from this ability to keep pushing through problems that nobody else could push through. For Chandra, it would be completely out of character to drop down to something he knows a whole bunch of us could do."

Chandrasekhar tends to agree. "If I cannot pursue a subject in earnest," he says, "I would rather not make the effort at all." It is tempting for him to stop after this book if only for aesthetic reasons, to end with a study of the black holes that seemed so absurd at the beginning of his career. It would be a nice finale, especially since he regards it as perhaps the most difficult work he has ever undertaken. Yet he also talks about going into still another new field, maybe this time cosmology. "That's my habit of life, and it requires enormous discipline to change a habit of life. I haven't decided."

Although he doesn't consider himself a Hindu anymore—he classifies himself as an atheist—he sometimes wonders if he should follow the Hindu tradition of retirement: renouncing all worldly connections and going into the forest for solitary contemplation. To him, of course, this simply means giving up science, the ultimate change of field.

"One of the unfortunate facts about the pursuit of science the way I have done it is that it has distorted my personality. I had to sacrifice other interests in life—literature, music, traveling. I've devoted all my time, every living hour practically, to my work. I wanted to read all the plays of Shakespeare very carefully, line by line, word by word. I have never found the time to do it. I know I could have been a different person had I done this. I don't know if regret is the right term for what I feel. But sooner or later one has to reconcile these losses. One has to come to terms with oneself. One needs some time to get things in order."

2

CARLETON GAJDUSEK

OUTRAGEOUS ARDOR

by Roger Bingham

In March 1957, Carleton Gajdusek, a thirty-three-year-old physician returning to the United States after working at the Walter and Eliza Hall Institute of Medical Research in Australia, broke his homeward journey in what was then the Australian territory of Papua and New Guinea. He expected it to be a brief visit; it lasted ten months. In that time Gajdusek became the central figure in the most intriguing medical detective story of recent years, setting off a chain of events that would lead him to a share of the 1976 Nobel Prize for physiology and medicine.

Within two days of his arrival, he wrote excitedly to the late Joseph Smadel (then associate director of the National Institutes of Health) that he had begun to study "so astonishing an illness that clinical description can only be read with skepticism." Early in April, in another letter, Gajdusek insisted: "I tell you, Joe, this is no wild goose chase but a really big thing. . . . I stake my entire medical reputation on this matter."

The disease that Gajdusek, together with a local physician, Vincent Zigas, brought to world attention was kuru. It affected a small, isolated population in the eastern highlands of New Guinea—the Fore, Stone Age people who still practiced cannibalism, and their neighbors, who intermarried with them. In the Fore language, kuru means the trembling associated with fear or cold. It is a fatal degenerative disease of the central nervous system that begins with shivering and tremors, then progresses through loss of coordination and speech to overall incapacitation. The victims are finally unable to swallow or chew and usually die within a year of the first symptoms.

When Gajdusek encountered kuru, it had reached epidemic proportions in the Fore, accounting for 50 percent of annual deaths.

11

The tireless attempts of Gajdusek, Zigas, and their coworkers to combat the illness in the most primitive of conditions make a heroic tale. But the importance of kuru goes far beyond a tantalizing case study in tropical medicine. In the years that followed, kuru was shown to be transmissible—the first chronic disease proven to be a "slow virus infection," an inexorable, wasting process caused by an agent that could incubate undetected in a victim's body for years before flaring up. In the wake of Gajdusek's discovery, researchers throughout the world began to hunt for evidence of similar microbial time bombs in illnesses ranging from multiple sclerosis, Parkinson's disease, and amyotrophic lateral sclerosis (ALS) to Huntington's chorea and chronic arthritis. Gajdusek's own team later discovered that a form of senility, Creutzfeldt-Jakob disease (CJD), was also transmissible and caused by a virus virtually identical to kuru. CJD occurs worldwide and may represent the tip of an iceberg of similar neurological diseases, all viral in origin. That possibility offers at least the prospect of developing vaccines to fight them.

As Gajdusek predicted in those first excited letters to Smadel, kuru has had far-reaching effects, catalyzing a global effort to open a new medical and microbiological frontier. But the kuru investigation is unusual in another sense: it is an exceptionally well documented example of science in the making. Because of the remote field location, Gajdusek carried on a lengthy correspondence with his colleagues at NIH and the Hall Institute. The letters cover everything from detailed pathological analyses, clinical descriptions, hypotheses, and false trails to scientific-political squabbles and humorous personal insights.

Two additional complementary sources also reflect the unusual style that Gajdusek stamped on the investigation from its inception. First, he set great store in cinematic records to document both the progress of the disease and the cultural setting. Over the years he has amassed an archive of almost twenty-five miles of clinical and nonclinical film. Second, there are Gajdusek's thirty-six field journals, covering 1954 to 1983. They are intensely personal documents, part travelogue, clinical diary, anthropological field notes, and confessional. Characteristically, they are alarmingly indiscreet, and Gajdusek's irreverent assessments of those who people his narrative have led to many of the journals not being widely circulated. All, however, have been published under the auspices of the National Institutes of Health.

The kuru story that emerges from this welter of material sounds at times like an epic Hollywood concoction: a bizarre, fatal disease; exotic location; a cast of Stone Age cannibals suddenly exposed to the wonders of modern medicine; and, always on center stage, the extraordinary and eccentric character of Carleton Gajdusek.

It begins with a report from Vincent Zigas, district medical officer, Department of Public Health in the Territory of Papua and New Guinea, dated December 26, 1956. On a field trip, Zigas wrote, he had found many natives suffering from "a probably new form of encephalitis attributed by inhabitants to sorcery and called 'Kuru.' . . ."

The Hall Institute expressed interest in the disease and made plans to dispatch an investigator. But while Zigas waited until the secretary of law in Australia decided what compensation might be appropriate for such an investigator in case of "attack by tribesmen," Gajdusek arrived.

Originally, he had planned a brief visit to continue his studies of child development in primitive cultures. As soon as he caught wind of kuru, however, he headed for the area of the epidemic, was shown some of the victims by Zigas, and fired off lengthy letters to the Hall Institute and NIH.

Predictably, before the month of March was out, Gajdusek had become a painful burr under the Australian administrative saddle. His presence was interpreted as another brash American invasion. On March 30, the acting director of public health sent a radiogram to Gajdusek, noting the imminent arrival of the Hall Institute representative: "Accordingly on ethical grounds request you consider discontinuing your investigations kuru."

"Intensive investigation uninterruptible," Gajdusek replied. "Will remain at work with patients to whom we are responsible."

The political maneuvering continued, with the hard-pressed Gajdusek composing mollifying letters to officialdom in his spare moments. Eventually, what the authorities viewed as his act of medical piracy was grudgingly accepted as a *fait accompli*. Hall Institute director Sir Macfarlane Burnet professed himself "still considerably irked by Gajdusek's actions, but there is little doubt that he has the technical competence to do a first-rate job." And later: "I have a sort of exasperated affection for Gajdusek and a great admiration of his drive, courage, and capacity for hard work. Also there is probably no one else anywhere with the combination of linguistic ability, anthropological interest, and medical training who could have tackled this problem so well."

It was a good point. Gajdusek was a tailor-made adversary for kuru. It is plain from his letters to Joe Smadel that he also knew instinctively that he had hit medical paydirt with kuru. But how exactly to refine it? Initially, he and Zigas hypothesized that the disease was infectious, perhaps a virus. And yet, all the clinical evidence argued against it: there was no fever, no inflammatory changes in the cerebrospinal fluid, none of the usual signs of infection. Gajdusek's colleagues at the Hall Institute (which was supplying invaluable laboratory backup, now that tempers had cooled) could discover no transmissible agent. It was baffling.

To add to the frustration, working conditions were primitive. In mid-May 1957, Gajdusek wrote to Smadel: ". . . we have had a kuru death and a complete autopsy. I did it at 2:00 A.M., during a howling storm, in a native hut, by lantern light; and I sectioned the brain without a brain knife." (In fact, as he explained later in a letter to Burnet, he used a carving knife.)

There were other clues, other leads to follow. The disease was found to affect all ages beyond infants and toddlers; it was common in male and female children and in adult females but rare in adult males. Why? No one entering the Fore region since it was opened up in 1956 had contracted the disease. Why? Kuru was restricted to an area of about 1,000 square miles in a region of steep, forested mountain valleys, 3,000 to 7,000 feet above sea level. Only the Fore people and their intermarried neighbors were afflicted, and yet 50 percent of all deaths in a year could be ascribed to the disease. Why? There were no answers.

Gajdusek considered possible genetic mechanisms, some form of lethal kuru trait, dietary factors, trace metals. Nothing seemed convincing. Moreover, the Fore were beginning to doubt Gajdusek's powers of healing. "They have decided that this magic is too strong for me and that my prolonging life by treating and controlling decubitus ulcers [bedsores] is no blessing at all," he wrote Smadel. "They want to die at home; and once fully incapacitated, they want to die as quickly as possible."

In September, Gajdusek received a report from Igor Klatzo, a senior NIH neuropathologist, who had been examining the latest batch of autopsied brains from kuru victims. The disease, Klatzo noted, seemed to resemble Creutzfeldt-Jakob disease (CJD). It meant little at the time but would later prove to be an astute observation.

After ten months in the field, Gajdusek finally returned to NIH early in 1958 with a mass of data, the initial phase of the investigation over but no solution to the mystery at hand. The first clue came in 1959 when Dr. William Hadlow wrote to the British medical journal *Lancet* pointing out the strong similarities between kuru and scrapie—a slow virus disease of sheep and goats. Gajdusek was impressed. With his longtime collaborator Clarence Gibbs at NIH, he resumed the search for a transmissible agent in kuru, gearing his research to look for parallel causes in other human degenerative diseases.

By 1963 Gajdusek and Gibbs were injecting kuru-infected brain tissue into chimpanzees. Their patience was rewarded when the first animals came down with the disease in 1965. (Since then they have transmitted kuru to a variety of nonhuman primates and non-primates, as well as from monkeys to monkeys and from chimpanzees to monkeys.) Three years later they repeated the success but with CJD inoculates, producing results virtually indistinguishable from kuru and corroborating Igor Klatzo's suggestion. The evidence was incontrovertible: the infectious disease hypothesis had been right after all.

The pieces began falling into place. But how was the infection transmitted in the Fore, and what caused the curious female-male ratio of mortality? The answer, according to Gajdusek, was cannibalism. In the Fore, dead kinsmen were consumed as a rite of mourning. Traditionally, the women performed the butchery, using their hands and sharp bamboo blades. Brain tissue (which, in a kuru victim, contains more than 10 million infectious units of virus per gram of tissue) was packed into bamboo cylinders and steamed. Pregnant women and children were given the primary honor of practicing cannibalism; the men participated to a lesser degree. Throughout this process, the younger children were constantly close to their mothers. Essentially, they were self-inoculated through mucosal tissues—eyes, nose, and mouth—and the ever-present open wounds of jungle sores, as well as through ingestion.

Though suspect at first, the actual consumption of flesh, Gajdusek argues, may not have been the important factor. His laboratory succeeded in the early 1980s in transmitting kuru and CJD orally to squirrel monkeys; but when the viral agent was put directly into the stomach of chimpanzees via a tube, bypassing the mucosal tissue of the mouth, no infection resulted. "We have no evidence that a chimpanzee or man could be infected by eating kuru-infected tissue," he says. "But scratch the skin, and one in ten can die. It was the cannibalism *rite* that caused the widespread contamination."

Recent statistics bear out the thesis. Since missionary intervention brought an end to cannibalism (roughly from 1957 to 1962, depending on the village), kuru has been gradually disappearing. No one born in a village since cannibalism ceased has ever developed the disease, although it continues to affect those born earlier. Of several hundred kuru orphans born since 1957 to mothers dying of kuru, not one has been afflicted.

"Kuru is gone," Gajdusek says. "All you have to do to avoid kuru is be born after they stopped opening up the bodies. You can still live in a house with a sister and mother who are incubating kuru, you can nurse at their breasts, you can eat with them, share food with them, copulate with them, stay and nurse them through their disease until they die . . . and never get kuru."

And yet the viral agent that causes kuru remains mysterious. Conventional viruses—those that cause measles and influenza, for example—operate by well-understood mechanisms and have clearly defined properties. Essentially, a virus is a package of genetic information—DNA or RNA—wrapped inside a protein overcoat. It cannot reproduce itself and functions instead as a microbial subversive, penetrating a cell, hijacking the cellular machinery, and substituting its own genetic blueprint. The commandeered cell's assembly lines become a factory, turning out new viruses.

There is, of course, a reaction to this invasion: the immune system manufactures combative antibodies. This immune response, together with inflammation and the other symptoms of infection, is characteristic of conventional viruses, which also show other common traits: they are visible under the electron microscope and are inactivated by high temperature, ultraviolet light, gamma radiation, and disinfectants like formaldehyde.

Kuru, on the other hand, is one of a group of four unconventional viruses—scrapie, CJD, transmissible mink encephalopathies (TME), and kuru itself—that so far defy classification. Gajdusek and Gibbs have dubbed them the subacute spongiform virus encephalopathies. They produce none of the usual signs of infection and reduce the brain to a spongy mass full of microscopic holes. The viruses are resistant to UV, gamma radiation, heat, and formaldehyde. Peculiarly, they seem to provoke no immune response. Despite every effort, no one has actually "seen" the kuru virus or characterized its structure.

There is another mystery: how did kuru arise in the first place? Gajdusek speculates that a spontaneous case of CJD may have occurred in New Guinea. During the cannibalistic rite, the original CJD virus became modified in the victims, to give kuru. There is more. Suppose, Gajdusek conjectures, that all four of these unconventional viruses are different strains of a single original virus, modified by their respective hosts. Scrapie, for example, might be the prototype. Mink feeding on sheep carcasses would develop TME. Humans, via kitchen or butchery accidents with scrapie-infected sheep, would develop CJD, which in turn would become kuru in New Guinea.

How realistic Gajdusek's notion of family relatedness between the various viruses will prove to be is anybody's guess. In recent experiments, though, goats inoculated with kuru and CJD derived from humans have developed a scrapielike disease. How extensively these and other agents are distributed globally, lurking at a subclinical level in the population, is another unknown. One thing is certain: Gajdusek's work with kuru has stimulated the widespread search for answers. Furthermore, three isolated incidences of accidental transmission of CJD to patients—via a cornea transplant from a donor with CJD or from use of CJD-contaminated surgical instruments— have prompted Gajdusek's laboratory to issue a paper detailing special precautions to be used with CJD patients.

Without Gajdusek's unique combination of characteristics, the various threads of this medical puzzle might never have been pulled together. In a handwritten note sent during the kuru incident to an angry senior Australian official, Hall Institute director Sir Macfarlane Burnet tried to explain the creative possibilities of Gajdusek's eccentric character: ". . . his personality . . . is almost legendary among my colleagues in the U.S. [John] Enders (Boston) told me that Gajdusek was very bright but you never knew when he would leave off work for a week to study Hegel or a month to go off to work with Hopi Indians. Smadel at Washington said the only way to handle him was to kick him in the tail, hard. Somebody else told me he was fine, but there just wasn't anything human about him.

"Actually, I got on better than I expected with Gajdusek during his fifteen months at the Institute. During the last four or five months, he did some first-rate work on autoimmune reaction; and we parted on excellent terms. My own summing up was that he had an intelligence quotient up in the 180s and the emotional immaturity of a fifteen-year-old. He is quite manically energetic when his enthusiasm is roused and can inspire enthusiasm in his technical assistants. He is completely self-centered, thick-skinned, and inconsiderate, but equally won't let danger, physical difficulty, or other people's feelings interfere in the least with what he wants to do. He apparently has no interest in women but an almost obsessional interest in children, none whatever in clothes and cleanliness; and he can live cheerfully in a slum or a grass hut. . . ."

Although there is plenty of testimony applauding his kindness and generosity, Gajdusek has no trouble playing the role of irascible exotic that is so often required by his legend. It is never entirely clear whether his more outrageous statements are to be taken seriously, or whether he simply lobs them, like grenades, into the conversation to shock his listeners.

He paces incessantly, punctuating his comments with a swooping, accusatory finger or theatrical flourishes of his glasses. He is a fast talker, but his mind sprints at Olympian pace. Sometimes there are traffic accidents as words collide, the vocal apparatus backed up with output from the cortex. He can be venomous and gossipy, drops names with total abandon, and dispenses braggadocio like Hemingway—"If I was a normal human being, as I would rather be . . ." he will say. Then he punctures the immage with a fruity chuckle and engaging Rabelaisian ribaldry.

"He's the kind of whirling carousel that wears people out," comments colleague Paul Brown. "Carleton is a driven man, and what drives him is the need to create. When he does not create—in his own judgment—he suffers."

Gajdusek's "specialness" was evident early in life, according to his brother Robert (Robin), professor of English at San Francisco State University. He tells of a visit that he and Carleton were taken on as children to the village of their paternal grandfather in Czechoslovakia. Carleton was five, Robin four. "Carleton would go out every morning, and he would scrub the pig," Robin recalls. "And the pig would wallow in the mud, and Carleton would scrub the pig. And the pig would wallow—and so on. I didn't know what that meant then.

"As Carleton grew older, he created clubs. The first group he ever organized went to the incinerating plant to see how they disposed of waste. First the pig, then the sewage. Then one day, he came here to watch my wife Linda throwing a pot on the wheel. His first question—I could have predicted it—was, Can you make a square pot on that wheel? Can you make a square pot? Can I keep the pig clean? This is a thirst for absolutism and idealism: I will *protest* the cycle of nature. I want a square pot from the wheel of nature, and I want to keep the pig—the eternal metaphor of the cyclicity of nature—clean.

"Now, when a kid of five tries to keep a pig clean, I knew he had to have a Nobel Prize."

Since 1970 Gajdusek has been chief of the Laboratory of Central Nervous System Studies, National Institute of Neurological and Communicative Disorders and Stroke (NINCDS) at the National Institutes of Health. He has also—since 1958—been director of NINCDS's Laboratory of Slow, Latent and Temperate Virus Infections and of the Program for the Study of Child Growth and Development and Disease Patterns in Primitive Cultures. These are titles of fearsome length: what they boil down to is that Gajdusek is at home in pediatrics, virology, epidemiology, neurology, and anthropology; sits at the hub of what has been called an empire of perhaps two hundred collaborating laboratories worldwide; and has a remarkable way with children.

His interest in pediatrics goes back to his days at Harvard Medical School. (He had already taken a degree in biophysics at the University of Rochester.) "I had not counted on my captivation with clinical pediatrics," he wrote in an autobiographical sketch. "Children fascinated me, and their medical problems . . . seemed to offer more challenge than adult medicine. I lived and worked within the walls of Boston Children's Hospital through much of medical school."

The pattern continued. Through a series of research appointments at Columbia College of Physicians and Surgeons, Caltech (working with Nobel Prize winners Linus Pauling and Max Delbrück), and Harvard (poliomyelitis virology with John Enders), he always held concurrent posts in pediatrics, and the stories of his devotion to sick children, of round-the-clock bedside vigils attempting to outwit nature, are legion.

The joint themes of childhood and aging recur frequently in Gajdusek's early journals. Here is the entry for September 9, 1957—his thirty-fourth birthday: "To me, everything beyond the twenties is 'aged'—and though I am well in the thirties myself, I consider it closer to senility than youth . . . I have always thought that to live to thirty was to live a lifetime; Christ and Alexander, and most of the 'greats' had proved this amply. All the years beyond thirty are bonus. . . ."

Now this from the journal for January 8, 1962: "I have never liked geriatrics, I have never enjoyed medical work with the aged, and I would not be a good doctor with old people . . . I do not make enough concessions to the decline of the human organism . . . to be properly humane with the aged."

It is no surprise that, on Gajdusek's trips to primitive cultures, the children—boisterously engaging life, full of promise and un-bridled sensuality—have always been drawn to him. As he noted in his journal for June 17, 1959: "I can still find no difficulties with my Pied Piper tunes, the sincerest notes in my repertoire! All else is but exercise for these tunes, and all work is but practice for the pipes."

In New Guinea the children helped to transport his cargo, sat at his feet as he typed by lantern light, functioned later as medical assist-ants. Over the years, he has adopted twenty-eight Melanesian and Micronesian boys, who have shared his home, looked after the im-pressive collection of artifacts that he has collected on his travels and deposited at the Peabody Museum at Salem, Massachusetts, and been educated through his generosity. "I have lived in a world of children and of child humor, child fantasy, and child passions for four dec-ades," he wrote on July 5, 1962. "If only I can grow old, foolishly old in this same world—if it is my fate to grow old, I shall be most fortunate!"

There is an irony in all of this. Kuru, which made Gajdusek the Pied Piper of Papua and New Guinea, has led to a close study of the senile dementias. "That's a beautiful way of the gods getting even with you," he jokes. "A person like me, who, with such great confidence, focuses entirely on childhood, picks a child problem, loads up the hospital with child patients, gets pulled into *geriatrics!*"

Gajdusek was born in Yonkers, New York. His paternal grandfather—a man who took three wives and sired twenty-five children—was patriarch of a Slovakian village. Gajdusek's father was a master butcher in Yonkers, a colorful, outspoken character well known in the neighborhood. The maternal side of the family—originally from Hungary—was, according to Robin Gajdusek, far more academic and genteel. "My father," Robin recalls, "simply could dance every woman in a dance hall off her feet in a polka. He was voluble, he was loud, he was gloriously exuberant, volatile and virile. My mother was a refined spirit who had somehow entered into this liaison with brutality and outrageous ardor."

There was another crucial influence in the household, Gajdusek's maternal aunt Irene, an entomologist. Through her connections, the precocious Carleton gained access to the Boyce Thompson Institute for Plant Research in Yonkers. By the time he was ten, he had already written an essay setting out his plans for a medical career and stenciled the names of famous microbiologists (beginning with Leeuwenhoek, Spallanzani, Pasteur . . .) from Paul de Kruif's classic book *Microbe Hunters* on the steps leading to the attic of the house where he set up a laboratory. His own name would not be out of place in their company now.

The names are still there: Gajdusek owns the house where he was born more than sixty years ago. For nearly twenty years—since the death of his mother—the house remained just as she left it, with her collection of pictures, crystal, and china intact (until 1980, when it was finally vandalized). "It's the one subject on which Carleton is absolutely immovable," comments Robin Gajdusek. "That house has to be left as it is. It is deeply, deeply embedded in the sense of home that he has been creating surrogates for. He'll go up to the house once in the winter and maybe six or seven times in the spring, and that will be his use of it for a year. But he wants it to *be there*."

Carleton Gajdusek has little use for cultural conventions and social niceties, easily wearies of structures and sameness, and is happiest when he is on the move. (His mood changes visibly, colleagues say, as soon as he is on his way to an airport.) His journals speak eloquently of Gajdusek's concern for his friends in primitive cultures—his extended family, of his sense of mission and of kinship. Here are his reflections after his first six months in the Fore region, written on September 6, 1957, at Uvai rest house: "I came into the Fore on

March 14th for a brief visit. Kuru has now kept me in so-called 'un-controlled' regions for almost half a year, much of which time I have been out on patrol. I have abandoned my French and Russian authors; my correspondence, which has fallen to naught but the voluminous scientific exchange about kuru and our three kuru papers, has afforded me little time to follow world news, literature or home events for these six months. I am a bit shocked when I consider how little all this bothers me and how little is my anxiety to leave. I know full well that I shall be walking the streets of Paris, Rome, London and New York and Washington again and that from these places the New Guinea jungles and the 'savages' are but remote museum pieces or subjects for arty cine films and literature—hardly the humans with whom I now live and sleep. To me they are, as were my friends of New Britain, among the warmest and closest friends I have had. I respect, admire and love them, and know that once I part from them, I may never see them or hear from them again. I am in no hurry."

In fact, hardly a year has passed since his first trip without a re-turn visit to Micronesia or Melanesia. When Gajdusek says, "I have more experience than probably anyone else in the world with Stone Age man," he has good reason. To the natives, *"Kaoten blong mipella"* (pidgin for "Carleton belong me fella" or "Our Carleton") has become something of a legend, a cross between Lord Jim and David Livingstone.

In some ways, the award of the Nobel Prize has compromised Gajdusek's mission. Celebrity militates against quiet creativity, and the demands on his time have increased enormously. Often he will simply take refuge at home, avoiding interruptions. (He also has a habit of answering mail several years in arrears after shipping it out to New Guinea to be dealt with at his leisure, or whim.)

Slow virus work, by definition, is a protracted business, but there are some intriguing, and at this point tentative, spin-offs that have captured Gajdusek's interest. In animals with kuru or CJD, for exam-ple, there is a distinct change in paradoxical sleep patterns (EEG recordings of brain waves associated with dreaming) as the disease progresses. "It's very exciting," Gajdusek says. "We're right down at the structure of the brain and how dreaming started on earth." And, he notes, the research may offer leads in the study of juvenile epilepsy, releasing him from geriatrics and senile dementias. The Pied Piper may have a chance to play his favorite tunes once more.

Perhaps the missionary image he holds of himself is closest to the truth. This is what Gajdusek wrote in his journal on July 10, 1960, aboard a Pan American Boeing 707:

"To bring this age of cosmology, atomic and nuclear structure, information theory in human communication and in the interpretation of biological continuity, in touch with its roots as they are still evident in so-called 'primitive' cultures, is my mission—with all the skepticism of anyone who has been shocked by the 'missionaries' of our history. To bring man in his diverse cultural experiments far removed from Western Semitic-Christian and Sino-Asiatic traditions into the awareness of modern man, of inter-nuclear force, intergalactic space and theory of knowledge complexity, and into rational and emotional contact with the nature of man, is all I can strive for . . . that I shall do with the zealousness of a foolish, comic, inspired, ridiculous—yet passionate—pediatric apostle."

Rick Friedman/Black Star

3

SHELDON GLASHOW

THE CHARM OF PHYSICS

by Arthur Fisher

In the jam-packed blue-and-green auditorium known as Science Center B, 450 students of Harvard core course A-20, From Alchemy to Quarks, watch their lecturer intently. A tall, solid man of about fifty, he is dressed in a blue blazer and gray flannels and wears thick-lensed horn-rims. He pauses in front of an assemblage of glass containers and rubber tubes. Beneath an unruly thatch of hair the color of tarnished silver, his face is puckish.

"If I were to be so foolish as to inhale one of these gases," he says, "the nature of the sounds made by my vocal cords would be very different from their sound in air. I will show that that is indeed the case." Much laughter and applause from the audience.

"I will now do my Bugs Bunny voice." His body assumes a Grouchovian slump. "I may collapse, and if I do, call the doctor." Appreciative hoots from the hall.

He grabs a rubber tube, inhales mightily, then speaks in a high-pitched squawk more like Donald's than Bugs's. "Do I sound any different?" Hilarious laughter and roars of approval.

The lecturer mugs. "It's addicting." Then, "Helium is one-seventh the density of air."

Next he tries sulfur hexafluoride, "for prevention of disease only." This time his voice issues, as if from the tomb, in a low, muffled boom. As the torrents of laughter subside, he explains, "Sulfur hexafluoride is four times denser than air."

Sheldon Lee Glashow, professor of physics, Nobel laureate, and irrepressible wag, is giving his "physics for poets" class a lesson in the gas laws they will not soon forget.

Particle physicists, like the enigmatic objects they dabble in, come in a fruit salad of flavors and colors from "strange" to "charmed."

25

There are those whose manner is grave and monastic, those whose genius is so constantly in evidence it stifles conversation, those so intent on some inner, recondite meditation they appear bumbling and distracted, those so defensive-aggressive they seem to carry a quark on each shoulder.

Glashow is none of these. In the classroom, with his colleagues, at home, even being interviewed for the $(n + 1)$th time he is, quite simply, funny.

The wit leavens but does not mask the very serious matters that are Glashow's intimate professional concern. Like many of today's theoretical physicists, he deals with first things and last ones, too, with the birth of the universe and its end, with the fundamental particles of nature, and with whether there is a fundament. His 1979 Nobel Prize in physics was awarded for contributions to the combined or unified theory describing two of the four basic forces of nature, the so-called weak and electromagnetic forces. The prize was shared with Abdus Salam and Steven Weinberg, a boyhood chum in high school and until recently also a professor of physics at Harvard.

That two Nobelists would share a common high school is no coincidence when it is New York City's Bronx High School of Science, a spawning ground for eminent scientists. The roots of Glashow's present flowering lie in a youth nurtured by caring parents and older brothers at home and fertilized by the ideas of bright young friends at school.

He described these experiences not long ago at his big, rambling, eighty-year-old house in Brookline, Massachusetts, just across the Boston city line, where he lives with his wife and four children. He sat in the sun-washed parlor, filled with potted plants—jade, fig, avocado—and overlorded by an elaborate mask and headdress from Zaire. As he chatted, he puffed on the stubby Swiss cigars called Stumpen.

Shelly Glashow was born in 1932 and grew up on Payson Avenue in the Inwood section of Manhattan, "across from a nice park just big enough to get lost in." His parents had fled Czarist oppression early in the century, and his father developed a successful plumbing business. His brothers were eighteen and fourteen years older than he. One became a doctor, the other a dentist.

When Glashow entered high school, he already knew he wanted to become a scientist, but he didn't know what kind. "My parents really wanted me to become a doctor, but they couldn't be too opposed— having one doctor and a dentist already was enough. At age fifteen I had a rather well-equipped chemistry lab in our basement, with a sink—no problem for my father—and all kinds of dangerous chemicals that I wouldn't go near now."

Glashow's qualities of mind were apparent early on, as revealed in a story told by classmates about an encounter between Glashow and Henry Stern, a former New York City councilman and now parks commissioner.

Glashow (then thirteen) to Stern (then eleven): "I have reached the age of reason. You have not."

Stern to Glashow: "When will I? How will I be able to tell?"

Glashow to Stern: "*I* will know."

At the Bronx High School of Science, Glashow helped start a science-fiction club ("Before I graduated to science fiction, I was a voracious reader of comic books") whose members were really more interested in talking about science than literature. It is unfortunate that there are no transcripts of the club's meetings or of the cafeteria conversations of Glashow and his friends; they would have gladdened the research of any historian of modern science. This remarkable collection of kids included, besides Glashow, Steven Weinberg, now at the University of Texas at Austin, Gerald Feinberg, now in the physics department at Columbia University, and others destined for great distinction in physics.

Glashow remembers that the physics and chemistry courses at Bronx Science were "okay, but not very stimulating, and I actually absorbed more physics by learning it from my friends, especially Weinberg and Feinberg. I read lots of College Outline physics books, but then someone would say, 'Hey, I learned some quantum physics last night, and it's not so hard,' and the other two of us would get so jealous we'd go out and get some quantum physics textbooks to learn it ourselves."

The math courses at Bronx Science were very good, Glashow says. "But," he adds with a look of wild indignation, "there was no *calculus*. I learned it in the lunchroom from friends, especially Dan Greenberger. It was this interaction with friends like Steve, Gary Feinberg, and Dan and others that made Science such a remarkable and important place. What you become in life depends partly on who you go to school with. I learned faster at Bronx Science that I did in college."

By the time he entered college, Glashow knew exactly what kind of science he wanted to do: elementary particle physics. "I was almost thirteen when the atom bomb was dropped and knew that it was using stuff I was interested in. I was glued to the radio. I remember reading about the curve of binding energy in *Astounding Science Fiction* magazine. Then, later, in high school, mesons were just becoming popular things. I remember going to a lecture in New York where I heard the Japanese physicist Hideki Yukawa speak. People were arguing about particle physics in words I couldn't quite understand—it was very exciting. It seemed clear that the most basic kind of science to do was elementary particle physics."

Ironically enough, Glashow's college application to Harvard was rejected. He chose Cornell over MIT and Princeton "because Cornell was prettier." Weinberg, too, went to Cornell.

"The student body was very good," Glashow recalls, "but the faculty was not terribly responsive. The physics department wanted us to take a lot of elementary courses we didn't need or want and frowned on us taking more advanced courses."

Glashow does not suffer foolishness in education lightly. "We were forced to take all kinds of revolting classes at Cornell. I remember showing up in a freshman history course when I was a senior. The teacher looked at me and said, 'You're the only senior in a class of freshmen. Why don't you just accept a grade of eighty-five and not come to class?'" Glashow smiles in a self-satisfied way and adds, "There were a number of courses that I took in this fashion. I spent a good deal of time in the poolroom. Most successful people in physics made it by going off by themselves and learning what they wanted to."

After Cornell, Glashow went to Harvard for graduate studies. His ferocious independence of mind and amused skepticism are reflected in the introduction to his Ph.D. thesis, with a quotation from that master iconoclast Galileo, which Glashow translates roughly as:

"It is necessary to say that poetic spirits are of two kinds, first, those who invent fables, and second, those who are disposed toward believing them."

The thesis is titled *The Vector Meson in Elementary Particle Decays*. "This was a highly speculative thesis," says Glashow now, "and the message from Galileo seemed appropriate."

Speculative or not, the thesis marked the start of a long trail that led, eventually, to a Nobel Prize in 1979. Glashow's thesis adviser was physicist Julian Schwinger, who was interested in combining the weak and electromagnetic interactions into a single complex mathematical theory known as a gauge theory. "My thesis," explains Glashow, "was an attempt to investigate that possibility. It was basically unsuccessful, but it did lead to the successful unification theory we have today for the electromagnetic and weak forces."

To penetrate this terminology and to understand why Glashow won his Nobel, one must know something of the course of particle physics over the last several decades. Briefly, its history can be described as a titanic struggle to impose some kind of order on a seeming jumble of entities and phenomena. One part of this effort was to arrange scores of subnuclear particles into some comprehensible pattern, in which there would be only a few "basic" particles that combined to form all others. Closely linked to that effort has been the attempt to develop a single mathematical structure that can describe the four different ways that particles of matter interact with each other. This has also been called the attempt to "unify" the four fundamental forces of nature—electromagnetism, gravity, and the strong and weak nuclear forces—with one coherent theory. The task has often seemed insuperable because of the utter disparity of these forces in magnitude, range of action, and dominion.

The strong nuclear force, for example, binds the occupants of the nucleus, acting over a range no larger than the diameter of a single proton. Gravity, on the other hand, exerts its way over infinite distances and affects every form of matter and energy. Yet the gravitational attraction between two protons in the nucleus of a helium atom, for instance, is some thirty-nine powers of 10 (10^{39}) times weaker than the attraction due to the strong force. The weak nuclear interaction, 100,000 times more feeble between these two protons than the strong, affects all kinds of subnuclear particles and is involved in a particular sort of radioactive decay called beta decay, which is an essential step in the production of energy by stars. And electromagnetism, the interaction responsible for attraction and repulsion among charged particles, creates a repulsive force between the protons that is 100 times weaker than the strong force binding them.

For the last thirty-odd years of his life, Albert Einstein was balked in his attempt to unify just two of these forces, gravity and electromagnetism. Each time his work led down a blind alley, he published his fruitless research "to save another fool from wasting time on the same idea."

Nevertheless, many physicists, including Glashow, now feel that a unification of at least three and perhaps all four forces may be attainable. Their confidence rests in part on the successful application of two seminal ideas in twentieth-century physics. One was advanced more than forty years ago by Hideki Yukawa. He suggested that when two particles exert a force on each other, they may be thought of as exchanging yet another particle that "mediates" the force. In this scheme, each of the four forces has its own exchange particle. In the electromagnetic force, for example, photons are the mediators. When two electrons repel each other by the electromagnetic force, the interaction may be thought of as one electron emitting a photon while the other absorbs it. Like a basketball player passing the ball across the court to a fellow player, the first electron recoils away from the second, which is nudged in the opposite direction when it "catches" the photon. The result: the two electrons are pushed away from each other.

The second key concept is the singular kind of quantum field theory called a gauge theory. In an intricate and subtle pattern, it weaves together three ostensibly unrelated sets of things: geometrical transformations in space and time; the symmetry of the laws of nature; and the internal symmetries that dictate the quantum characteristics of particles. It depends on a complex branch of mathematics called group theory, once described by James R. Newman as "the supreme example of the art of mathematical abstraction" but an everyday tool of physicists.

It turns out, Glashow says, that "nature has chosen a gauge theory —this highly specific version of a quantum field theory—not once but three times: for the electromagnetic, the strong, and the weak forces." In fact, Maxwell's classical theory of electromagnetism, which describes the two forces of electricity and magnetism as one, is the earliest gauge theory.

By 1960 Glashow had contributed much to what now constitutes the gauge theory, which provides a combined description for the weak and electromagnetic forces, often called the electroweak theory. There was, however, a major theoretical kink. Quantum physics demands that the mass of an exchange particle be inversely proportional to the range of the force it mediates. Because electromagnetism has an infinite range, the photon must therefore have zero mass. But the weak force has an infinitesimal range; its exchange particles must be very massive. They and the photon are thus "unlikely siblings," as some physicists have put it, and seemed impossible to crowd into one happy, unified family.

Glashow was unable to eliminate the paradox. But in 1967, Weinberg, then at Harvard, and a year later Abdus Salam of London's Imperial College and the International Center for Theoretical Physics in Trieste, independently developed a gauge theory unifying electromagnetism and weak interactions in a way that overcame the mass problem. It did so by means of a concept called symmetry breaking, a construct that has assumed towering importance in modern particle physics.

Put simply, symmetry breaking accounts for the difference between the way the physical world acts at the relatively cool temperatures and calm conditions of today and the way it would act in a situation similar to the first instants of its existence, when temperatures were enormously high. At conditions of extremely high energy, according to various unified theories, all the forces are equal and indistinguishable—a grand symmetry. As the universe cooled into its present state, however, that symmetry was broken.

The concept of symmetry breaking explains how the supposedly unified interactions of electromagnetism and the weak force can use two very different kinds of exchange particles: the massless photons on the one hand and the three massive carriers of the weak force on the other, the W^-, W^-, and $Z°$. The idea is that such differences between the forces appear only at low, everyday energies and would vanish if the universe could be returned to its primordial, high-energy state. The specific means by which Weinberg and Salam applied symmetry breaking to the electroweak theory demanded the existence of yet another particle, the Higgs boson.

Glashow treats some of these ideas with mocking levity. "I'm responsible for symmetry," he says, "Steve Weinberg is responsible for symmetry breaking. I invented $SU(2) \times (U1)$ [the mathematical structure upon which the electroweak theory is based]; he broke it." And about the somewhat inelegant Higgs mechanism, "The Higgs boson is like a toilet. Everyone has a toilet inside the house, but it's not necessarily an object of pride and beauty. It is essential, though. And that makes Steve Weinberg the Thomas Crapper of twentieth-century physics."

In the 1970s, the Weinberg-Salam-Glashow electroweak theory rapidly gained support as a number of indirect tests of its predictions were confirmed in the entrails of particle accelerators. And in 1979, the three men shared the Nobel Prize for physics for their work in constructing a successful unification theory for two of nature's four forces.

But in 1979, no one had actually detected the W^-, W^-, and $Z°$, the three massive particles that were an essential ingredient of the electroweak unification. "The Nobel committee really put its reputation on the line," says Glashow, "by awarding the prize for a theory whose principal prediction had not yet been confirmed. It shows they were pretty confident."

Glashow certainly was. At a seminar for science writers held in Cambridge, Massachusetts, in November 1982, he buoyantly forecast the detection of the still theoretical W particles. The forecast was one in a series of "invented tomorrow's headlines for science writers," he explains, "with realistic dates." Datelined December 1982, Geneva, Switzerland, the article read, "Intermediate vector bosons seen by two large collaborations working at the proton-antiproton collider at CERN. According to Carlo Rubbia . . ."

The rest, as they say, is history. In January 1983, a beaming Rubbia announced that his team at CERN, the European Center for Nuclear Research, had indeed found evidence of the W particles— with the mass predicted by the theory. By the spring, not only had the CERN scientists confirmed their observation of the Ws, they had found the predicted Z particle, as well.

One of the other "future headlines" Glashow flashed at science writers that November has not proved so prescient. Datelined February 1983, Ann Arbor, Michigan, it said, "Scientists from Irvine, Michigan, and Brookhaven working at the Morton-Thiokol Salt Mine in Ohio claim 'Diamonds are not forever,' " an epigram coined by Glashow himself some years earlier. It refers to the prediction that the proton, and thus all matter—diamonds, physicists, and galaxies—is unstable.

That prediction, in turn, stems from a number of theories that attempt to combine the electroweak and strong interactions, which would unify three of the four forces, leaving out only gravity. These efforts are known as grand unified theories. The simplest one, invented by Glashow and Howard Georgi at Harvard in 1974, calls for the proton to live to a ripe old age, 10 quadrillion quadrillion years on average—but finally perish. "That's a very long time," says Glashow, "considering the universe is only some ten billion years old."

There are, however, ongoing experiments to test that eventuality, tests that are feasible because they amass enormous numbers of protons and look for the statistical probability that every so often one out of the zillions will be caught decaying. The Ohio experiment, for example, which started in 1982 uses 8,000 tons of water, containing 5,000 quadrillion quadrillion protons. A second three-year-old experiment is underway in a Utah silver mine. And last fall a group of Japanese scientists began their own project.

That "Diamonds are not forever" headline did not appear last February, but Glashow is not dismayed. In November, the Japanese announced preliminary indications of a single proton's decay. If that finding doesn't pan out, Glashow says he is willing to extend his dateline into 1985. "If they don't see any definite events by then, it pretty much rules out the [grand unified theory] in its original form. So I would give the theory, just like a doctor to his patient, one more year."

Asked to survey the present state of the discipline, Glashow says: "This is a very curious time for fundamental physics. We have two guiding principles. One is that the only good theory is a gauge theory. The other," he says with an impish grin, "is that anything is allowed that is not expressly forbidden—like sex in Scandinavia.

"On the one hand, we have this great and generally conceded synthesis. We have a unified electroweak theory and a good [separate] theory of the strong force. This is a revolutionary development. When I first came into physics, we didn't even know what the strong force was. On the other hand, when we try to superimpose on this structure a grand unified theory, we have to go well beyond the energy level of present experiments before we can detect anything interesting."

In essence the grand unified theory predicts the existence of specific new particles and new rules for their interactions—none of which will be manifest until physicists can ram particles together with far greater energy than they can now, transforming some of that energy into these new bits of matter. This infertile interval between experiments conducted at an energy of roughly 500 Gev (billion electron volts) and a grand unification level of one quadrillion Gev has been called "Glashow's desert."

But an accelerator powerful enough to reach beyond the desert would have to be several light-years long and consume the power of more than one sun. "That certainly wouldn't get through the Reagan administration," says Glashow, "and might not even get through a Democratic one.

"What we're learning is that some of nature's secrets may be hidden away at energies that are too high to get at directly. So it will take some tricks—like the proton decay experiment and some others —to find out what's going on. These experiments are windows into the world of very high energies. The most depressing thing would be to learn that nature has no more surprises. I hope that's not true.

"We need to design a next generation of experiments with machines capable of higher energies, to test whether the desert is a mirage, pardon the metaphor, whether there is actually an oasis in the desert, some new and interesting flora to tell us the desert isn't barren. You've got to build bigger machines if only to see that there isn't anything more to see.

"What the world needs, and I'd just as soon have it in this country, is a particle collider like CERN's proton-antiproton collider but with collision energy of twenty thousand Gev instead of five hundred Gev. It's obligatory for this country to have such a machine."

In an address given last year at Texas A&M University, Glashow proposed that just such a device be built in Texas, "because people in Texas think big." This "Texatron" would be about a hundred miles around and cost several billion dollars, rivaling, as one observer put it, the construction of the pyramids, the cathedrals, and the manned space program. Since he proposed it, Glashow has been actively lobbying for the idea and consulting with a consortium of three Texas universities interested in the project. "I'd like to see such a machine within ten years," he says. "It's ridiculous that the Europeans are so far ahead of us."

What Glashow perceives as the dangerously laggard state of American science, technology, and science and math education is a theme he hammers at lustily. "We're living in a technological society, and the people are accustomed to the rights and privileges of high technology, but they are technologically ignorant. We used to be the unquestioned technological hub of the world, but now much of our industry is in terrible trouble. Forget about steel, ships, shoes, stereos, sewing machines. We even buy Polish robots.

"I blame much of this on the quality of math and science teaching in this country. I have many students in my core course at Harvard who are so afraid of anything to do with mathematics or even just numbers that it's like an allergy. You think dyslexia is a problem? This hidden disease of being unable to deal with numbers is both more prevalent and much more serious . . . My oldest son's algebra book has lots about how to multiply and divide polynomials, but at no point does it indicate that you might actually encounter a polynomial in a real situation. The books are awful. When I testified before the House Committee on Science and Technology, I learned that there was a poll among U.S. high school science teachers, asking them whether they felt their undergraduate training prepared them to teach their own courses. Fifty-one percent said no."

Glashow puffs furiously on his cigar, glares at some poor wretch of a teacher who is fortunately not present, then continues:

"When I was a kid, my father told me that he had seen Halley's Comet in 1910. He explained to me that I would see it when it returned in 1985. After 1910, he witnessed a technological explosion in this country—not just telephone and electricity but radio, TV. He told me with great pride that he was sure the Americans would send a probe into space and solve the mystery of what Halley's Comet really was. Had he lived"—and here Glashow pauses for a moment—"had he lived, he would have been very unhappy to know that there will be a Russian, a European, and a Japanese space probe to meet Halley seventy-five years after he saw it, but not an American one."

"Physics in my high school was atrocious," says Glashow. "We used a book that was actually called Dull."

Standing in front of a cramped classroom, Glashow lectures a group of high school physics teachers who have come to sharpen their skills. The lecture is billed as a general overview of physics, but it is obviously more than that. As he leaps to and from the milestones of the past century, he is passionate, his hands are conjuring, his eyes are smiling, and he spouts a constant stream of anecdotes and one-liners.

He recasts Rutherford's discovery that the atom is a relatively airy thing with a small hard center as "The Parable of the Peach," in which a little boy sitting under a peach tree—"or perhaps one of the little boy's graduate students"—infers the existence of the pit by shooting BBs up into the tree.

He calls the official panel that establishes international units of measure "filthy pigs" for having chosen two unrelated sets of units for electric and magnetic fields—which are really parts of a single phenomenon.

Toward the end of the two-hour performance, he suggests a couple of classroom experiments guaranteed to get students excited. "One of my favorites involves dropping a basketball with a tennis ball poised on top of it. What happens every time is spectacular. After one bounce the tennis ball hits the ceiling!" And then there's a neat and simple stunt showing how gases of different densities affect the vibration of vocal cords. "All you need," says Glashow, "is a little helium . . ."

4

MARGARET MEAD

AN INDOMITABLE PRESENCE

by Boyce Rensberger

Margaret Mead wouldn't have been fazed for a minute. Not by this charge that she made some serious mistakes in her very first anthropological study, a book she wrote more than half a century ago. Mead spent her whole life wading eagerly into controversial issues. She preached peace and harmony, but she could never stay out of a juicy intellectual fray.

Were she alive to hear these new criticisms, raised by Australian anthropologist Derek Freeman, her reaction would be predictable. She would listen as long as she could, her head propped against the back of one hand. The fire would begin to burn in her eyes. Her tongue would dart out in quick, serpentlike licks. Finally, the ever-present forked stick would shoot up to draw the audience's attention.

"Oh, fiddlesticks!" she would interrupt, like a grandmother who had heard enough from impudent children. "Just plain fiddlesticks!"

She could win over the whole house like that—win their hearts first and then, having established her advantage in age with a deliberately antiquated expression, she would work on their minds.

Nobody liked to cross Margaret Mead. She was, after all, a legend in her own lifetime. She was perhaps most widely known as a champion of the causes of the youth movement in the sixties, but she had been a major force in anthropology from the beginning, ever since 1928. That was when she published *Coming of Age in Samoa,* the book Freeman now says is all wrong.

The issue for Freeman, as it happens, is not so much Margaret Mead herself as it is the controversy that launched Mead's career—the intellectual debate that sent Mead to Samoa. This was the question of whether the patterns of human social behavior are innate, fixed in the genes like bipedalism or speech, or whether these patterns are created anew in each generation, shaped into distinctive forms by local customs and teachings. This was the original nature-nurture debate, and Mead's book, her anthropological debut, would become one of the most powerful weapons used to silence the genetic determinists and inaugurate the long domination of cultural determinism in Western thought. The rise of sociobiology in recent years, reasserting a role for genes in human behavior, has only rekindled that old debate. The original controversy was in full cry early in the century when a twenty-one-year-old Margaret Mead was working on a master's degree in psychology.

During her senior year at Barnard College, Mead had taken an anthropology course from Franz Boas, a charismatic, German-born physicist who switched to anthropology and imposed a new degree of scientific rigor on a previously undisciplined field. For one thing, Boas insisted that anthropologists ought to collect data by visiting other cultures and not merely spin theories based on reports of explorers and tourists. Boas was a leader in the battle against the new genetic determinist movement that had arisen shortly after the rediscovery of Gregor Mendel's pea-breeding experiments. Early Mendelians insisted that all human traits, including broad behavioral patterns, were genetic, rooted in nature. Boas argued to the contrary, stressing the richness of cultural diversity, which he said was evidence that behavioral differences were rooted in nurture.

Mead was greatly impressed by Boas and by his teaching assistant, Ruth Benedict, who herself would become one of the giants of American anthropology. One day Mead asked Benedict for advice on whether to become a psychologist, a sociologist, or an anthropologist. "Professor Boas and I," Mead remembers Benedict saying, "have nothing to offer but an opportunity to do work that matters." That was all Mead needed to hear. From her childhood in rural Bucks County, Pennsylvania—her father was a professor of economics at the nearby University of Pennsylvania, and her mother had a degree in sociology—Mead had developed a strong interest in the peoples and events of the larger world. In college Mead was interested in feminism and radical politics. She *wanted* her life to matter. Mead set to work on her doctorate in anthropology under Boas—Papa Franz, as his followers called him.

During the 1920s, the nature-nurture debate grew ugly, as many geneticists embraced eugenics, a movement that sought to improve the human species through selective breeding. Eugenicists advocated such things as sterilizing "inferior" individuals, preserving "racial purity," and restricting immigration of "less developed" ethnic and racial groups. Boas opposed the eugenicists vigorously, but he needed more ammunition, and in Margaret Mead he saw a way to get it.

Boas knew that adolescence was widely considered to be an inescapably difficult phase of life, a time of psychological crisis and behavioral turbulence. If he could cite some other culture in which children were raised differently and then sailed effortlessly through adolescence, it would be very difficult for the eugenicists to maintain that all behavioral patterns were innate and unchangeable. Boas asked Mead to look for such a situation among American Indian tribes.

Mead was willing, but she had her heart set on Polynesia. She already realized that to make a name for herself in anthropology, she had to have her own "people," a culture no other anthropologist had yet studied. Boas thought a remote Pacific island was too risky for a young woman. He refused permission; Mead refused to yield. At this impasse, Mead tried a tactic that years later she would acknowledge was a deliberate attempt to manipulate two powerful men into serving her own interest. She told her father that Boas was trying to force her to do research in which she was not interested. Mead's father offered to pay for a trip around the world with time for a lengthy stopover in Polynesia. When Boas realized that Mead would make the trip anyway, he relented.

In the summer of 1925 Mead got her shots, packed her clothes, a portable typewriter, notebooks, carbon paper, and a camera. She also vacationed with the husband she had married two years earlier but from whom she became emotionally estranged. As Mead tells the story in her autobiography, *Blackberry Winter,* Luther Cressman was her childhood sweetheart; they were engaged for five years, but after barely two years of marriage, they drifted apart.

Just twenty-three years old, Margaret Mead set sail for Samoa and her first visit to another culture. After a few weeks at a hotel in Pago Pago, learning a smattering of the Samoan language, Mead moved to the smaller island of Ta'u for her studies. She lived with the family of an American medical officer at the local dispensary. Each day she went about the village, looking for adolescent girls who would tell her about their sexual behavior. Nine months later, Mead went back to New York, accepted a post at the American Museum of Natural History—which remained her base of operations until her death—and wrote her report.

Coming of Age in Samoa was like no other anthropologist's report, and it was to change not only Mead's life but the course of American anthropology. It could have been written by a novelist:

> The life of the day begins at dawn, or if the moon has shone until daylight, the shouts of the young men may be heard before dawn from the hillside. Uneasy in the night, populous with ghosts, they shout lustily to one another as

they hasten with their work. As the dawn begins to fall among the soft brown roofs and the slender palm trees stand out against the colorless, gleaming sea, lovers slip home from trysts beneath the palm trees or in the shadows of beached canoes, that the light may find each sleeper in his appointed place. Cocks crow, negligently, and a shrill-voiced bird cries from the breadfruit trees. The insistent roar of the reef seems muted to an undertone for the sounds of a waking village.

This is hardly the usual language of anthropological science, and it certainly was not in 1928 when it was first published. Along with such idyllic descriptions, Mead described the lives of Samoan young people, focusing largely on the sexual freedom she said young people enjoyed. Mead wrote:

> Familiarity with sex, and the recognition of a need of a technique to deal with sex as an art, have produced a scheme of personal relations in which there are no neurotic pictures, no frigidity, no impotence, except as the temporary result of severe illness, and the capacity for intercourse only once in a night is counted as senility.

One reason Samoans knew nothing of sexual problems, Mead said, was that they never really got deeply involved with their sexual partners. "Samoans rate romantic fidelity in terms of days or weeks at most, and are inclined to scoff at tales of life-long devotion," she wrote. In fact, Mead claimed Samoans had no intense feelings about much of anything.

This easygoing way of life led to an adolescence quite different from that of American youth, but it was precisely the kind of adolescence Papa Franz needed to make his case. Mead wrote:

> With the exception of the few cases to be discussed in the next chapter, adolescence represented no period of crisis or stress, but was instead an orderly developing of a set of slowly maturing interests and activities. The girls' minds were perplexed by no conflicts, troubled by no philosophical queries, beset by no remote ambitions. To live as a girl with many lovers as long as possible and then to marry in one's own village, near one's relatives and to have many children, these were uniform and satisfying ambitions.

Mead did find some examples of "deviant" and "delinquent" young people, but these were put into a separate category and quite disregarded in Mead's overall conclusions. She wrote:

> The Samoan background which makes growing up so easy, so simple a matter, is the general casualness of the whole society. For Samoa is a place where no one plays for very high stakes, no one pays very heavy prices, no one suffers for his convictions or fights to the death for special ends.

Coming of Age in Samoa easily gave Boas the "negative stance" he needed to counter the eugenicists. The book became a major weapon in the battle, helping to weaken support from intellectuals. But Mead won broader acclaim from the anthropological world both for her methods in probing so deeply into the Samoan mind and for her focus on the way children are brought up. Until Mead went to Samoa, children and women were largely ignored by anthropologists. The question of how a society inculcates its values and traditions in its new members was hardly even asked.

Indeed, though Mead never again studied Samoa, the die was cast. Major themes in the rest of Mead's scientific career would include the ways in which children are brought up, the role of culture in shaping personality, and, on a broader scale, how whole cultures cope with the transition to modern technologies and values.

Outside anthropology *Coming of Age* had an even greater effect. It became a best seller, aided, no doubt, by its frank advocacy of sexual freedom, couched in a scientific context. The book thrust Mead into prominence in American intellectual affairs, a position she would occupy for the next half century. In the book, Mead drew direct contrasts between Samoa and the United States and suggested that Americans consider adopting some of the ways of Samoa. These were the Roaring Twenties, and people who were already deep into the growing revolt against Victorian attitudes on sexuality and child rearing welcomed Mead as a scientific backer of their cause. Anthropologists tended to dismiss these parts of the book, one calling it "pedagogical sermonizing."

Derek Freeman's attack on this fifty-five-year-old book, then, is more than a footnote to anthropological history. It is a challenge to what was once hailed within academe as part of the scientific basis for cultural determinism and, in the larger world, for the sexual revolution of the 1920s and 1930s.

Where Mead saw an adolescence of ease and tranquillity, Freeman saw teenagers every bit as rebellious and troubled as those of the industrialized world. Where Mead saw a sexual freedom that banished everything from impotence and frigidity to rape ("The idea of forcible rape," Mead had written, "was completely foreign to the Samoan mind"), Freeman saw a puritanical attitude toward sex and even a cult of virginity in a society where rape was twice as common as in the United States. Freeman's data refer to a more modern Samoa, but, he says, if Mead were interested in Samoan rape, she should not have missed the *Samoan Times*'s regular reports on rape cases in 1925 and 1926, the years Mead was there.

On the central question of the nature of adolescence—the reason Mead went to Samoa—Freeman finds some of the evidence to refute Mead's conclusion right in her own book. These were the girls Mead counted as exceptions and relegated to a separate chapter where they would not interfere with the book's broad conclusions.

"Mead," Freeman writes, "was at error in her depiction of the nature of adolescence in Samoa, just as she was in her portrayal of other crucial aspects of Samoan life. This being so, her assertion in *Coming of Age in Samoa* of the absolute sovereignty of culture over biology is clearly invalid."

Freeman attributes Mead's conclusions to youth and inexperience. Mead once acknowledged that Boas had given her only a half hour's instruction in field methods before she set sail. Freeman also cites Mead's preexisting belief in Boasian cultural determinism. He thinks that the young girls Mead interviewed—her main source of information—simply told their young visitor what they thought she wanted to hear.

Mead was well aware of these problems *after* she wrote the book. Many anthropologists have challenged *Coming of Age,* though none as broadly as Freeman. Mead was also aware that her interpretation of Samoa differed radically from that of others. In a 1969 scientific paper, not one written for popular consumption, she conceded that it was hard to reconcile the "contradictions" between *Coming of Age* and evidence from "other records of historical and contemporary behavior." But she always refused to revise the book. "To revise it would be impossible," Mead wrote in the preface to the 1973 edition.

It must remain, as all anthropological works must remain, exactly as it was written, true to what I saw in Samoa and what I was able to convey of what I saw." Mead adds that the books was "true to the state of our knowledge of human behavior as it was in the mid-1920s," and in an apparent allusion to the uglier threats of the eugenics movement, Mead said the book was "true to our hopes and fears for the future of the world.

Mead did, however, recant her assertion in *Coming of Age* that "a trained student can master the fundamental structure of a primitive society in a few months." In later life she conceded this would actually take decades.

It is rather common for cultural anthropologists to arrive at differing interpretations of the same culture. Each comes with distinctive preconceptions that filter perceptions in the field. One classic contradiction involved the Mexican peasants of Tepoztlan. Robert Redfield's 1930 study said their society was easygoing, unflappable, harmonious. Oscar Lewis studied the same people in 1951 and found them preoccupied with interpersonal strife and serious crime. Because of such problems, many social scientists regard most cross-cultural studies as tentative at best.

For Margaret Mead, however, such matters were second-generation issues, questions that occur to followers, not leaders. Even before *Coming of Age* was published the first time, Mead had already moved on, personally and professionally. Had she never gone to Samoa, any of her next few books would have established her as an anthropologist of the first rank.

On the long boat trip back from Samoa in 1926 Mead met a young New Zealand psychologist, Reo Fortune, whom she would later marry. From this point on, Mead's style of fieldwork changed. No longer would she take on a new and strange culture alone; she would work in partnership—first in New Guinea with Fortune and, six years later, in Bali with Gregory Bateson, her third and last husband.

One of the interests Mead shared with Fortune was psychology, in particular Sigmund Freud's idea that the minds of adults in "primitive" societies are like those of children in "civilized" societies. Civilized adults, the theory goes, outgrow the belief in magic and other nonrational thinking processes that are typical of children. It was a widely accepted theory.

But, Mead realized, it had never been tested. If it were true, what would primitive children be like? It seemed a logical extension of her work with Samoan adolescents, but Mead and Fortune chose to try a different society, the Admiralty Islands off the New Guinea coast, home of the Manus people. To study the mental processes of children, Mead pioneered the use of psychological tests—making certain kinds of drawings, in this case. She found no hint of magical or irrational thinking either among the children or the adults.

After six months, Mead and Fortune finished their work at Manus, and to the mournful beat of funeral drums—traditionally sounded at the loss of a great person—they were paddled away in canoes. Her interpretation of Manus culture would become another book, *Growing Up in New Guinea*. Twenty-five years later, Mead would return to Manus, beginning a series of five emotional revisits over the years —scenarios that gradually lost their narrow anthropological significance as they took on a more personal meaning for Mead and *her* people.

As an anthropologist, Mead moved from one pioneering innovation to another. She was the first anthropologist not only to study how children grow up but to compare child-rearing practices and other roles of women in various cultures. She was a founder of the "culture and personality" school of anthropology, which examines the ways a culture shapes an individual's personality. And she was a major force, along with Bateson, in the development of visual anthropology—the use of photography, and eventually video, to document vanishing cultures.

At the time, however, Mead's origination of new methods and concepts stirred controversy and sometimes resentment among her scientific colleagues. So did the easy-to-read, jargon-free writing style of her books, which numbered some two dozen. From the first, Mead reached beyond her profession to the public at large, especially to Americans and to young people.

Mead's appeal to the young alarmed conservative parents with its advocacy of legalized marijuana, greater sexual freedom, and even two-stage marriages. In fact, her role as guru to the youth movement ran deeper. She saw all the world's cultures evolving to an unprecedented stage in which the young rightfully had as much to say about their futures as their parents, if not more. Until modern times, Mead observed, young people could anticipate a future rather like that of their parents. Social change was that slow. Now young people face futures for which their parents' culture cannot prepare them. The young, she said on campus after campus, must create the future themselves. It was a message in which the youth of the sixties and seventies could find respect and hope. And it was all the more rewarding because Mead, rather than identifying with the young, spoke as a wise grandmother.

As Mead grew older, she grew busier. She became such a frequent guest on radio and television shows that she joined the American Federation of Television and Radio Artists, guaranteeing herself union-scale pay for each appearance. She gave scores of lectures every year on almost every conceivable subject—there was nothing she would not talk about, friends say. A partial list of subjects includes world hunger, pollution, mental health, the women's movement, tribal customs, military duty, alcoholism, city planning, child development, population control, art, and, of course, sex. A covert philanthropist, Mead channeled most of the earnings from her books and lectures into the foundation she started to help struggling young anthropologists, the Institute for Intercultural Studies. In the last years of her life, the Institute received nearly $40,000 in royalties from her books alone.

Through the fading days of October 1978 Mead lay dying in a private room on an upper floor of New York Hospital. She liked the room because from the window she could see, twenty-three blocks to the south, the United Nations headquarters—meeting place of the world's cultures, nucleus, she liked to think, of the "global village" she had long prophesied. Mead had been told that she had cancer of the pancreas and that her time was short.

Word spread quickly among Mead's inner circle, and many traveled to her bedside for a last visit. What some of them saw when they entered the hospital room has largely been hushed up during the four years since. Hovering over the patient, who not only had become one of the world's best known scientists but was once elected leader of the entire American scientific community, was a Chilean woman touching, softly massaging the diseased regions of Mead's body.

The woman was a faith healer or, as some preferred, a psychic healer. She was a friend whom Mead had asked to perform her mysterious rituals even as the seventy-six-year-old scientist lay in one of medicine's premier hospitals. Mead considered the Chilean woman a modern equivalent of the shamans and witch doctors that she had known in so many traditional cultures.

After fifty-three years studying exotic rituals and strange ways of thinking, Mead was turning her skills as a "participant observer" to the ultimate human act, her own final rite of passage. "My mother always tried to observe her own actions objectively," recalls Mary Catherine Bateson, Mead's only child, "but I think it's fair to say that she had difficulty facing the fact that she was dying."

By the time Mead entered the hospital, her cancer had progressed so far that even the doctors did not recommend heroic measures. Mead, however, was not finished with life. She reached out to every source of hope, as well as scheduling her visitors and her work periods for the lucid hours between periods of pain and knockout doses of pain-killers.

"Margaret was hoping she would live," recalls Wilton Dillon, an official of the Smithsonian Institution who was a close friend and one of the pilgrims at her bedside. "She was assuring herself she would live. She was pouring all of her faith into the future—even planning another trip to the South Seas. But all the while she wasn't being fooled for a moment."

Dillon says some of Mead's friends were afraid her scientific reputation would be damaged if it got out that she was consulting a faith healer. "There are people who didn't want this known publicly," Dillon says, "but I think it was a case of Margaret being willing to tolerate any source of information or help."

On November 15, the first day of the 1978 annual meeting of the American Anthropological Association and the day the *World Almanac* named her one of the world's twenty-five most influential women, Margaret Mead died.

5
GERALD WASSERBURG

TIMEKEEPER OF THE SOLAR SYSTEM

by Leo Janos

The Charles Arms Laboratory of Geological Sciences is almost lost in a jumble of imposing brick and glass structures on the campus of the California Institute of Technology in Pasadena, California. It is a diminutive building of gray stone, more nearly resembling a Victorian gentlemen's club than a center for geology and planetary studies. Above double doors in the center of its second floor hallway is an engraved brass sign boldly announcing: THE LUNATIC ASYLUM. In front of the doors are six or seven pairs of empty shoes patiently awaiting their owners, who are locked inside. The asylum's keeper arrives with three dozen keys linked to his belt. He is a dark-haired, intense, middle-aged man with a paunch and a slight stoop to his strong shoulders.

"Shoes off," he commands, and leads his visitor directly into the men's room on the left. "Wash up," he orders. "Special nonalkaline soap. There's more particles of silver, magnesium, or God knows what on your hands and shoes than we investigate in a year," he says. The right key turns in the lock, and the moment the door to the asylum opens, instead of an alarm, the sound of a Bach fugue fills the hallway. "Music," the keeper says, "is the best security device there is." Moments later we stand togged in white nylon, hands gloved, head capped, ready to enter the clean rooms of the most famous rock-dating laboratory in the world.

Gerald Wasserburg, keeper of this self-proclaimed asylum, opens the door to a gleaming, sterile lab. "Our moon-rock room," he says. Sealed inside plastic containers, the small fragments of moon rock brought back from six Apollo and three Soviet unmanned missions look like pieces of ordinary basalt. Wasserburg calls attention to a glass cabinet where there are several sealed beakers no larger than salt shakers.

"Stardust," he says proudly.

High-flying *U-2* aircraft from NASA, equipped with special fly-paper devices, have brought back from the thin reaches of the upper atmosphere samples of interplanetary dust. These barely visible particles are believed to be the spoor of comets that coincide with or predate the formation of the solar system. Wasserburg and other "inmates" of his lunatic lab are analyzing such grains of stardust hoping to determine precisely when and how the solar system was created.

Many scientists now believe that the solar system may have been seeded by the explosion of a supernova star some 4.6 billion years ago. Shock waves from this gigantic burst of energy are thought to have compressed vast clouds of interstellar gas and dust into the clumps of matter out of which comets, planets, moons, and our own sun formed. Some of this supernova stardust and gas, chiefly the heavier elements, became trapped in the nascent planetary material. The discovery of this anomalous matter by various scientists led directly to this new theory of solar-system birth.

For example, in 1980 one of the scientist-"inmates" of the Lunatic Asylum, Franz Niederer, announced the first finding of a peculiar form of the metal titanium, which is believed to have originated within the solar system's parent supernova. This material is 2 to 3 million years older than the oldest rocks ever found, even the 4.5-billion-year-old rocks gathered on the moon. With characteristic enthusiasm for the quest he pursues, the Lunatic Asylum's keeper describes this work as "probably the most exciting thing any of us will ever work on."

The asylum is acknowledged by the scientific community to be the best of its kind in the world. Simply put, Wasserburg and his colleagues have become the precise timekeepers for the milestone events in our solar system. Over the past fifteen years, Wasserburg's lab has produced some of the most accurate and significant measurements in the history of geophysics, including dating the earth, moon, meteorites, and the birth stages of the solar system.

The basis for the dating system lies in the natural process of radioactive decay. At the turn of this century, the founders of nuclear physics discovered that nearly all atoms come in several forms called isotopes.

Some of these isotopes are radioactive and spontaneously disintegrate into new atoms. The key for dating purposes is that this decay takes place at a fixed pace that does not vary because of

chemical or physical changes that the element might undergo. Once
a radioactive atom is created anywhere in the universe, it begins to
tick away like a finely tuned clock. In order to read this clock one
must count the number of new atoms, called *daughter* elements, that
have been created from the old atoms, the *parent* elements. Once this
daughter-to-parent ratio is established, Wasserburg and other masters
of the dating game use the known rate of radioactive decay to
calculate backward to the time when there were only parent atoms
in a sample. That is when the sample's radioactive clock started; in
other words, its birth date.

Or so goes the theory. In practice, it is far more difficult. For
example, the first radioactive process used to date earth rocks was the
decay of uranium into lead. But lead from other, earlier sources may
be present at the time the rock formed, complicating the issue. Also,
if the sample has remelted since it first was created, daughter elements can escape from the sample and thus yield an incorrect age.
In earth rocks, water can dissolve some of the lead produced by
uranium decay and carry it away, leading to an underestimate of the
rock's age. Other daughter products are gaseous, and the gas can
diffuse out of a rock, again leading to a false age for the sample.
Thus, the need for selecting samples in which the radioactive clocks
have not been reset must be coupled with absolute precision in every
step. It is a tough, nerve-racking game.

The Lunatic Asylum's measurements of bits and pieces of meteorites and minute cosmic fragments have significantly altered theories
about the solar system's creation. This new evidence indicates that
the sun and planets were created in an astonishingly brief period—
within 3 to 10 million years.

"Working small allows us to think big," say Wasserburg, professor
of geology and geophysics. "If our measurements and interpretations
are correct—and our measurements surely are—then the solar
system was formed from a dense cloud that had over sixteen thousand
hydrogen atoms per cubic inch. Secondly, large stars—twenty times
larger than our sun—were exploding like superfirecrackers, filling
enormous volumes of space with debris. And all of this happened not
for a period of some one hunderd and sixty million years, as
previously supposed, but practically overnight. Now that's a mighty
potent story derived from a few specks and grains of dust and rock,
but that's where we are."

The irrefutable numbers flowing from Wasserburg's lab are challenging theoreticians in a half-dozen scientific disciplines to provide
a new text to the solar system's Book of Genesis. Pet theories are
simply no match for Jerry Wasserburg's sophisticated machines,

which can precisely analyze the trace constituents of pieces of matter as small as three microns. One micron is one millionth of a meter, the width of a blood corpuscle. Wasserburg's new and vastly improved versions of the old mass spectrometer, originally developed in the 1920s, have revolutionized the field. The spectrometric process measures amounts of radioactive atoms in a sample by converting them to charged particles and accelerating the particles through a magnetic field that deflects them according to their charge, mass, and speed.

As a physics and geology student at the University of Chicago in the early fifties, Wasserburg used prototype machines invented for the Manhattan Project—the World War II atomic bomb program. Crude by today's standards, they sufficed for more than two decades. After President John Kennedy vowed to man the moon by the end of the 1960s, the lure of being able to examine lunar rocks prompted Wasserburg, along wih coworkers Victor Nenow, Curt Bauman, and Dimitri Papanastassiou, to devote six years of intense labor to building a new and highly refined spectrometer.

"From late 1963 until the switches were turned on in 1969, I was nothing but a plumber," says the scientist. "But all the detailed, tender loving care in assembly resulted in perfection. The machine hasn't been improved on yet."

Wasserburg's new and improved model of the mass spectrometer is an invention whose appearance belies its dramatic results. Two of them sit on tabletops in one equipment-cluttered room of the Lunatic Asylum, looking like pairs of oversized pressure cookers connected by shiny tubes passing through a large magnet, painted fire-engine red, and plugged into banks of electronic controls and computers. A tablet on the base of one in the far corner of the room proudly proclaims, "Lunatic I." Soon after *Apollo 11* returned from the moon, this spectrometer was fed a few grains of lunar rock and rewarded science with the precise age and early history of the earth's nearest neighbor.

"The Holy Grail" is how Wasserburg describes the 800 pounds of rock returned by the Apollo missions. It was, in fact, the laboratory's first published paper on its analysis of the lunar samples that led to the naming of the Lunatic Asylum. "This was a big-deal historic paper of the first magnitude," Wasserburg says, "and I was stymied to find a way to credit a total of ten coworkers that wasn't self-consciously alphabetical. Then it dawned on me that the late Curt Bauman had nicknamed our first new spectrometer 'Lunartic,' anticipating its use dating moon rocks. Well, we work in a nuthouse and were affected by the moon, so I decided to call ourselves the

Lunatic Asylum. I sent the paper to *Science*. The material dated the moon at 4.45 billion years, same age as the earth. Not a trivial paper, but they were very unhappy about the 'Lunatic Asylum of the California Institute of Technology. The inmates are . . .—' that's how I listed the credits. Well, I told them what I've told every other publisher since. That's our name, and if you want to run the paper, you'll use it. I now get mail from around the world addressed to the Lunatic Asylum, California."

"The important point about Jerry," says Caltech nuclear astrophysicist and Nobel Prize winner William A. Fowler, "is not only that he built a truly great lab but that he knows what to do with it. He chooses the significant problems and produces the most accurate and important measurements for addressing these problems. His accomplishments are incredible."

Nevertheless, Wasserburg seethes at past snubs. "One of my colleagues once said about me, 'Well, he's not doing great creative science; he's just worried about making equipment.' That's a goddam insult. I've been called a machinist and a pipe fitter. My spectrometer cost $200,000 to build, and the National Science Foundation turned me down for a grant at the time, thinking the project was an extravagance. The snobbishness in science that places ideas completely over technology impedes real growth," he grouses with typical irreverence.

Installing a Wasserburg instrument is no guarantee of producing Wasserburg results. "The point often lost about his dating of the lunar samples," says Arden Albee, chief scientist at NASA's Jet Propulsion Laboratory and a lunar-sample collaborator of Wasserburg's, "was that Jerry's skill with a microscope enabled him to select the critical samples for analysis. He is a great scientist."

The success of the Lunatic Asylum is in its totality of skills. Measured against the craft and dedication necessary for working expertly with minuscule specks, precision apparatus is almost incidental. Imagine sitting at a microscope for a week to pick out individual crystals from a snippet of rock no bigger than a grain of salt and efficiently separating the brown ones from the whites ones, without contaminating the sample. Next, complex and sophisticated chemical procedures must be performed to separate the particular kind of elements to be studied. The smaller the sample, the better the chance to avoid contamination. Routinely, Wasserburg's lab uses the surface tension of a droplet as a mixing beaker. "We work with things that are harder than most people want to work with," he says. "Frankly, working small can be emotionally repugnant in its tension and demands."

Wasserburg neither appears nor acts like a casting office concept of someone who is director of the world's most prestigious rock-dating laboratory. "He looks like he's coming apart," says his friend William Fowler. "Here's this rumpled, prickly cactus, wearing a Western string tie, smoking with an FDR cigarette holder, cussing like a drill sergeant, ogling pretty women, exploding like a string of Chinese firecrackers, who also happens to be the most precise measurement maker in the world." All who know him well acknowledge the depth of Wasserburg's warm and emotional nature.

Both of his offices, at home and at the lab, are obviously the preserves of a pack rat, hoarding mounds of papers and rebelling against the self-imposed neatness and precision of his clean laboratory rooms. To get from one office to another, Wasserburg travels in a 1966 skyblue Mercedes-Benz with a large, silver Star of David above the grill, a surprise birthday gift from his wife, Naomi. His home office, a fifteen-minute drive from the Caltech campus, is a two-room suite separate from the large, rambling house and overlooking a modest swimming pool. On one wall are the framed certificates of his numerous honors, including NASA's highest award given to people outside of the agency, its Distinguished Public Service Medal, awarded to him in 1972 and 1978.

The first time Wasserburg won, he was called out of an earlymorning shower in a motel near the Manned Spacecraft Center in Houston to receive the telephoned news from Washington. "I stood dripping wet and bare-assed in front of a full-length mirror and cried," he told a friend at the time. "I felt I was so lucky." He still is unable to speak about the NASA awards without a quaver in his voice. Five years of his life were devoted to helping to plan the science of the Apollo space programs, and he is generally credited with having won the most significant victories after staging the bloodiest battles to ensure the continuation of the Apollo missions and the ample scientific returns from those missions. "At times," he admits, "I was ruthless, and the battles severely tested my determination and character."

Wasserburg's volatile temper is legendary, and heading the list of incendiary devices certain to ignite his two-micron fuse is the misspelling of his name. More complex than any isotopic anomaly, Wasserburg is disarmingly candid, if not unnecessarily harsh, in assessing his personality. "I'm an egomaniac . . . I'm scientifically compulsive. When I achieve something important, I get a high that lasts exactly two weeks; then depression sets in, and it's time to get back on the treadmill. Bad toilet training, I guess. I'm unconstrained; when I think somebody is full of crap, I say so. My scientific career has caused my family to suffer more than I can ever imagine. Besides being gone for long periods of time, my mind is off in space even when I'm at home. My wife has put up with a lot. Our two sons must feel a kind of lonesome hostility mixed with their respect for my accomplishments. At work, I'm a very difficult SOB, and that's not a character recommendation I'm particularly proud of. I feel guilty very often, but I'm so difficult that no one works for me unless they're good enough and tough enough. I explode all the time. I'm like the office plague; I snoop into everything, and everyone wishes I'd stay out so I don't screw it up. But that lab is my baby."

Wasserburg's colleagues rate him extraordinarily high as a selfless scientist. Many of his numerous lobbying trips to Washington are on behalf of projects in which he has no direct vested interest. His efforts on behalf of NASA's space telescope, for example, amount to a single-minded crusade. While Caltech students who do not know him may tremble at the mention of his name, Wasserburg's research fellows, comprising the best and brightest graduate students from seven or eight countries, regard him as a lovable tyrant. "He's like a very demanding father," one of them says. "His expectations for my success transcend even my own. Everyone who's recruited is told, 'This is the best damn lab in the world, doing the most exciting stuff in the world. If you're not famous by the time you leave here, it will be my fault."

"Big deal" is one of Wasserburg's favorite expressions, and he uses it mostly in its enthusiastic rather than cynical context, as, for example, "Right now, in our meteorite studies, we're trying to find iron atoms that originated deep inside a large star that was not our sun. Now that's a big deal." He tackles only big deals. "I want to lay out the evolution of the solar system and the cosmic connection of the solar system to the galaxy. I can die happy if I make a substantial contribution." Chances are, he will.

These not inconsiderable ambitions were formed during a lonely, troubled boyhood, growing up as a lower-middle-class Jewish kid in the small New Jersey town of New Brunswick. Einstein, then at nearby Princeton, was Wasserburg's moral and intellectual hero. Early on, he became fascinated with rock collecting, inspired by a Rutgers geology professor who took neighborhood children out on collection trips. "By ten, I was hooked. My collection was my little piece of private beauty in a world that wasn't too pretty." Hot-tempered and rebellious, he enlisted in the army and, after returning from combat in Europe, spent time in a stateside prison stockade for insubordination. Authority, it seems, always rankled. He returned home with gallantry decorations determined to be a hard-rock geologist and applied to Rutgers under the G.I. Bill. But Wasserburg was at first thwarted by an aptitude test that purported to disclose that he had no scientific aptitude whatsoever.

"I sat under a tree on the Rutgers campus—I was a combat vet, no longer a child—but I wept like a baby," he recalls. "Then I got furious at this ridiculous psychologist who had administered the test. I charged back into her office and told her that I didn't give a damn what she said. I was going to be a geologist, and she could take her test and shove it. They finally agreed to let this crazy psycho into the program.

"I flunked geometry three times in high school," he admits, "and I dropped out of qualitative analysis at Rutgers. Just damned awful. I'm not a very good chemist even now." Ultimately, he transferred to the University of Chicago, then at the height of its golden age, and decided to earn his first degree in physics. "The idea was to learn this stuff so I could solve important problems in geology."

This was in the late 1940s and early 1950s. His professors included Enrico Fermi, Harold Urey, and Edward Teller. Willard Libby was dating with carbon 14, and Harrison Brown was speculating about the formation of the solar system. "There was a sense of excellence, of tough front-rank stuff, where the cutting edge was." Nobel Prize winner Urey and another mentor, Mark Inghram, suggested the subject of Wasserburg's doctoral thesis, which was a major advance in how to measure the age of meteoritic rocks by analyzing the daughter products (argon) of radioactive potassium.

By the time he graduated from Chicago, Wasserburg's career was rooted in mass spectrometry, experimental physics, and chemistry and immersed in the basic problems of the solar-system time scale. He was recruited for Caltech, where a geochemistry group was being formed. Since that time, Wasserburg and his asylum colleagues have been responsible for more than four hundred research papers, all of them stamped with the hallmark of precision, many of them milestones of geophysical advances.

Without question, one of the most important events in Wasserburg's life occurred in the fall of 1969, while he impatiently waited for the first lunar samples to arrive. A giant meteor lit the skies over northern Mexico and rained down on a small hamlet named Allende. Quickly told of the event by a NASA friend, Wasserburg drove to the Los Angeles airport to pick up his mother, who was arriving for a visit. He deposited her at home, hurriedly packed his bags, and low on traveling cash, smashed his sons' piggy banks. "Ma," he said, "lend me two hundred bucks." She agreed but first made him sign an IOU. He was off to Allende.

"Mind blowing," he recalls. "The biggest deal imaginable."

Wasserburg and many other researchers laboriously recovered two tons of meteoritic debris that had scattered over 100 square miles of the Mexican landscape. The meteorite was of a rare type known as a carbonaceous chondrite, containing large amounts of carbon and peculiar inclusions (small, embedded particles). "The minute I picked up a chunk, I knew it was special," recalls the scientist. "There were pink and white inclusions. God, seeing a fresh fall is a very big deal. You spend all your life laboring on materials from museum collections, and to actually discover a chunk in a backyard, to pull it out of the ground and see where the grass was pushed in under it— absolutely a thrill of a lifetime. Meteorites are busted pieces of stained-glass windows—windows that let you look back in time."

Returning to Pasadena with sixty pounds of Allende meteorite, Wasserburg barely had time to examine it before the first lunar samples arrived. In 1973, he and his brilliant, longtime collaborator, Athens-born physicist Dimitri Papanastassiou, offered the first detailed analysis of the Allende meteorite and showed it to be the oldest known object in the solar system. "It took us two years, but by strontium isotopic data we clearly demonstrated that it was older than 4.6 billion years; we couldn't measure backward to say exactly how old, but it had to be between two and ten million years older than anything found before.

"The moment you move back a couple of million years, the possibilities explode and expose a new world," says Wasserburg.

Evidence of radioactive elements such as aluminum 26 could be found in the meteorite. The common form of aluminum, aluminum 27, has an additional neutron and is stable, not radioactive. The significance of aluminum 26, explains Wasserburg, is rooted in one of Harold Urey's old puzzlements: how were the small planets melted? The logical explanation would be a rapid melting caused by an abundant, short-lived radioactive element that gives up heat as it decays. Aluminum 26 was a prime candidate, since its half-life, the time it takes for half of a radioactive isotope to decay into its daughter elements, is extremely short, only 740,000 years. Hence, it gives up its heat very quickly. But since the element was thought extinct, it was relegated to pure speculation. Magnesium 26 is the daughter of the decayed aluminum 26 parent. The problem confronting researchers over the years is that very few atoms of the total magnesium in nature are produced by aluminum decay. But in 1976 and 1977, Wasserburg, Papanastassiou, and another coworker, Typhoon Lee, found enough magnesium 26 in a piece of the Allende meteorite to prove that aluminum 26 did indeed exist at the time some objects were forming in the early solar system.

The significance is that in order to produce such effects, vast quantities of nuclear matter, such as aluminum 26, would have had to be freshly manufactured in a presolar-system supernova and injected very rapidly into the nascent planetary cloud. It also means that the small planets would have to have formed very quickly, before the aluminum 26 decayed. "The amounts are such that the radioactive aluminum has to be the dominant source of making charged particles in the interstellar medium," says Wasserburg. Further discovery, with William R. Kelly, of a palladium isotope thought to be extinct showed that there was a bonanza of rare nuclides yet to be found. This isotope has now been shown to be widespread in small planets, confirming that they did, in fact, form rapidly. "The isotopic and astronomical discoveries of the past decade dovetail perfectly," says the scientist.

Wasserburg also has tried dating the earth. In 1974, accompanied by his son and four other geologists, he launched Operation Oldstone, a geological expedition to Greenland. Renting a thirty-foot retired police cutter piloted by two Danish smugglers, they braved the rough and rocky western coast searching for a possible connection between rocks from the lunar highlands and the Greenland variety. They found no similarity. Aside from a hassle with the police when a not-quite-sober Wasserburg joyously fired a flare gun and nearly ignited a church in a small fishing village, the real highlight of the voyage was a large rock now in the possession of the Smithsonian Institution. From lead studies on this artifact, it was shown that the earth is actually 4.45 billion years old, not 4.55, as previously believed. "This," he says "is the best age we have for the earth and the moon, and is about fifty to seventy million years younger than meteorites."

In 1979, Wasserburg surprised the earth-sciences community with a study of lava samples from land and ocean bottom. The findings argued for the existence of a two-layered model of the earth's mantle, each layer isolated from the other for billions of years. The deeper mantle is the unaltered, unmelted original material from the earth's beginnings. "It's hard to believe," he concedes, "that despite all of the vigorous convections of the earth's mantle, which keep things stirred up, the deepest core of the interior remains unaltered and houses the original juices and elements. But the evidence indicates this is precisely the case. We can infer this from the relative abundance of different isotopes of atoms, such as neodymium. There is a definite leaking of gases from inside the earth which can occur only if the earth had not been outgassed. In essence, the juvenile material is still being burped from the deep interior, out of a primary reservoir.

That means that inside our planet are materials that remember the beginning of earth's formation."

Wasserburg grins in audacious pleasure. "We're building a new generation of fairy castles and myths for the next generation to play with. I suppose we'll be proven just as wrong or right as we were before. But more important, we've started a new generation of facts and ideas about the earth-moon-solar system origins that are different. Speculations will have to include processes which we now know took place and are no longer subject to dispute."

He continues: "A fair jab at the scientific community would be to ask: 'Now that you know all of this, tell us how the earth, moon, and planets were really formed.' The trouble is that unless you were there recording creation with a movie camera, it is awesomely difficult to prove who did what to whom. It's like trying to eat a whale: the best you can do is take one bite at a time.

"Now the next question is how do you date the gasbag planets like Jupiter? That is a really big deal. But damn it, I think we can do it. If you walk through the doors of the Lunatic Asylum with a bucket of Jupiter gas, I have a funny feeling we will be able to give you a precise number."

How I Measured the Age of the Moon

To start with, the chances are quite high that rock samples collected on the moon by the astronauts during the Apollo missions have been contaminated with materials that may confuse the dating process. The rocks were exposed to the astronauts' tools and equipment, the environment of their spacecraft, and the processing in NASA's lunar receiving laboratory outside Houston. Our guiding principle is to keep this contact with potentially contaminating materials to a minimum.

In our studies of meteorites, the samples usually are obtained from museums throughout the world. On very rare occasions, as with the case of Allende, scientists have harvested their own samples immediately after a fall. The number and variety of meteorites greatly exceed those of the lunar samples. Since meteorites are believed to originate from quite disparate parts of the solar system and are not replenishable except by their random falling to earth, they are exceptionally valuable. I do not believe meteorites are treated with sufficient respect.

Lunar samples arrive at the laboratory sealed in double Teflon bags. The outside bag is cut open before the inside bag is transferred into the controlled environment of the moon room. The sample is removed from its container, weighed, and inspected under a microscope. The exterior of the rock fragment is cleaned with a blast of freon gas to remove the moon dust. Then its outer layers are carefully "peeled" using a tungsten carbide chisel and stainless steel hammer. This exposes an uncontaminated interior surface of the rock, which is used for the ensuing analysis.

A fragment of this newly exposed interior is crushed in a mortar and pestle made of pure sapphire. The pieces are sifted through stainless steel mesh to separate the various mineral grains in the rock. The samples are placed under a microscope, and individual grains are selected for study. A special micromanipulator is used with extreme delicacy to pick up the grains and place them on new slides, dividing the original sample into different mineral types.

Sometimes still more elaborate procedures are required. After the sample is crushed, it is poured into a magnetic separator that segregates grains on the basis of their magnetic and mechanical properties. The material may be separated even further using a centrifugal force. It is spun at high speed in a tube of high-density liquid.

The more difficult analyses depend on grains of "quintessence," which are samples rich in the radioactive elements crucial to the dating process. Several hundred of these tiny, ten- to forty-micron-sized grains must be picked from the separated sample; some are mounted in plastic and polished. Using a petrographic microscope (one specially modified for the classification of minerals) and an electron microprobe (which identifies the distribution of elements in rock crystals by shooting an electron beam into the sample), a representative sample of the grains is analyzed for chemical properties and purity. The remaining grains are then stored for later use.

The next stage is separation of the elements to be used for age determination, using a sophisticated set of chemical procedures. Most of the chemicals used in this process of preparation and analysis are manufactured in the laboratory to assure purity. The attention paid to water, acids, and chemical reagents must be as great as that paid to the lunar or meteorite sample. Each bottle of purified water is labeled and analyzed for all possible contaminants. The allowable level of lead impurity in lab water, for example, is the same as the concentration of lead in normal air. The lab's work would be set back a year if our water were accidentally contaminated.

The sample is placed in a Teflon beaker containing a few drops of acid. The beaker goes into a covered Teflon pot, and the apparatus is heated until the mineral sample dissolves. Filtered nitrogen gas is passed through the pot during the cooking procedure to flush out volatile chemicals without allowing contaminants into the beaker.

The aim is to find the number of atoms of each isotope in this solution. To do this, a set of tracers is added, each a pure isotope of the chemical element of interest. This added isotope permits the determination of the relative number of atoms of the other isotopes. The different chemical elements then are separated from one another using devices known as ion exchange columns. For example, rubidium may pass through the column readily, while strontium becomes chemically bound to the special resinous material in the column. Another acid is added to permit the strontium to pass after the rubidium has filtered through. The end result is drops of solution containing the key elements and their tracers. These are collected in Teflon beakers and dried in a "pot." The dried drops form very thin patches of material—the largest are only the size of a pinhead—which appear as barely visible stains in the bottom of the beaker.

Finally, the atoms in the sample are "counted" with the mass spectrometer. A small drop of acid is added to the stain in the beaker to dissolve it. The droplet containing the sample then is loaded onto a clean metal filament under a microscope and gently heated in air until the drop dries. The sample is placed into the mass spectrometer and heated to 2,800 degrees Fahrenheit in a vacuum to evaporate the atoms and convert them into ions (charged particles). The ions are accelerated by a series of electrical lenses, then passed through a magnetic field that deflects them into different paths depending on their mass. Lighter particles are deflected more easily than heavier ones. Each mass forms a physically separate ion beam, which is then detected.

The result is a recorded computer signal equal to the

number of ions of particular mass in each beam. The magnetic field automatically switches every second to count ions of each mass, and after a certain period starts the process over until all the ions in the sample are counted. Sometimes the process takes as long as an entire day to analyze one sample. The final calculation of the number of parent atoms that remain today and the number of daughter atoms that accumulated defines the age of the sample.

That's all there is to it.

G. J. Wasserburg

6

ROBERT TRIVERS

BIOLOGIST OF BEHAVIOR

by Roger Bingham

Once upon a time, when the world was new, there lived in the Howling Desert a dog, an ox, a horse, and a camel (which then had a straight back just like the other animals). The dog, ox, and horse worked diligently for man, but the camel simply said, "Humph!" whenever it was suggested that he carry a burden.

Eventually, the other overworked animals complained to the Djinn in charge of All Deserts, and he taxed the camel with the problem. "You've missed three days' work," said the Djinn. "You'll have to catch up." "Humph!" replied the camel. And magically his back began to puff and swell into a giant excrescence. "*There's* your humph," said the Djinn. (We call it a hump nowadays.) "Now you can work for three days without eating."

And that, according to Rudyard Kipling, is "How the Camel Got His Hump." Like his other *Just-So Stories*, Kipling's treatise on the camel is a dubious proposition in evolutionary terms. That is also one of the charges leveled against sociobiology, the discipline that claims genes help determine social behavior, officially born with the publication, in 1975, of Edward O. Wilson's *Sociobiology: The New Synthesis*.

Although hailed as a scholarly tour de force by most scientific reviewers, the massive tome prompted an acrimonious debate. Wilson's antagonists argued that talk of a genetic basis for animal behavior was all very well up to a point. But to extend the theory by little more than analogy along an evolutionary continuum to explain human sociality savored of "biological determinism." There is, they insisted, no evidence of gene-based behavioral traits. In effect, they saw Wilson as the Kipling of evolutionary biology and his explanations of a genetic basis for such behavior as altruism, spite, xenophobia, and homosexuality were dismissed as a new crop of dangerous *Just-So Stories.*

By now, much of the smoke has cleared, though the embers still smoulder. Burning Wilson in effigy may have seemed the best way to cauterize the new discipline, but the evidence suggests that everyone simply went to the wrong fire. Wilson, after all (despite an impeccable reputation for his studies of ant behavior and the undoubted achievement of *Sociobiology* as a work of scholarly synthesis), was basically a messenger who became, like one of Shakespeare's messengers, infected by the nature of the bad news he brought. Only time will tell if the news was bad or good. Meanwhile, the theoretical work upon which the whole sociobiological edifice has been erected is seen by many students of behavior as a revolution, the most important advance since Darwin and Mendel.

One of the principal theorists of the sociobiology revolution, and certainly its most controversial, is Robert Trivers, lately of Harvard and now at the University of California, Santa Cruz. Trivers built upon the work of George Williams, a zoologist at State University of New York, Stony Brook, and especially William Hamilton, a British biologist now at the University of Michigan. The deeds of Williams and Hamilton are, sadly, largely unsung outside their disciplines. But Trivers, the youngest of the three, is such a colorful individual that he has inevitably attracted a great deal of attention.

Far from a disembodied theorist, Trivers is at once uncannily perceptive and unpredictably moody. Like the nursery rhyme girl with a curl, when Trivers is good, he is very, very good; when he is bad, take cover. His personal background and his evolutionary theories seem to feed each other to a degree rarely seen (or at least acknowledged) in a scientist, and his mercurial personality is inseparable from the equally flamboyant examination of human nature that his work addresses.

How Robert Trivers Came to Be an Evolutionary Biologist reads, at times, like another Just-So story. His childhood was troubled, marred by parent-offspring conflict (the subject of one of his best-known papers). His years at Harvard were dogged by a series of breakdowns, diagnosed (if the word can be properly applied to such an imprecise condition) as acute undifferentiated schizophrenia. He is married to a Jamaican, Lorna Staple, and spends as much time as possible at the Staple family home in Southfield, Jamaica, with his wife and four children. Clearly, Trivers lives well off the track of academic orthodoxy.

In May 1979, he joined the Black Panther party, largely as a result of his friendship with Panther President Huey Newton (now godfather to one of the Triverses' twins). At the time, Trivers described Newton in the party's newspaper as "a man of very rare intellectual talents, a bona fide genius. At Harvard . . . I dealt with a lot of light and middleweight minds. . . ."

Trivers's rejection of the pressure-cooker intellectual environment and what he viewed as elitism at Harvard and his enthusiastic espousal of black culture—from his Panther party membership, to his fluency in Jamaican patois and his wearing of a tam (the woolly cap that Rastafarians use to confine their braided "dreadlocks")—make him, as his Santa Cruz colleague Burney Le Boeuf puts it, "the blackest white man I know."

All in all, Trivers appears to be an outrageous invention, as though some enterprising public relations man had set out to fabricate a scientific maverick, an *enfant terrible* of sociobiology. Yet, however infuriating he can be, however challenging in his judgments and actions, he is no poseur. For beneath the occasionally extravagant personality lies an acute, encompassing mind. As one of his colleagues puts it, "Trivers has always perceived himself, it seems, as being threatened by other people in the race to assume authorship of ideas. But he has little to worry about. He's one of the great brains in this business."

Add the personality to the output of brilliantly original scientific papers—on, for example, the evolution of reciprocal altruism, parent-offspring conflict, parental investment, and sexual selection, and his current work on social evolution and theories of mate choice and of deceit and self-deception (he is also coauthoring a book on the subject with Newton)—and it becomes a little clearer why he has been described as the man who has been boldest in applying the gene-based view of social behavior to humans. He is also someone who lives and breathes his own theories.

Trivers came to evolutionary biology by an unusual route. Initially an undergraduate studying mathematics at Harvard, he switched to U.S. history, intending eventually to take a law degree. But in his junior year he suffered a breakdown and was refused admission to law school.

After graduating in 1965, Trivers took a job writing an educational text on animal behavior (a subject he knew nothing about). It brought him into contact with two men who greatly influenced his thinking on sociobiology: Irven De Vore, a noted anthropologist, and William Drury, who worked for the Massachusetts Audubon Society.

Those contacts led to what Trivers considers one of the most important intellectual experiences of his life: rejection of the theory of group selection. This conversion took place as a result of studying altruism, the most vexing problem in the evolution of social behavior. In Darwinian terms, altruism seems to make no sense. Why should an organism jeopardize its own fitness, its survival and reproduction, in favor of another? Why, for example, should kamikaze bees die in defense of the hive? Why should ground-nesting birds risk their necks performing a distraction display at the approach of a predator? Why should some soldier termites detonate themselves spraying fluid at enemies? And why should individual birds in a population faced with food shortage lower birth rates?

According to the British biologist V. C. Wynne-Edwards, who addressed this last question in his classic study "Animal Dispersion in Relation to Social Behavior," the answer was simply this: for the good of the species. Individual sacrifices made sense because they improved the overall fitness of the group. This, in condensed form, was group selection.

But there is another explanation, one that jibes more closely with the original Darwinian notion of individual survival and reproductive success. In his "Population Studies of Birds," the evolutionist David Lack tackled Wynne-Edwards's example from a different perspective. In times of food shortage, he argued, an individual bird will reduce its clutch size for what might be called *selfish* reasons, not for the good of the group. The bird wants to produce as many potentially successful reproducing survivors as possible. Quality overrides quantity, and a reduced optimum number of eggs is laid.

In 1966, Trivers recalls arguing the question with Drury, who suggested he read and reread both Wynne-Edwards and Lack. "I did it for three straight days, and each one reconverted me. Then Wynne-Edwards's hold, which had been weakening, finally let go. That was the end of group selection, species-advantage thinking in my life. . . . From then on I knew that natural selection referred to individual reproductive success. I was *inflamed* with the truth."

Six months after he experienced his conversion, Trivers learned from Ernst Mayr, then director of the Museum of Comparative Zoology at Harvard, of the work Hamilton had published in 1964 in the *Journal of Theoretical Biology*. Initially, Trivers recalls, he read it "without knowing what the hell it even meant." But at length, he came to appreciate it as "the appropriate expression of this great theory. . . . [Hamilton] was worthy of the idea—and that's saying an awful lot, because it is *the* most important idea." Hamilton's kinship theory was what so excited Trivers.

Essentially, Hamilton addressed the problem of altruism from a mathematical standpoint, providing a theoretical base for the genetic evolution of social behavior. His kinship theory revolves around the concept of inclusive fitness, which is the cornerstone of sociobiology.

To estimate the fitness of an individual, Hamilton argues, it is not enough to consider it in isolation. You must also take into account the survival and reproduction of kin (those organisms with some degree of genetic relatedness). For example, in human beings, a mother has on average half her genes in common with her offspring and a quarter with her grandchildren. Siblings share half their genes, cousins one-eighth, and so on.

Suppose that an apparently altruistic act, an act of sacrifice that destroyed an individual organism, nevertheless increased the survival and reproductive prospects of related individuals carrying some of the same genes. If the cumulative increase in fitness of the survivors exceeded the total loss of the "altruistic" organism, it could still be said to have struck a good bargain. According to this calculus of self-interest, enough of its genes would survive for the sacrifice to be worthwhile. Hamilton's work took the altruism out of altruism, showing it to be genetically self-interested: the maximization of inclusive fitness through natural selection.

The immediate consequence of Trivers's discovery of Hamilton's work was that it gave him a springboard to extend the altruism argument to unrelated organisms and to those from different species. An organism helps another, Trivers argued, because it expects help in return (a delayed-return benefit) and because cheating—which in this context means simply a failure to reciprocate and carries no moral connotation—will be selected against. The theory of reciprocal altruism propounded by Trivers is offensive to many people. For according to it, such "noble" qualities as charity, loyalty, and sacrifice can be interpreted as genetically ordained strategies for amassing biological brownie points that can later be cashed in as increased fitness and viability.

The human altruistic system, according to Trivers, is sensitive and unstable. There are many occasions when subtle cheating will pay off. As a result, he argues, a complex psychological system has evolved favoring ever subtler forms of cheating—and of detecting cheating. He even thinks that escalation of this deceit and anti-deceit weaponry—a kind of biological cold war—may have contributed to the enlargement of the human brain during the Pleistocene. Friendship, gratitude, trust, sympathy, and suspicion can derive from reciprocal altruism.

For those who prefer ascribing man's more exalted qualities to a humanly, species-specific cultural overlay, evolutionary biology seems morally bankrupt, and theories like reciprocal altruism are greeted with dismay. Trivers acknowledges, "There is no direct evidence regarding the degree of reciprocal altruism practiced during human evolution, nor its genetic basis today," but he clearly believes that it would be irrational to take the evolution of human social behavior out of the genetic arena.

In the foreword to Richard Dawkins's 1976 book *The Selfish Gene*, Trivers wrote:

> The chimpanzee and the human share about 99.5 percent of their evolutionary history, yet most human thinkers regard the chimp as a malformed, irrelevant oddity, while seeing themselves as stepping-stones to the Almighty. To an evolutionist this cannot be so. There exists no objective basis on which to elevate one species above another. . . . Natural selection has built us, and it is natural selection we must understand if we are to comprehend our own identities.

The basic message of the Dawkins book—put in very crude fashion—is this: the only thing that matters is the survival of individual genes. We are their temporary residences, their mobile homes. When we die, they live on—through reproduction—in the next generation of mobile homes. The genes direct us in a way that maximizes their own survival. If subtle cheating behavior is a successful method of ensuring that the gene machine keeps rolling along, then subsequent generations will have the same genetic predisposition to selfish deceit. The selfish gene theory seems to work in other species, so why not in humans? As the British philosopher Mary Midgley puts it: "We are not just rather like animals: we *are* animals." There is a paradox here. Although the current emphasis is on the gene as the basic unit of selection, it is obvious—as Paul Sherman, a biologist at Cornell University, puts it—that "genes don't run around naked: They exist, cooperate, compete, within phenotypes [individuals]. We have yet to test the power of the individual against that of the gene."

Of course, no sociobiologist would deny the speed and power of human cultural evolution, the oddly Lamarckian transmission of acquired "characteristics" (learned information, values, and so on). But, for Trivers, a refusal to come to grips with the possibility of a genetic component of behavior is tantamount to moral and intellectual cowardice; at the very least, a dereliction of the scientist's duty. If we have been selected for our selfishness and subtle cheating, then the fact should at least be faced. Without such understanding, cultural evolution—no matter how successful it may be in overcoming negative traits—operates in a vacuum. Evolutionary biology has long been burdened by the hoary nature-nurture debate (in some ways, sociobiology is an old play on a new stage), which did the discipline a disservice by setting up apparently competing hypotheses when the true picture is one of complementarity. Behaviorally, humans are neither totally in thrall to their genes nor totally emancipated from them. That message, Trivers believes, is now well established. And within that framework many evolutionary biologists now see the theories of Hamilton and Trivers as representing a new paradigm.

Trivers was born in 1944 in Washington, D.C., and lived as a child in a suburb in Maryland, with spells abroad in Denmark and West Berlin. His father, a Harvard graduate with a doctorate in philosophy, spent five years as a student in Nazi Germany. He later became an American foreign service officer and was partly responsible for developing a postwar classification system that was used as a basis for de-Nazification.

Of his father, Trivers says, "He came from a deeply authoritarian and patriarchal tradition and in his lifetime moved away from it. I have continued in that direction, so we share a common pattern of resistance to our past and to change." Today he acknowledges that his theoretical work was "very strongly influenced" by the conflict with his parents and that his affection for black people contains a strong element of identification with the underdog. "I don't think there's any question about that. It goes way back. I identified with black people when I was a child, and I don't know why. It was partly a matter of justice. I'm sure, intuitively, that I knew the system I grew up with in Maryland was unjust."

It is perhaps not surprising, then, that Trivers developed such an affinity for Jamaica, its people and culture; to the point that he describes himself as "Jamaican in my soul or spirit" (although there are many people who would argue that the warmth and affection has not rubbed off). He first visited the island in 1968 with a Harvard zoologist to begin a project on anoline lizards in Kingston. Shortly afterward, he met a member of the Staple family, and when the Kingston study area was destroyed, he moved his base to Southfield.

Unwittingly, he won his future wife's affections when he defended her mother's honor in a fracas with a local farmer. As Trivers tells it —playing the various roles in patois—the story is a hilarious farce, with the farmer drawing a knife, Trivers grabbing an ice pick and "throwing myself insincerely at the people separating us." Trivers has a store of such Jamaican tales and obviously relishes the cunning deceit, internecine conflicts, and the seamiest kind of arcane knowledge they contain. (If you ever need to know how to walk a dead man along a street in Kingston, Trivers can tell you.)

Burney Le Boeuf has been taken by Trivers to after-hours dives in the rougher parts of Kingston and Panama ("I was scared as hell," he recalls) and to a transvestite bar in San Francisco. "We were on our way to talk about the deceit and self-deception book with Huey Newton. The symbolism didn't escape me. Deceit and self-deception. Here you had it in the flesh!"

Trivers's fascination for this shadowy demimonde distances him from the culture he grew up in and which surrounded him at Harvard. In many ways, he's a renegade, proud of his ability to walk on the wild side. In black communities, the tam and patois are his passports. Most visitors are irritated, even intimidated, by the street people who try to sell you ganja or cocaine in Montego Bay. Not Trivers. He stops and talks; he knows the Rastafarian religion, and he knows about ganja cultivation. These are *his* people. For Trivers, Jamaica is an antidote to what he calls "effete old Cambridge where you go and sleep with your best friend's girl friend, and your best friend's not supposed to be angry because that's a sign of immature character development. It's refreshing to be down here where the cards are more out on the table."

Irven De Vore remembers Trivers returning to Cambridge after visits to Southfield and talking constantly of Miss Nini (Lorna's mother) and her extended family, which he had effectively adopted as a surrogate kin structure. "It was obviously a sort of psychological Shangri-La, completely away from the pressures at Harvard," De Vore says. "That grew on him through the years, and his marriage to Lorna was a way of making that real and manifest."

Harvard has become something of a *bête noire* for him. As soon as he joined the faculty in 1973, Trivers says, his standard of living dropped, and his work load increased. Soon afterward, he married Lorna and began a family. His papers were becoming widely appreciated, and he applied for tenure. Harvard asked him to wait. Trivers pressed his case—but with the same result. Finally, Trivers left for Santa Cruz, infuriated by the Harvard process: "Lecture on reproductive success and not be paid enough to have any of my own? I was outraged!" Once again, Trivers lived his own theories.

However turbulent the Harvard years, they were immensely productive for Trivers. Hot on the heels of his theory of reciprocal altruism came his paper on "Parental Investment and Sexual Selection" (1972). Parental investment (PI), as Trivers defines it, is "any investment by the parent in an individual offspring that increases the offspring's chance of surviving (and hence reproductive success) at the cost of the parent's ability to invest in other offspring." The relative PI of the sexes in their offspring, Trivers argues, governs the operation of sexual selection. In most species, the parenting relationship is asymmetric, or unequal, from the outset: the egg is a comparatively rare commodity and nutrient rich; sperms are produced in vast numbers and are little more than DNA with a propeller. Eggs are expensive; sperms cheap. In general (although there are species where role reversal is common), the female continues to bear the brunt of nurturing; male PI is limited or absent. Some—like Dawkins—have argued that female exploitation begins precisely with this disparity in the sizes of egg and sperm.

Differences in parental investment provide fertile ground for conflict to develop. The male wants to keep his investment low and impregnate as many females as possible to spread his genes. The female is more interested in extracting the maximum investment from the male. Seen in these overly simplistic terms, a sexual partnership is an exercise in mutual distrust and exploitation. Other factors must be considered. In the male's case, for example, costs accompany the benefits of unabashed philandering: offspring left in the care of an abandoned mate may not survive, and competition with other males may become deadly.

The coy female develops tactics designed to establish how faithful a suitor might be—she demands precopulatory feeding and nest building, for example. At the same time, the male tries to minimize the possibility of being cuckolded and investing in offspring that carry none of his genes. Trivers suggests that courtship is less a "romantic" cooperation than a case of sexual one-upsmanship. The coy female has a chance to assure herself that she has hooked a high-resource, high-investment mate. The male isolates the female from competitors, patrolling her to satisfy himself that she is not already pregnant and attempting to dupe him into a genetically worthless investment.

The implications of this battle of the sexes are far-reaching. The theory once led Trivers to consider optimum times for one partner to desert, leaving the other—literally—holding the baby. And he has looked at the ways in which female choice might operate as an evolutionary force—how it could lead to adaptations in the male and to what extent it is responsible for male-male competition. In fact, Trivers has been attacked as a male chauvinist but argues that his logic is symmetrical, regarding the two sexes.

In 1972, Trivers accompanied Irven De Vore on an ethological odyssey that took them to Brian Bertram's lion studies at Serengeti, Sara H'rdy's langurs in India, and the Van Lawick-Goodall baboon and chimpanzee studies at Gombe Stream Reserve in Tanzania. De Vore remembers the trip as "physically exhausting and mentally exhilarating"—almost *too* exhilarating for Trivers. At Gombe, watching baboons, Trivers recalls suddenly realizing "there was a conflict over socialization of the child. When I saw that, it was like a thunderbolt—seeing that all the machinations Freud imagined going on early in life had reality (which I had formerly disbelieved) but that he had misinterpreted it. For two months I had what you could call a brainstorm. Night and day I thought about nothing else and worked out endless implications, including a lot on deceit and self-deception. I ended up in the hospital for two weeks with a very mild kind of breakdown. Then I drew back a bit and said, 'Let's be cautious.' Eventually the parent-offspring paper came out."

The theory, published by Trivers in 1974, adopted a revolutionary position. Classically, parent-offspring relations have been viewed from the standpoint of the parent. Trivers, in a sense, championed the offspring, arguing that they were not simply "passive vessels into which parents pour the appropriate care." What is appropriate to a parent, he suggested, may be inappropriate and inadequate to a child. Conflict develops as a result. Conflict of individual interests is invariably the stress point that Trivers looks for, the point at which he begins to apply theoretical leverage.

The parent-offspring relationship is clearly asymmetrical in some ways: parents have a monopoly on resources and physical strength. But, Trivers argues, the offspring have a battery of psychological weapons at their own disposal.

Consider weaning. When the benefit to the offspring begins to be outweighed by the cost to the mother (in terms of her reduced ability to bear, or care for, other offspring or kin), she will opt for weaning. The offspring resents the withheld source of easy nourishment. A dissatisfied offspring cries for more; when satisfied, it smiles, wags its tail—whatever is the appropriate species response. In other words, Trivers says, selection should have favored parental attentiveness to signals that alert parents to the offspring's condition.

If the system of communication is "honest," all will be well. But suppose, as Trivers does, that an offspring has been selected for its ability to "cheat." The offspring knows how hungry it is; the parent can only guess. Are the child's screams genuine cries for hunger or deceitful manipulation—which will eventually lead to parents becoming adept at spotting deceit? Is regression in offspring simply a tactic to induce the kind of parental investment that would have been forthcoming at an earlier stage of development? How subtle a cheat should an offspring be, when *too* much selfishness could be harmful to its kin and reduce its inclusive fitness?

In essence, parents want their offspring to be more altruistic; the offspring tend to be egoistic. Yet *both* parties are acting out of self-interest, to maximize their inclusive fitness. "Conflict during socialization need not be viewed solely as conflict between the culture of the parent and the biology of the child," Trivers argues. "It can also be viewed as conflict between the biology of the parent and the biology of the child."

Only time will tell if sociobiology has been the biggest revolution in evolutionary biology since Darwin's original theory. Although the immediate applications are, almost by definition, confused and confusing, Trivers believes that his own work is fundamental. But he is less interested in offering pat prescriptions about the various ways of interpreting feminism, homosexuality, single-parent families, and so on than he is in alerting people to the possibilities:

"I want to change the way people think about their everyday lives. How you think is going to affect who you marry, what kind of relationship you establish, whether and in what manner you reproduce. That's day-to-day thinking, right? But they don't even teach courses on that stuff. . . . Life *is* intrinsically biological. It's absurd not to use our best biological concepts."

He knows of one case where his theory was put into practice. A graduate student, in her late thirties, had herself sterilized a week after reading "Parental Investment and Sexual Selection." "She'd been thinking through relations between the sexes from a feminist perspective—and the titanic injustice of it. . . . She was seized with rage and went and had herself tied." It is a sobering tale, as Trivers tells it. He is too sensitive to be untroubled by the implications.

For him, reproductive success, conflict, friendship, mate choice, the investment of resources, deceit, and self-deception have an added, at times burdensome, dimension. He sees an underlying genetic imperative, and right or wrong, it has changed the way he interprets human nature. Psychology, law, economics, anthropology, psychiatry, psychology, and sociology would all benefit, Trivers argues, from a strong injection of evolutionary thinking.

As for long-term prospects, "the only fantasy I have is the Grand Old Man fantasy—that if I educate a generation with these books, they'll have a special feeling for me. So twenty years from now, they're going to be willing to hear my thoughts on religion and all sorts of crackpot stuff at national meetings."

So: Trivers the missionary? "Sure! Definitely! Only a minor one, though. Not winning souls for eternity, which is the big league. Just winning minds for Darwin."

7

KURT GÖDEL

MASTER OF THE INCOMPLETE

by Rudy Rucker

I didn't know where his office door was, so I knocked on a glass patio door. It looked out on a little pond and the peaceful woods of the Institute for Advanced Study in Princeton, New Jersey. It was a sunny day in March, but the office was dark. I couldn't see in. Did Kurt Gödel want to see me?

Suddenly he was there, floating up before the long glass door like some fantastic deep-sea fish. He let me in. I took a seat at his desk.

Gödel (rhymes with hurdle without the *r*) was unquestionably the greatest logician of the century. He may have been one of the greatest philosophers, too. When he died in 1978 at the age of seventy-two, the mathematician Simon Kochen at his memorial service compared him to Einstein—and to Kafka.

Like Einstein, Gödel developed a structure of exact thought that forces scientists to look at the world in a fresh way. Although Einstein was twenty-seven years Gödel's senior, the two came to know each other well in Princeton during the 1940s. They often walked together in the fields near the Institute's Fuld Hall. Gödel was given to severe depressions, and those who knew them both say that Einstein cheered Gödel by teaching him the general theory of relativity.

The Kafkaesque aspect of Gödel's work is expressed in his famous incompleteness theorem, which he published in Vienna in 1931 when he was twenty-five. Its reasoning was so novel and complex that it was unintelligible even to many mathematicians. Yet it has become a landmark of twentieth-century thought.

Although the theorem can be proved in a rigorously mathematical way, it ironically suggests that rational thought can never penetrate to the ultimate truth: certain mathematical propositions can never be proved or disproved; mathematics is necessarily incomplete.

More precisely, the incompleteness theorem shows that mathematicians can never formulate a correct and complete description of the set of ordinary whole numbers (0, 1, 2, 3, 4 . . .). They are thus left, like Kafka's K in *The Castle,* unable to escape from the imprisoning passageways. Endlessly, they hurry up and down corridors meeting people, knocking on doors, conducting their investigations. But nowhere in the castle of science is there a final exit onto absolute truth.

On the surface, Gödel's proof does seem terribly perplexing. Understanding it, paradoxically, bestows on mathematics students a kind of liberation akin to a religious experience. This is partly because Gödel's reputation is immense but also because understanding the labyrinthine nature of poor K's castle is to be free of it.

Certainly Gödel seemed to have freed himself from the mundane struggle. I visited him in Princeton three times in 1972, and my clearest memory is of his curious laughter. His voice had a high, singsong quality. He frequently raised its pitch toward the end of a sentence, lending an air of questioning incredulity to his conversation. At other times his voice trailed off into an amused hum. His English was good and his German accent heavy, but his bursts of rhythmic laughter, combined with his rich conversation and instantaneous grasp of what I was saying, made encounters with Gödel almost hypnotic.

The first time I visited him in Princeton I was writing my Ph.D. thesis in logic and set theory at Rutgers University in nearby New Brunswick. I was particularly interested in Cantor's continuum problem of 1873, which posed a question about his bizarre notion that there are different levels of infinity. I had acquired a copy of a copy of a paper that Gödel had written on the problem but had not yet published. I deciphered the faint squiggles and thought about Gödel's ideas for a month. Finally, I wrote to him.

I had no great hopes that Gödel would reply to my letter on Cantor's continuum—Gödel almost never answered letters—but I happened to be attending a weekly seminar at the Institute with Gaisi Takeuti, an eminent Japanese-American logician who was at Princeton for a year. Gödel knew this, respected Takeuti, and invited me for a visit.

His office was dim and unlit, but there was comfortable carpeting and furniture. His desk was clean except for a glass that had contained milk. Gödel was dressed exactly as he appeared in all his photographs—a dark suit, warm woolen vest, and a necktie. He worried a great deal about his health and was always careful to bundle up in cold weather. In the winter, he often wore a scarf wrapped around his head like a ski mask, exposing only his eyes, nose, and mouth to New Jersey's bitter winds.

He encouraged me to ask questions, and feeling like Aladdin in a treasure cave, I asked him as many as I could think of. He was tremendously fast and experienced. He had already thought through every philosophical problem I posed.

He talked with zest and openness. When I said something particularly stupid or naive, his response was amused astonishment. It was as if, during his years of monastic isolation, he had forgotten that the rest of the human race was not advancing along with him.

No one seems to know why Gödel chose to live his later life in such splendid isolation, his only regular companion his wife, Adele. As a young man, Gödel took an active part in the intellectual life of Vienna, but he made almost no public appearances after moving to Princeton. He spent his later years in ever-deepening silence. A difficult and enigmatic man.

The first time I saw Gödel, he invited me; the next two times, I invited myself. I wrote several times. Finally, I telephoned. "Talk about what?" Gödel replied testily to my suggestion that we meet. He agreed, but when I arrived at his office, he wore an expression of real distaste. Finally, annoyance gave way to interest, and after I asked a few questions, the conversation became friendly and spirited. Still, toward the end, as he grew tired, a mixture of fear and suspicion played across his face.

We talked some about Gödel's central credo—that he did "objective mathematics." This concept, known as Platonism, holds that we do not create the mental objects we talk about. They actually exist on some higher plane; all mathematicians have to do is to find them.

The philosophy of mathematics that is antithetical to Platonism is called formalism. According to formalism, mathematics is an elaborate set of rules for manipulating symbols.

Platonists and formalists agree about what constitutes a correct mathematical proof but disagree on what sorts of proofs are interesting or important. The difference between the two viewpoints shows up clearly in Cantor's continuum problem—the question of which infinite number best represents the number of points in space. Thanks in part to Gödel's work, we know that Cantor's continuum problem is undecidable on the basis of today's theories of mathematics. For the formalists, this means that the continuum question has no definite answer. But for a Platonist like Gödel, this means only that we have not yet looked at the continuum hard enough to see what the answer is.

In one of our conversations, I pressed Gödel to explain his Platonist philosophy—what he meant by the "other relation to reality," which allows one to see mathematical objects directly. He replied that the same possibilities of thought are open to everyone, so the world of possible forms is objective and absolute. Possibility, then, is not dependent on an observer; it is therefore real because it is not subject to our will.

I asked him how best to perceive pure abstract possibility. He said three things: (1) First one must close off the other senses, for instance by lying down in a quiet place. It is not enough, however, to perform this negative action; one must actively seek with the mind. (2) It is a mistake to let everyday reality condition possibility and to only imagine the combinings and permutations of physical objects. The mind is capable of directly perceiving infinite sets. (3) The ultimate goal of such thought, and of all philosophy, is the perception of the Absolute. "When Plato could fully perceive the Good," Gödel said, "his philosophy ended."

Gödel shared with Einstein a certain mystical turn of thought. The One has variously been called the Good, God, the Cosmos, the Mind, the Void, or—perhaps most neutrally—the Absolute. No door in the labyrinthine castle of science opens directly onto the Absolute. But if one understands the maze well enough, it is possible to jump out of the system and experience the Absolute for oneself.

Another favorite subject of Gödel's was time, and we talked a good deal about that. One of his lesser-known papers, "A Remark on the Relationship between Relativity Theory and Idealistic Philosophy," probably influenced by his conversations with Einstein, attempts to show that the passage of time is an illusion. The past, present, and future of the universe are just different regions of a single vast space-time. Time is part of space-time, but space-time is a higher reality existing outside of time. In order to destroy the time-bound notion of the universe as a series of evanescent frames on some cosmic movie screen, Gödel actually constructed a mathematical description of a possible universe in which one can travel back through time.

In one of our meetings, we discussed the traditional paradoxes inherent in time travel. What if one were to travel back in time and kill one's past self? If one's past self died, then there would be no self to travel back in time, so one couldn't kill one's past self, after all. But then the time trip would take place, so one *could* kill one's past self. And so on.

In the same vein we also discussed the future: if the future is already there, then there is some sense in which our free will is an illusion. Gödel believed that. I objected that if there were a completely accurate theory predicting one's actions, then it would be possible to prove the theory false, by learning it and then doing the opposite of what it predicted. Gödel replied, "It should be possible to form a complete theory of human behavior, that is, to predict from the hereditary and environmental givens what a person will do. If a mischievous person learns of this theory, however, he can act in a way so as to negate it. Hence, I conclude that such a theory exists but that no mischievous person will learn of it. In the same way, time travel is possible, but no person will ever manage to kill his past self." Gödel laughed his laugh then and concluded, "The *a priori* is greatly neglected. Logic is very powerful."

On another occasion, I asked, "What causes the illusion of the passage of time?" Gödel did not speak directly to this question but to the question of what my question meant, that is, why anyone would even believe that there is a perceived passage of time at all. He went on to relate the idea of getting rid of the passage of time to the struggle to experience the One Mind of mysticism. Finally, he said this:

"The illusion of the passage of time arises from the confusion of the given with the real. Passage of time arises because we think of occupying different realities. In fact, we occupy only different givens. There is only one reality."

Later, he said, "There is no contradiction between free will and knowing in advance precisely what one will do. If one knows oneself completely, then this is the situation. One does not deliberately do the opposite of what one wants."

The last time I talked to Kurt Gödel, in March of 1977, he had been studying the problem of whether machines can think, and he concluded, "The human mind is incapable of formulating (or mechanizing) all its mathematical intuitions . . . On the other hand, it remains possible that there may exist (and even be empirically discoverable) a theorem-proving machine, which in fact is equivalent to human mathematical intuition."

This seems to imply that it is impossible for a person to program a computer to be as smart as himself but that such a program could perhaps evolve spontaneously. Any machine that behaves like us, however, must of necessity be so complicated that we can never fully understand how it works.

What had struck me was that if a machine could mimic all of our behavior, both internal and external, then it would seem that there is nothing left to be added. Body and brain fall under the heading of hardware. Habits, knowledge, self-image, mind, can be classed as software. All that is necessary for the resulting system to be alive is that it actually exist.

In short, I had begun to think that consciousness is really nothing more than simple existence. By way of leading up to this, I asked him if he believed there is a single mind behind all the various appearances and activities of the world.

He replied that, yes, the mind is the thing that is structured but that the mind exists independently of its individual properties.

I then asked if he believed that mind is everywhere, as opposed to being localized in the brains of people.

Gödel replied, "Of course."

I wanted to visit Gödel again, but he told me that he was too ill. In the middle of January 1978, I dreamed I was at his bedside. There was a chessboard on the covers in front of him. Gödel reached his hand out and knocked the board over, tipping the men onto the floor.

The chessboard expanded to an infinite mathematical plane. And then that, too, vanished. There was a brief play of symbols, and then emptiness—an emptiness flooded with even white light.

The next day I learned that Kurt Gödel was dead.

8

BERND HEINRICH

AN OBSESSION WITH INSECTS

by William Jordan

As the lead runner approaches the finish line, his eyes stare straight ahead in a state just preceding physical exhaustion. Sweat plasters his hair to his head, glues his shirt to his chest, and drips from his shorts. Although he still runs with the pumping stride of a trained athlete, it is clearly his will that propels him. He stumbles through the tape and lurches forward like a rubber mannequin, collapsing into the arms of the bystanders. He has just won the 1981 Chicago ultramarathon, 100 kilometers of relentless running, and set a world record for the masters category—six hours, thirty-eight minutes, twenty seconds. A year earlier he won the masters category of the 1980 Boston marathon. The runner is Bernd Heinrich, professor of zoology at the University of Vermont.

The thrill of competition and the challenge to the will attract this man as they do all top performers, but running to Heinrich is more than an athletic feat. It is an extension of the work that has earned him ranking with the world's top ecologists. His area of research, known as physiological ecology, relates an animal's physiology and body structure to the style of life it leads. So when Heinrich runs, he is also asking questions: How does it feel to run in heat? How much work do you save by trimming all the excess rubber from your shoes? And, most interesting, how does the body avoid overheating? Such questions contribute, at least indirectly, to his knowledge of insect energetics, the study of how insects use energy. It is a field Heinrich pioneered.

For his work in this field he has studied a variety of insects, but the one that brought him public attention is the bumblebee, the "supreme endurance athlete" whose power output, he says, "is twenty to thirty times that of a world-class marathoner." In years of research on this creature, he has made some remarkable discoveries. The bumblebee, for example, is "warm-blooded" in the sense that it cannot fly until its wing muscles reach a temperature of about 85 degrees Fahrenheit. Its small body contains a physiological structure that allows it to hoard heat in the precise area, the thorax, where the muscles are housed. Even so, to maintain this temperature while getting enough food to perpetuate the colony, the bumblebee must forage constantly. And it does this on its own: in searching out their nectar, bumblebees do not cooperate as honeybees do. Rather, each individual is driven throughout its life in an endless, frantic search for the nectar that forms the basis for what amounts to an intricate economic system.

Heinrich is a reserved, thoughtful man in his forties. He is lean and sinewy and in top physical condition. His calm green eyes tend to stare unblinkingly when he speaks, as if what he's saying is not what he's thinking about. He speaks softly in the flat, nasal twang of Maine, with just a hint of his native German. Sometimes you find yourself cupping your ear to catch each word.

Heinrich began his bumblebee research in 1970 while visiting his parents on their Maine farm. He had just completed his Ph.D. at the University of California at Los Angeles. It was springtime, and frost still covered the ground in the early-morning hours. But even then, Heinrich noticed, bumblebees were actively flying from flower to flower. Such behavior almost certainly indicated a warm-blooded physiology. Having just studied temperature control in sphinx moths, Heinrich still carried a needle-probe electronic thermometer for taking insects' body temperatures. He netted a bee, grabbed it in one heavily gloved hand, and jabbed the needle into the insect's thorax. The readout settled at 95 degrees Fahrenheit, even though the air temperature stood near freezing.

From work he had done with moths, Heinrich knew that this ability to elevate body temperature would require many biological concessions. The insect's physiology, body shape and internal design, behavior, social structure, and ecology would all reflect the problem of maintaining a body temperature higher than the surrounding air. The bumblebee looked like a good subject for studying these problems.

The first question was how the bumblebee conserves heat. The smaller the body and the cooler the air, the faster heat escapes—and a bumblebee is little larger than a grape. But Heinrich found that its energy losses are minimized through the special structure of its circulatory system.

The bumblebee has three sections—the head, the thorax, where the flight muscles are housed, and the abdomen. Bumblebee blood flows forward through a large artery from the abdomen into the thorax. The blood carries sugar to the flight muscles there, picks up heat generated by the work of flight, then flows back to the abdomen again. The abdomen, however, has no need for an elevated temperature, since it plays no direct part in powering the wings, and any excess heat arriving there is simply dissipated. But to lose so much heat, generated at the cost of great time and effort collecting nectar, is an unacceptable extravagance.

An elegant bit of morphological design helps the bee conserve heat. The two channels that carry cool blood into the thorax and hot blood out to the abdomen lie in contact in the narrow "waist," or petiole, of the bee. In such close proximity, heat from the warm blood is partly absorbed by the cool blood, acting like a heat exchanger to carry heat back into the thorax.

Further, the bee is able to reverse this condition when necessary by simply alternating the two blood flows so that they do not pass each other. It pumps a pulse of heated blood to the abdomen, and when that has passed through, it pumps a pulse of cool blood to the thorax. Thus, instead of returning to the thorax, heat is "dumped" by the abdomen. This allows the bee to fly on hot days without overheating.

This ability to regulate body temperature did not end with the individual bee; Heinrich found that the body heat was also used to heat the nest. In order for the eggs to hatch and the brood to develop normally, he learned, the bees must maintain a nest temperature of at least 80 degrees Fahrenheit. If the temperature drops below this point for too long, the developing bees will not only grow slowly but could also end up with wrinkled wings and deformed bodies. How is it possible to keep the nest warm, especially in the cold northern spring when a single queen is starting a new colony and night temperatures often drop below freezing?

To find out, Heinrich captured entire nests, queen included, and took them into the lab where he could control the air temperature. He discovered that instead of attempting to heat the nest's interior, the queen heated only her brood clump—a wax envelope that holds eggs, pupae and larvae—incubating them in the same way as a hen. She used her abdomen as a sort of flatiron, pressing it against her brood and pumping heated blood from her thorax back into her abdomen. To generate heat, she uncoupled her wings from her flight muscles and worked the muscles against themselves in dynamic tension, a process commonly known as shivering. When enough of her offspring had hatched, they took over the heating of the nest by shivering while they bustled about at other chores.

Maintaining the nest at high temperatures was a relentless problem: it required tremendous amounts of nectar. So Heinrich's next question was how, precisely, these energy demands affected foraging behavior. Leaving his lab, he followed bees on their foraging trips and kept detailed records on the flowers they visited, the techniques they used to tap the nectar sources, the rate at which they worked, the weather, the air temperature, and the amount of nectar gleaned.

Heinrich made two fundamental discoveries. The rate of foraging is critically important (in general, the faster the bee worked, the greater its nectar profits), and this foraging rate is directly linked to the insect's thoracic temperature. Stalking and jabbing hundreds of bees with a probe, Heinrich found that with a muscle temperature of 86 degrees Fahrenheit, a worker could visit about ten blueberry blossoms per minute; at 96.8 degrees it could visit twenty. By raising its temperature only a few degrees, all else being equal, the bee could double its harvest, at the expense of only a few extra calories.

By now a plot of bumblebee life was beginning to take shape. It was not the romantic poet's idyll of bees droning lazily from pretty flower to pretty flower. In Heinrich's meadow, bumblebees were locked in bondage to their warm-blooded flight and driven by their need for a heated home. Not only were they *able* to forage from dawn to dusk, in good weather or bad, they *had* to do it.

Heinrich published his findings on physiology and behavior in the April 1973 *Scientific American*. The article reached far beyond the audience of scientific specialists that he usually addressed and stimulated public response, some from rather unexpected sources. One, a letter from an editor of *The New York Times*, was to shift his outlook on energetics and change the course of his research. Could he, the editor asked, write an essay comparing the world of the bumblebee to the human world?

"I was not ready to compare bumblebees and mankind," he admits now, "but the idea kept nagging me. Energy is always limiting in the natural world." Finally succumbing to the allure of human-insectan comparisons, he wrote the piece. The result, according to Heinrich, was a misinterpretation of what he was trying to say. "There it was," he recalls, "complete with a cartoon of a monstrous giant (a capitalist?) rolling barrels of oil that gushed black and horrible across a beautiful landscape. The picture implied, 'Ah—if only we could be like those beautiful bees, living in harmony with the flowers!' I guess the message didn't get across, because I meant to say that we are, like the bees, exploitative without regard to long-term consequences. That is the problem."

Subsequent pieces for the *Times* caught the attention of the editor of *Business and Society Review*, who requested him to do yet another piece, possibly entitled "The Limits of Adam Smith's Theory of Greed."

"I had never heard of Adam Smith," says Heinrich, "but I didn't tell the editor that. I got *Wealth of Nations* and found it to be one of the most fascinating books I'd ever read. It made me think about competition in bumblebee foraging. All previous analogies between human and bee societies had been along communistic lines . . . you'd get the idea that the bees sat around in their hives and decided who should forage on what flowers, all for the good of the hive. But competition *had* to be an almost inevitable fact when there were large populations of bees and they had only a limited area with a limited number of blossoms to forage on."

Wealth of Nations turned Heinrich's interests to the next level of biological complexity—social structure and the way it was crafted along lines of energy use. Capturing a new nest in the spring, he placed it in a box that he could plug with a cork. Then he enclosed part of the meadow behind his parents' barn with wire screening stretched over a framework of poles.

Uncorking the hole, he would release a single worker and follow it on its foraging trips inside the enclosure. As the insect fed, he observed and recorded its choice of flowers and its foraging routes. When the worker returned to the nest box, Heinrich would unplug the opening to let the first bee in and a second out. From dawn to dusk, each day for the entire summer, he pursued the experiment, with a persistence that did not make for domestic tranquillity. "My [first] wife would come out at noon and bring a sandwich. . . . I could eat, but I couldn't take my eyes off the bees. There is no stopping in the middle of an experiment."

The results bore out Heinrich's feelings on the nature of bumblebee life: the bees work entirely on their own initiative and do not recruit their nestmates to new nectar sources as honeybees do. They run the risk of duplicating their efforts by visiting and revisiting the same blossoms, a seemingly counterproductive competition from the standpoint of the welfare of the nest. But in fact this behavior leads to an overall benefit.

Each of the bees, Heinrich found, specializes in one or just a few flower species. On the first few trips of their foraging careers, the young workers visit a wide variety of species until they find the ones that yield the largest profits. From then on they visit that kind more or less exclusively until it is depleted or dies out. This increases the rate of foraging, since most of the species have complex lips and petals that act as barriers to all but the bees that have the skills to pry them open. With practice, speed increases dramatically. And although the workers are competing for the same high-yield flowers, the net result is a greater nectar profit for the colony: they will gather far more nectar than if they were to "divide up" the species so that some bees concentrated on low-yield flowers.

Heinrich also noticed some amusing sidelights to the bees' behavior. "The bumblebees starting out their foraging careers were flexible and open to change," he says. They searched until they found the flower with the highest rewards, and when that one dried up, they quickly switched to the next most rewarding species. "However, the older they got, the less able they were to switch their profession. . . . Not only did these bees conform to Adam Smith's model of competition for optimum functioning of society; they also seemed to conform to some human weaknesses."

As the season draws to a close, the flowers die out, the nectar sources dry up, and the insects face the ultimate crisis in energy. On the other hand, to die out at the end of the season is actually the bumblebee's strategy for survival in the long term. Its entire thrust is to produce as many young queens as possible by season's end. These survive the winter in hibernation and start the cycle again the following year.

In 1979, Heinrich published his collected findings in *Bumblebee Economics*. With its scientific graphs and charts on the one hand and its nontechnical prose sprinkled with the terms of economics on the other, it was an eccentric little book that fell somewhere between the lay and the scientific communities. But precisely because it combined economic and ecologic terms, it pointed out the real, logical connections—the energy base—between natural systems and the realm of human activities we had come to assume was a system aloof from nature.

Cautioning that "insects can tell us nothing about human problems," because we are rational beings capable of reasoned choices, Heinrich nevertheless found the comparison of systems fascinating. Bumblebees, he observed, seem to exhibit "individual motivation, as each individual bee tries to optimize its foraging success. And this success results in the good of the whole colony, as if the individuals were led by an 'invisible hand.' In this sense, a bumblebee hive bears some interesting resemblances to the economic model outlined by Adam Smith in *Wealth of Nations*. Smith proposed that 'the uniform, constant, and uninterrupted effort of every man to better his condition, the condition from which public and national, as well as private opulence is originally derived, is generally powerful enough to maintain natural progress of things toward improvement.' Smith . . . felt that individual initiative was the most potent force for public good. In bumblebee society, other things being equal, those colonies whose foragers exercise the most individual initiative in finding and skillfully exploiting the most rewarding flowers will be the ones producing the most new queens and drones."

The New York Times Book Review and *The Wall Street Journal* both raved about the book. Twice it was nominated for the American Book Award in science. Most surprising, the scientific community also received it with accolades.

The book is unusual in that it crosses the boundaries of several research areas. In an age of strict specialization, this can be a risky practice that brings with it the charge of spreading yourself too thin. But Heinrich has another characteristic that transcends this risk. George Bartholomew, professor of biology at UCLA and Heinrich's research adviser during his graduate studies there, sums it up this way: "Bernd has always had the ability to perceive the central issue. Most of us have to learn this, but he's always had it naturally."

Heinrich's productivity is legendary among those who have worked with him. Harvey Lillywhite, professor of biological sciences at the University of Kansas and a student with Heinrich at UCLA, tells about the time Heinrich took his dissertation data to Bartholomew for review and was informed that he needed some more information in a particular area. "It was work that could have taken several weeks. So the next morning, there is Bernd, waiting at Bart's door with the data! He had stayed up all night to get it."

Taken as a source of productivity, this intensity of mind is an admirable trait, but it has a social price. "He always carries his projects with him," says Bartholomew. "He never puts them down. This sometimes makes it difficult for the people near him."

It is his running, though, that most clearly reflects the incredible force that drives the man. "I have always run," he says, "even in the late fifties when anyone in shorts was a spectacle. When I was a child in Germany, my family called me Wiesel [weasel] because I was always running through the forest. It feels easier than walking, and it's faster." He also uses running, occasionally, to continue his research. He once decided, for instance, to test the bumblebee method of using sugar. Bumblebees drink nectar and then begin to metabolize it almost immediately when flying. The radically different human physiology, on the other hand, does not allow such immediate access to sugar. "Just for the hell of it," Heinrich says, "I calculated how many calories

I'd need to run a marathon. It came to about two jars of honey, which I spooned down and ran out the door. Let's just say my time was not good. Sometimes I try to be as wrong as I possibly can. It gives me a real sense of my limits."

Running is still part of his daily life; in a normal week he runs nine or ten miles a day, then goes on a twenty- to thirty-mile run "to purge myself." The ultimate purge came on September 3, 1983, when Heinrich set yet another masters world record. Running continuously for twenty-four hours, he covered nearly 157 miles—and landed in the hospital with severe dehydration. The medical attention, however, provided him with a wealth of scientific records in the form of medical reports—all relevant, in the final analysis, to his work.

His curiosity and his drive are enormous, but there is a more basic side to Heinrich's makeup that has set the overall course of his life. It is a deep sense of communion with nature. This is something he was born to, since his father was one of the last of the naturalists in the classic, nineteenth-century tradition. Papa Heinrich spent his life collecting birds and other specimens in the tropics for the world's great museums of natural history, and it was only natural that he should encourage his son's wonder at wild creatures. Heinrich's own love of nature was reinforced, ironically, by World War II.

As German resistance broke down, the Heinrichs fled the family estate in Poland, keeping barely ahead of the Russians advancing from the east. To the boy of four, the experience made a deep impression—the whine of strafing fighters, the thump of distant bombs, the black silence of underground shelters, the ragged columns of refugees trudging doggedly over the snow toward the West behind horse-drawn carts, are images still strong in his memory. There was a hair-raising escape aboard a crippled bomber onto which "Papa" had bribed passage with a flask of schnapps carried specifically for this purpose. Just as fuel ran out, the pilot found an unoccupied airstrip and landed safely. A few days later "Mamuscha," who was a Polish national, managed to negotiate her family's passage across the East-West border.

Arriving in the Hamburg area, they took up residence near the *Hahnheide*, a nature preserve. For the first few months they lived in a cow shed that was open at one side and still used on occasion by cows. Later, they moved into a tiny cabin owned by a local nature club and spent the next five years living almost exclusively off the land. They collected most of their food from the woods and earned their only cash by brewing moonshine for sale to the local burghers. "If the gamekeeper dropped by for a chat when the still was going, he was informed that he couldn't go inside because 'the ladies were taking a bath.' "

The *Hahnheide* years left an indelible mark on the young Heinrich's mind, acquainting him with the intimacies of nature that can only be felt as a child. "I had no playmates, and I never owned toys. But I had no need for toys. There were so many things around me . . . insects, especially the large carabids. Some were larger than a shrew, and they looked like six-legged knights in black, shiny armor with a beautiful metallic polish."

In 1951, the Heinrichs moved farther west, this time to the United States, where they settled on an old farm in central Maine. One of the barns had decayed beyond the point of repair, and the forest was creeping back into the pastures, but to the ten-year-old Heinrich, this was "heaven on earth. Every time I discovered a new nest, it was so exciting it nearly took my breath away."

This fascination with nature became the guiding interest in his life. After entering UCLA to take a Ph.D. in cell physiology, full-time work in the laboratory—"with ether fumes in a cloud above my bench"—left him disoriented and unfulfilled. He joined Bartholomew's group of physiological ecologists, a decision that led to ten years on the entomology staff at the University of California at Berkeley. According to those closest to him, however, he always talked about going back to Maine.

Most assumed it was idle talk, this yearning for some forest in New England. So in 1980, when Heinrich resigned his prestigious position as a fully tenured professor, many in the field were astonished. When he accepted a $5,000-a-year cut in salary to join the University of Vermont, a school devoted to teaching, with no research reputation, more than a few of his peers assumed that Heinrich had slipped off the path of sanity.

"I felt like the Birdman of Alcatraz [at Berkeley]," says Heinrich. "I was doing good work, only as a substitute for the freedom of the land. Hearing the robin in spring sends shivers down my spine— it sends vibrations through my brain, right into the remotest memory traces."

A prime advantage of teaching in Vermont is being within reach of the piece of land where he grew up in Maine. He goes there each summer, and most of the problems he chooses to undertake arise from his observations during these months. This has the effect of making his scientific inquiries an intimate part of his domestic life.

It also leaves him little time to worry about what his peers think or to consort with a faculty of world-class researchers. "I couldn't see where any stardust was going to rub off on me by staying at Berkeley.

I still had to do my own work." Says Bartholomew, "Most of us need the contacts and facilities of an institution. . . . Most of us pretty much follow the orthodox ways and stay within the scientific establishment, but Bernd does science his own way."

His way cannot be appreciated without a visit to Heinrich's experiment station, as he calls it. An old hunting camp, the 300 acres covers a wide range of habitats, stretching from the top of a mountain down to a trout stream at its base. There are no modern conveniences here, no electricity, no running water, no gas, no telephone, no radio. Heat comes from a wood-burning stove, water from a twelve-foot cistern a quarter of a mile down the path. There is no vehicular access from the highway a half mile below.

Heinrich arrives here with his wife, Margaret, at the end of April each year to take up residence in the cabin that doubles as a laboratory. They stay until the fall semester calls him back to the university —a few brief months to answer the myriad questions that life in the woods brings to mind. Summer is a time, therefore, of total immersion in work and nature. Using a few simple tools—a laboratory balance of the type used in high school chemistry, several hand-held calculators, his needle-probe thermometer—Heinrich carries on his research. He checks out everything, from the spiders that nest on the windowsills and the ants that scurry along the baseboards to the yellow jackets that gather at the remains of a rabbit the cat has killed. Nothing escapes Heinrich's trained eye. All warrants at least a cursory investigation for possible further study. Ultimately, it will come back to a question of energy economics, for in the wild anything that exists take energy, and energy is a cost that must be paid. It is the "invisible hand" that organizes all of nature.

Each day begins early, with Heinrich writing for several hours. Margaret rises a bit later, lights the stove, and fashions a breakfast of scrambled eggs and flapjacks doused with the syrup Mamuscha Heinrich rendered from a winter tapping in the maple grove on the family farm fifty miles down the road. A former zoologist turned computer scientist, Margaret often works with her husband. The two stalk through the meadow, scanning the wildflowers, alert to each foraging worker. Heinrich wields the net and the thermometer. Margaret records data from the electronic display as her husband snatches the furious insects between leather-protected forefinger and thumb and inserts the steel temperature probe.

Most afternoons Heinrich slips off on one of his runs, to observe, to work out solutions to old questions, to test the principles of energy physiology on his own body, to "check out some bees on the next hill."

There is a balance to this life in the woods and a restorative simplicity. But the simplicity is by no means mundane. "There is nothing more magical, mysterious, than nature," says Heinrich. "But the real magic, the art, is in the design and execution of just the right experiments and procedures that somehow translate these mysteries into tangible realities." To the scientist who understands this, even the bumblebee will yield its secrets.

9

FRANK OPPENHEIMER

ON THE BLACKLIST

by Paul Preuss

In February 1949, Frank Oppenheimer found himself partway up a tree in a jungle ravine, high in the Sierra Maestra of southern Cuba. Tangled in the branches far above him was a parachute attached to a thirty-inch aluminum sphere. Oppenheimer was determined to retrieve the sphere before a cold night or another sweltering tropical day could ruin the photographic emulsions inside.

Oppenheimer was thirty-six years old, an intense man with blue eyes and a mop of curly black hair. For more than a year he and his colleagues at the University of Minnesota and the University of Rochester had been studying at high altitudes the high-energy particles called cosmic rays, using balloon-borne cloud chambers and stacks of special nuclear-emulsion photographic plates. The origin of cosmic rays had been unclear for two decades. Oppenheimer's team found the tracks of heavy nuclei in the radiation, which indicated that the sources of cosmic rays might include such phenomena as exploding stars. Now, with help from the U.S. Navy carrier *Saipan,* they were extending their research to the tropics to study how the rays were affected by the earth's magnetic field.

In 1949 cosmic-ray research was still at the forefront of particle physics, though it was not long until, as Philip Morrison of the Massachusetts Institute of Technology recalls, "the great accelerators put the cosmic-ray people out of the business." Some nuclear physicists went where the Big Machines were; others, like Morrison himself, concentrated on astrophysics. Frank Oppenheimer, whose record of ingenious work with accelerators, particle detectors, and other devices of high-energy physics had brought him recognition as one of the country's leading experimentalists, was never given the choice. Even as he was struggling to retrieve data from the Cuban jungles,

Oppenheimer was aware of the increasing attentions of the House Un-American Activities Committee back in Washington, D.C. Less than two years earlier, not long after joining the faculty of the University of Minnesota, he had falsely denied sensational but essentially truthful newspaper acounts of his prewar membership in the Communist party.

The cosmic-ray project, complicated enough without political interference, had been plagued by glitches from the beginning. Because many of the aluminum spheres had been lost in previous flights, every experimental package became more precious. When a search party spotted the treed experiment from a helicopter, they needed the help of local Cuban guides to reach it before nightfall. The climbing spikes Oppenheimer had commandeered from the navy were made for telephone poles, not mahogany trees, and he couldn't get up the slippery trunk.

Then one of the local men stepped forward cautiously: "Will it explode?" Oppenheimer assured him it would not, whereupon the fellow scampered up the tree and plucked the metal fruit. The scientists returned to their helicopter in darkness, their path lit by torches that the Cubans fashioned from flammable vines.

A few days later, the last balloon's payload was lost at sea, and back in Minnesota Oppenheimer typed up his personal notes: "I have just returned from a trip to the Caribbean with my spirit completely broken. . . ." It was an exaggerated sentiment, compounded of exhaustion, self-mockery, and possibly real fear, as well. Four months later, Frank Oppenheimer and his wife, Jackie, were made to appear before HUAC's hearings on "Communist Infiltration of Radiation Laboratory and Atomic Bomb Project at University of California, Berkeley [sic]." The committee questioned the Oppenheimers about their Communist party affiliations during the 1930s. Frank and Jackie answered most questions fully but refused to discuss the political affiliations of people they had known. For whatever reason, the committee did not see fit to hold them in contempt for their refusal to testify. However, Frank was immediately fired from the University of Minnesota. Despite the efforts of friends, he was not to work in physics again for ten years.

His gaze is still piercing, though his wiry hair is now sparse and gone to gray; he only intermittently leans on a cane to relieve a painful hip. (He almost as often uses the cane as a pointer or baton.) Today Frank Oppenheimer is widely known as the founder and director of the Exploratorium, San Francisco's innovative and much-imitated museum of perception, science, and art. Some people know him as

J. Robert Oppenheimer's kid brother. He is known to relatively few as a gifted experimental physicist whose career was disrupted in its prime.

"Blacklisting wasn't a fabrication," says Jon Else, the film maker who came to know Oppenheimer while producing *The Day After Trinity*. "Job offers were withdrawn, his passport denied—Frank took a worse beating than Robert. . . . He paid a higher price for his beliefs." Part of that price was blatant harassment by J. Edgar Hoover's FBI, harassment that continued for a decade. "Finally, after all these years, I have gotten wise to the fact that the FBI isn't trying to investigate me," Oppenheimer wrote in the early 1950s. "It is trying to poison the atmosphere in which I live. It is trying to punish me for being left wing by turning my friends, my neighbors, my colleagues against me. . . ."

Oppenheimer was born in New York City in 1912, far from the West, where he was to spend much of his life. His father was a successful merchant, his mother an accomplished painter. He was a bright student, a fine sailor and horseman, a gifted flute player. His brother Robert—eight years his senior—was already deeply involved in communicating the revolution in quantum mechanics to the United States when Frank entered Johns Hopkins University in 1930. Already a difference in style and intellectual temperament between the brothers had become evident. Robert was given to abstract thought (and was to become fabled for his mechanical ineptitude), while Frank valued direct experience, loved to tear things apart and rebuild them, and had a way (as his brother wrote to him in 1930) of "reducing a specific and rather complex situation to its central irreducible *Fragestellung* [statement of the problem]."

Oppenheimer fondly recalls the explosion of artistic, technological, and social advances during the 1930s. He was particularly intrigued by the political experiment in "industrial democracy," the Soviet Union. "On all these fronts there was the sense that I could make a difference and my friends could make a difference."

He graduated from Hopkins in three years, Phi Beta Kappa, and went to work in Europe, first at Rutherford's lab at Cambridge, where the neutron had recently been discovered, and then at the Institute di Arcetri in Florence, Italy. The mid-1930s was a time of revolutionary discoveries in nuclear physics; the neutron, the neutrino, the meson, and a range of antiparticles had recently been discovered or proposed, or were about to be, and Oppenheimer's work in electron spectroscopy and particle detection was highly pertinent. While in Florence, he spent his spare time in an activity that was eventually to prove as important to his life as physics was: he haunted art museums, spending so much time at the Uffizi Gallery that he memorized the collection. His favorite painter was Giotto, a pre-Renaissance artist whose paintings were direct, earthy, and sensual. He found later artists too slick.

Returning to the United States in 1935, Oppenheimer spent four years at the California Institute of Technology, earning his Ph.D. with work in the new field of artificially induced radiation. In California, he met and married Jacquenette Quann, a student at Berkeley.

Jackie rekindled Frank's social conscience. A few months after their marriage, they clipped coupons from a socialist newspaper and applied for membership in the Communist party. In Pasadena, in the 1930s, party membership meant demonstrating on behalf of farm workers, raising funds for the Loyalist cause in Spain, and attempting to integrate the city swimming pool. ("They let blacks in only on Wednesdays, and they drained the pool on Thursdays," Oppenheimer recalls.)

In the summer of 1937, he met young Victor Weisskopf, newly arrived from Europe, who tried to discourage the Oppenheimers' collective naiveté about the Soviet Union, without immediate result.

Oppenheimer did postgraduate work at Stanford, but for once his mechanical artistry deserted him. "I was supposed to build a neutron spectrometer with some old junk. . . . I wasted a year trying to make that goddamned tube work so [physicist Felix] Bloch could have some neutrons." Oppenheimer admits one cause of his failure may have been the distraction of Communist party activities; Stanford grew leery of him, and his fellowship was not renewed. "Basically, I was fired," he says, noting that outright persecution of professed Communists was rare at the time but that social discrimination was common. Ironically, Frank and Jackie had already abandoned the party, fed up with its insincerity. For several months he was without a job.

Through his brother, Frank had come to know Ernest O. Lawrence, inventor of the cyclotron, founder of the Radiation Laboratory at the University of California, Berkeley, and, some would say, creator of Big Science. Lawrence liked Oppenheimer and soon put him to work modifying the "Rad Lab's" older thirty-seven-inch cyclotron to prove that uranium isotopes could be electromagnetically separated.

The project was successful: a natural mixture of uranium ions, when accelerated across a magnetic field, was separated into concentrations of the heavy, abundant, nonfissionable isotope U-238 and the lighter, fissionable isotope U-235. Delighted, Lawrence exclaimed, "This is going to change the whole picture." It would, in other words, speed up construction of the bomb. He mounted a scaled-up program that made use of the huge magnet of the lab's unfinished 184-inch cyclotron.

In December, the Japanese had bombed Pearl Harbor, diverting the lab's basic research. American scientists and their allies became absorbed by the technological challenges of building a fission bomb, a theoretical possibility known to the Germans and Japanese, as well. Frank Oppenheimer was a key figure in getting the first uranium isotope separators at the immense plant in Oak Ridge, Tennessee, into working order. By 1945, he decided to join his brother in Los Alamos, where he was made deputy to Kenneth Bainbridge, the physicist in charge of the plutonium bomb test. "I was sort of in charge of safety at the test site," says Oppenheimer—in retrospect, an awesome responsibility, which involved everything from moving soft-hatted military officers out from under falling wrenches to calculating whether low-lying clouds would trap fallout. (He correctly concluded that the bomb would have punched a hole in the inversion layer.) "He knew the subject," says Victor Weisskopf, the theoretical group leader at the test site.

Frank Oppenheimer witnessed Trinity firsthand. He later wrote, "Its thunder continued as though it would never cease, as echo upon reecho reverberated through the valley of the Jornada." He remembers only relief—simple, quiet relief that "the damned thing worked."

Scientists had begun raising questions about "the impact of the gadget," in Robert R. Wilson's phrase, before the Trinity test. Wilson, youngest of the Los Alamos group leaders, remembers, "I had been a pacifist, Frank was interested in helping people, we both recognized the irony . . . but we both worked very hard, day and night," to make the bomb project a success. Like the rest of them, Frank found his voice only after Hiroshima and Nagasaki, when he became an outspoken advocate of international control of atomic weapons. "Virtually all atomic scientists were socially or politically involved during this period," he has written. And yet those "who did not drop out on principle or by indifference were in one way or another sucked into the processes of the war machine and were either corrupted, frustrated, or destroyed by it."

Frank Oppenheimer returned to the Berkeley lab after the war. They were exciting years for doing physics. The 184-inch Berkeley cyclotron was the largest accelerator in the world. More important, it included a revolutionary phasing principle that remarkably increased the energy of the accelerated particles, which allowed scientists to watch the interactions of a whole new class of subatomic matter. Frank Oppenheimer and Luis Alvarez designed the first experiment used in the new machine. Oppenheimer also worked with Alvarez and Wolfgang Panofsky on the construction of the world's first powerful proton linear accelerator.

For all the good physics, Berkeley was a different place; Ernest Lawrence had been one of the men "sucked into the processes of the war machine," and after the war Lawrence's conservatism had soured into intolerance of divergent political views. Nevertheless, says Oppenheimer, "Lawrence was basically apolitical. He didn't like politics in the lab because it interfered with physics." A hoped-for teaching job at the University of California failed to materialize, and Oppenheimer accepted an offer from the University of Minnesota. Ernest Lawrence put his arm around Frank's shoulders and warmly wished him well. It was 1947. A little over a year later, events had moved Lawrence to inform his staff that Frank Oppenheimer was no longer welcome at the Berkeley Radiation Laboratory. To this day, Oppenheimer doesn't know why has old friend turned his back on him, although he suspects that Lawrence was either upset by his denial of newspaper accounts of his Communist party membership, which Lawrence and almost everyone else in the scientific community had long known to be true and hardly worth a lie, or by vicious rumors of Oppenheimer's continued left-wing activities. One would not have had to look far for the source of these false rumors.

"Has Frank Oppenheimer arrived yet?" a visitor asked the head of the University of Minnesota's physics department, who replied that he didn't even know if Oppenheimer had left Berkeley. "Oh, he's gone all right," said the visitor—an FBI agent.

In the summer of 1948, Frank and Jackie Oppenheimer shared a ranch house with Robert and Jane Wilson in the valley of the Rio Grande below Los Alamos. To protest postwar policies, Wilson had refused to apply for renewal of his security clearance. "We had a constant stream of visitors, many intense discussions," says Wilson. The topics included secrecy, disarmament, a political climate perverted by fear of communism and the Russians. "Frank had not been completely candid with the people at the University of Minnesota. . . . We had a discussion about what he ought to do," Wilson remembers.

On one of his long pack trips with Wilson, Oppenheimer found a ranch near Pagosa Springs, Colorado, which he and Jackie later bought for a vacation retreat. In the fall of 1949, forced to leave Minnesota, they became full-time cattle ranchers.

"It was excruciatingly difficult," says Philip Morrison. At the unusually high altitude, the winters were long and cold; "Jackie would sit in the cabin with binoculars and watch cows ready to give birth in the snow. They'd have to run out to keep the newborn calves from freezing." And frequent visits from FBI agents made life no less difficult. Neighbors and townspeople were asked: "Is Oppenheimer doing any research?" "Do they have any radios?" If the neighbor allowed as how he hadn't seen any radios on the place, the agent would persist: "But have you been in *all* the buildings?"

Despite the FBI's harassment, the neighbors judged the Oppenheimers as they found them and in due time elected Frank Oppenheimer president of the local phone company (the local phone line had only thirteen subscribers), chairman of the soil conservation board, and representative of the county cattlemen's association (in which capacity, surely not oblivious to the irony, he testified before the U.S. Senate).

Most important, Oppenheimer's Western neighbors made him science teacher of tiny Pagosa Springs High School, which had fewer than 300 students and only one science teacher for all the sciences in all the grades. "In some ways, I was a better biology teacher—I could think of simple things I didn't know the answer to and design ways to find out." Two students, gifted in math, won the state science fair; another winner went about investigating the peculiarities of algae species living in nearby hot sulfur springs and is now a biochemist at Rockefeller University.

A neighboring rancher's son was impressed by several things about Oppenheimer—his wild hair, his fluent swearing (which was loud enough to echo throughout the basin whenever a cow gave him a hard time), and his imaginative teaching. Oppenheimer conducted one science class in the local automobile junkyard, showing students spark plugs, distributors, and condensers to teach them some principles of mechanics, heat, and electricity.

During his two-and-a-half-year tenure at Pagosa Springs High, Oppenheimer introduced the new Sputnik-inspired physics curriculum to his classes, which called on students to use their powers of analysis rather than rote memorization. He was perhaps the only teacher in the state who understood the innovative curriculum. He was invited to conduct a teacher-training institute at the University of Colorado.

The University of Colorado harbored others whose political beliefs or penchant for speaking their minds had brought them into conflict with the witch-hunters. Among them were David Hawkins, a philosopher, mathematician, and official Los Alamos historian, and E. U. Condon, former head of the National Bureau of Standards and past president of the American Physical Society, who, in 1948, had been absurdly accused by HUAC of being "one of the weakest links in our atomic security." With the support of these men, and especially George Gamow, the noted astrophysicist, Frank Oppenheimer got a post at the university—first as a research assistant and finally, five years later, at his former academic rank as professor of physics and astrophysics.

"I got back into research, but it was hard," Oppenheimer admits. He showed ingenuity and verve befitting a man twenty years his junior, organizing a "users' group" of investigators who, lacking an accelerator to call their own, borrowed thousands of bubble-chamber photos from Berkeley to study the properties of K-mesons, produced in collisions between high-energy neutrons or protons. K-mesons decay in one hundred-millionth of a second, making them difficult to analyze. However, they leave a path in a bubble chamber that can be photographed to reveal something of their energy and mass.

But Oppenheimer's years as a teacher had fired his imagination with the challenge of science education. He spent the decade of the 1960s not only doing research but pursuing the varied strands of experience that were to knit themselves into his unique invention—the Exploratorium.

The Oppenheimers moved to San Francisco in the late 1960s, with the concept of this unique hands-on museum already clearly in mind. What made it a reality, however, aside from Oppenheimer's bold conviction that somehow it would be done, were his friends. They included Panofsky, Wilson, and Weisskopf, the builders and directors of the world's most powerful high-energy physics labs. Philip and Phyllis Morrison spent a summer building exhibits on perception for the fledgling museum, and E. U. Condon, who seemed to know everyone in the national scientific establishment, wrote dozens of letters on its behalf. A typical missive, addressed to the head of the Westinghouse research laboratories (where Condon himself had been director of research), was graceful but pointed: "I expect you have some excellent material in storage. Could you lend us some?" NASA loaned an exhibit, as did the U.S. Coast and Geodetic Survey. Panofsky chipped in some chunks of his enormous electron linear accelerator, originally shown at the Stanford Art Museum to exhibit "the aesthetic dimensions of science." But there would have been no place to display these borrowed goods had it not been for Oppenheimer's local pals, representing every hue in the Bay Area's political spectrum. With such help he secured the use of a section of the renovated Panama-Pacific Exposition hall, a fanciful structure originally built in 1915 and located in one of San Francisco's most fashionable neighborhoods.

In the fall of 1969, a few bewildered visitors wandered into the vast and mostly empty space. "We didn't tell anybody we were opening—we just opened the doors," says Oppenheimer. Today the place is crammed with hundreds of thousands of visitors a year and more than five hundred exhibits. But even the most sophisticated exhibits still look rough-and-ready. Giottolike, they eschew an excessively skillful finish. Says Wolfgang Panofsky, "Visitors are expected to interact, even occasionally to break them. It takes the fake glamour out of science. That's deliberate. Science is fun but grubby."

"You can't build a place like this without a real knowledge and interest in science itself," says Oppenheimer. But an understanding of science, by itself, is insufficient. "I don't think I could have done this without having done all the other things that I've done in my life."

Jackie Oppenheimer died in February 1980, having devoted her energies, convictions, and considerable skills to the success of the new museum. Oppenheimer directs virtually every aspect of the place, moment to moment, day in and day out. He has the help of a large and skilled staff. Nevertheless, in the words of film maker Jon Else, "The Exploratorium is like the inside of Frank Oppenheimer's brain —that building is a very tall Frank Oppenheimer."

10

MICHAEL McELROY

A LOVE OF THE FRAY

by Tracy Kidder

Mike McElroy likes the big questions. The origin of life, for instance. He's dabbled in it on and off for the past ten years. McElroy sits in one of Harvard's prestigious chairs of chemistry and enjoys the enviable freedom—the research money, the apprentices, the autonomy—to indulge his eclectic tastes. Listening to him muse about the beginnings of life is a marvelous way to pass a quiet afternoon in the dead of a New England winter.

About 3 billion years ago, relatively suddenly and, most scientists agree, because of the blossoming of life, oxygen appeared in the earth's atmosphere. It is not clear just what the air was like before then, when the earth was devoid of life. McElroy, whose specialty is the atmosphere of planets, first approached that mystery by trying to conjure up the prebiotic atmosphere. But that tack, he felt, confined him to blind guesses. So he turned in the opposite direction. "Let me imagine that life was terminated, totally, completely, on the earth and that the atmosphere relaxed to a postbiotic condition. What would its chemistry be then? And can I see in that instabilities or peculiarities that might cause life to start again?"

In McElroy's imagination, the earth's air undergoes successive alterations, gradually losing oxygen. Ultimately, nitrogen remains the dominant gas, as it is now, but second place is occupied by carbon dioxide or water rather than by oxygen.

This state allows for another development. It has long been known that lightning oxidizes atmospheric nitrogen: among nitrogen, carbon dioxide, and water, lightning can initiate reactions that turn nitrogen into nitrite and nitrate, oxygen-bearing compounds that are the principal sources of nutrition on earth today. In water, these oxides of nitrogen become very stable. So on McElroy's postbiotic earth, where there is no biology to consume the oxides of nitrogen that lightning continually produces, the oxidized nitrogen entering the oceans simply accumulates there. Within about 100,000 years after the end of life, the dead oceans hold about as much nitrite and nitrate as they do today. Does oxidized nitrogen just go on accumulating, its constituents never returning to the air? McElroy says he asked himself that question and reckoned something would have to occur to balance the system. "My thought then was: if you didn't have life, you'd have to invent it."

McElroy and a young scientist named Yuk Yung, then apprenticed to him, published this curious theory in March 1979. For McElroy, the matter rested there awhile. Then he heard about the discovery of the extraordinary rifts in the ocean floor known as deep-sea vents. The deep ocean is dark and cold and holds little life, but the vents create oases. Life flourishes in their vicinity in spite of the absence of sunlight there. Bacteria occupy the bottom link in the chain of being around the vents. They get sustenance from chemicals in the hot water pouring out of the vents and have an enzyme that allows them to oxidize these chemicals. But they also harbor another enzyme, one they don't seem to use anymore, and here lies the "Aha!" in McElroy's tale: the unemployed enzyme, scientists have found, would allow the bacteria to use oxides of nitrogen in the process of their nutrition. It would let them use exactly those compounds that McElroy figured lightning would make abundant in lifeless seas.

Most theories about the origin of life posit a beginning in the atmosphere, with sunlight providing the energy for getting matters underway. Sunlight plausibly helps create complex compounds; it is also plausible that sunlight would destroy precursors to life. Deep-sea vents would, by contrast, provide safe harbors. McElroy imagines that the complex chemistry that occurs at the vents, coupled with reactions involving oxides of nitrogen, would eventually form organic material. McElroy acknowledges at this point that he's moved onto shaky ground; he admits it directly and also, perhaps, by stating his argument with increased force. "The key is at those vents. They're the most probable environment for the origin of life."

Here McElroy is building on the ideas and work of other scientists. But McElroy dreamed up many of the pieces of the theory and also constructed the narrative of ideas. The hypothesis remains at crucial points half-baked and could, of course, be wrong. But it isn't any less ingenious for that. Here is a chemist whose imagination functions on a planetary scale.

From time to time over the past decade, the press has focused its attention on atmospheric chemistry, and partly for that reason the field has known contentiousness. Safe to say that McElroy has helped to stir things up.

"One way of doing science," he says, "is to work something out slowly in private, and the other is to jump in and challenge your peers to refute what you've said, and I think the second way is an exciting and enjoyable way to do it. I think it's a faster way to get to the truth. I don't want to be taken as a Harvard professor, as a statesman who is thoughtful, kind, always a gentleman. I want to be taken as someone in the trenches with a bayonet." McElroy recounts, with obvious relish, a dispute he once had with an eminent scientist. Asked if he enjoys arguments with the eminent, he replies, "Sure. Because otherwise there's not much challenge in the whole thing. I can't imagine that Ted Williams would have enjoyed going back to American Legion ball. He would have hit a hell of a lot of home runs. But would he have enjoyed it?"

McElroy has unusual and, to some, abrasive ways. His style hardly partakes of cool, dry rationality, but it's not unpremeditated, either. Told that he seems to scare some other scientists, he smiles and says, "I hope it's true. And I hope it's good for them." One of McElroy's peers maintains that if a scientist is the first to stake out a given area of research, most others feel obliged to stay away. But McElroy doesn't play by that rule, says the peer, adding, "I'm glad there's a vulture around. Otherwise, all the turkeys would hoard their carrion."

Opinions on McElroy vary, but his influence and his force of personality are such that most of his peers do not wish to have their names attached to any unflattering opinions they might have of him. Some of them loathe him and disparage his work: "He's just gone out of his way to take advantage of, to misuse, others' research. . . . He hasn't made terribly important contributions to atmospheric chemistry." Some praise his science while to varying degrees disapproving of his style: "He's a very imaginative and innovative scientist. He *has* said some foolish things publicly. He's somewhat of a showman. In many ways, that's effective, but it kind of annoys some scientists." There are also some—and this number includes many of McElroy's protégés and apprentices—who offer wholehearted endorsements. Steve Wofsy, a young scientist who works with McElroy, says, "He scares people, sure. Because intellectually he's with the best in any field. Also because he so much enjoys a sharp exchange. Some people mistake that for aggression, but science is a sport to him. He plays it as you would a real sport."

McElroy went to Harvard as a full professor in 1969, when he was only twenty-nine years old. Today he has acquired a scientific team that numbers about thirty, including engineers and technicians, but also a dozen or so Ph.D. candidates and full-fledged but youthful scientists. One day early in 1983, several members of the team gather, as they often do, to talk about new ideas and work in progress. The first topic is water vapor on Venus. A Russian scientist named Moroz has published some conclusions on this subject. The Russian is wrong, McElroy believes, but he hasn't spotted the sources of the presumed error. McElroy has told the newest scientist on his team to settle the matter. McElroy and three of his other scientists interrupt a lot to ask questions. Their questioning is sharp and insistent but not notably combative. Then McElroy steps to the blackboard.

He is trim and tall, about six feet. He wears a jacket and necktie. He looks neat, contained, and for all of that a little wild, probably on account of his hair. It's cut conservatively, it's brushed, and still it looks unruly. It's also flaming red. Reviewing the issues at hand, he speaks rapidly and emphatically. He seems intent on whetting his apprentice's appetite for returning to the issue. But McElroy doesn't talk about the importance or fascination of the science involved, though it has enough of both for him. Instead, he talks about the Russian scientist, Moroz.

"There are a lot of sloppy Soviet planetary papers, but Moroz, if he were here, would be a leader in this business," says McElroy. "Moroz is sure about this water-vapor profile. And he's good. Very good."

This is, it seems, McElroy's idea of a pep talk, building up the adversary to add luster to the contest. Mike Prather, a young scientist who has been with McElroy for several years, explains, "There's always a hunger for interesting fights around here."

McElroy was born and raised in Belfast, in northern Ireland. His father managed a bank. McElroy got no science in high school. In college, he turned to it in rebellion from the antiscientific philosophy his teachers professed. It took him only two years to get his Ph.D. in physics, but the field soon looked too venerable, too populous, and too well developed for his taste. He went to the United States to work in theoretical chemistry. He found that dull. Finally, an opportunity arose for him to go to Kitt Peak and participate in the exploration of the solar system. The time was the early 1960s. "Space was exciting then," says McElroy. It was also a brand-new field. A young scientist in the planetary business could hope to make a name for himself without undue delay.

McElroy involved himself, most notably, in the attempts to describe the chemical characteristics of the atmospheres of Mars and Venus. His nicest work was an explanation of how oxygen escapes from Mars. The paper describing it relies on just a few equations, a fact that suggests elegance. In 1968, while still at Kitt Peak, McElroy won the James B. McIlwane Award. Back then, the International Geophysical Union gave this prize each year to one scientist under the age of thirty-five. McElroy was singled out for general contributions in the understanding of planetary atmospheres. He was twenty-eight years old.

Scientists who have seen McElroy at work, both enemies and allies, agree that he is a fast thinker, one who can scan a computer printout of experimental data and draw persuasive conclusions quickly. A scientist doesn't need the gift of speed in order to achieve profundity, but in the 1960s, in the planetary field, quickness had advantages for a theoretician. Each new body of data that came in from a spaceship could alter all previous calculations. McElroy is remembered dashing in and out of computer rooms, running and rerunning his photochemical models.

"A small number of people were controlling the data," McElroy remembers. "I certainly was aggressive about getting information. I wasn't going to wait for the experimentalists to get their papers into the literature. And as that game progressed, some experimentalists got very wary about what I would do to them. Once, one of them insisted that I speak before him at a presentation, even though it was scheduled the other way around. People know that I'm pretty fast on my feet. He knew I could have analyzed his data more thoroughly between speeches than he could have done in a week. Yes, that's the way I play the game. But I don't cry. In that case, I spoke first, and because I could guess what was coming, I changed my talk."

The early days of space exploration were heady ones for scientists in the planetary program. Those scientists were some of the first explorers of the solar system, and the press followed them around. "I grew up in the space program," says McElroy, "where there was a press conference every day. . . . I think that if science is to be funded by public money and if the media are interested in something a scientist is working on, you have a responsibility to talk to the reporter."

By 1969, when the invitation to Harvard arrived, McElroy accepted gladly. There he began to shift his attention to the earth's atmosphere. The first and perhaps the most exciting days of the space program had ended. The opposite was true of atmospheric science. McElroy went where the new data were, and as it happened, so did the press.

Fluorocarbons are the stuff once used to propel the contents out of spray cans. In the mid-1970s, scientists found reason to believe the increasing release of fluorocarbons would diminish the stratospheric ozone layer, the unstable girdle of molecules that protects life on earth from the harshest of the sun's ultraviolet radiation. In sheer volume of newsprint, this fluorocarbon theory ranks among the biggest of all stories about science. The theory aroused the press, which aroused Congress, and Congress looked to scientists for information, and also for advice. Scientists had only just begun to explore the chemistry of the stratosphere, however. Abundant room for disagreements existed, especially about what to do, and some disagreements degenerated into acrimony. McElroy got deeply and quite visibly involved.

The fluorocarbon theory originated with two chemists, F. Sherwood Rowland at the University of California at Irvine and Mario Molina, now at the Jet Propulsion Laboratory in Pasadena. After it got aired, McElroy talked a lot about it, both to reporters and to Congress. He consistently acknowledged the theory's scientific soundness, and his own theoretical calculations suggested that the threat should be taken seriously. But while some scientists urged Congress to ban at once some uses of the chemicals, McElroy argued publicly that many scientific issues still lacked resolutions and that further research should precede any banning. To some, it seemed that McElroy adopted the fluorocarbon industry's point of view.

Scientific reputations and a great deal of money were at stake. Not surprisingly, the real, scientific issues were often submerged in hyperbole from all sides. In retrospect, McElroy's view seems to have been reasonable, but then he, too, committed hyperbole. At a meeting of scientists, when the fluorocarbon issue still burned, McElroy suggested that some nations might use bromine, another ozone-eating chemical, as a weapon. McElroy says he didn't know a reporter was listening, he thought he could speculate freely. Clearly, though, he didn't help the case for moderation. To some of his peers, it looked like a case of wounded vanity: McElroy, they felt, was playing down the importance of the fluorocarbon theory because he had not invented it, and he was exaggerating the threat from bromine because he'd thought of that one himself.

A rumor suggesting worse circulated: McElroy was on the take from the fluorocarbon industry. No credible evidence stands behind this notion. Moreover, it's implausible. As one scientist who knows McElroy well—and who does not like all facets of the McElroy style —points out, "That's not what motivates him. He's not even in the top fiftieth percentile of humanity in terms of greed for money. Besides, he's not stupid."

Things quieted down gradually. Looking back, McElroy seems

to harbor some regrets about his part in the fluorocarbon affair. "The field was moving very rapidly, and a number of large egos, including my own, were involved. It was a public ventilation of science. The exposure of that moment stereotyped people. But personalities aren't like that. People change."

Few of the principal actors came away without some bruises and some expenditure of spleen, but a number of laboratories stay heated, and a number of young scientists draw salaries because of the furor over fluorocarbons. Money has flowed freely into stratospheric research ever since, and even McElroy's critics allow that he helped bring money into the field with his gifts for public speaking, for attracting attention. The spectacle wasn't decorous, but some good, important science came out of it. McElroy did some of that science.

After the fluorocarbon theory had made headlines, McElroy looked assiduously for other possible threats to ozone. There was, first, the question of bromine; McElroy was right in calling that chemical a possible threat, albeit he could have found a less sensational way of saying so. Then there was nitrogen, the subject of what may be his most important work so far.

Early on in the ozone affair, chemist Harold Johnston, at the University of California at Berkeley, and atmospheric chemist Paul Crutzen, then at the National Center for Atmospheric Research in Boulder, correctly postulated a cycle in which oxides of nitrogen destroy stratospheric ozone. Human beings could perturb the ozone layer dangerously, the scientists realized, by injecting directly large amounts of oxidized nitrogen into the stratosphere. The SST and nuclear weapons, for instance, were cited as possible sources. In the early 1970s, leaning on work done in the 1950s, McElroy and others published nearly simultaneous papers showing that oxides of nitrogen also get up into the stratosphere *indirectly*. They showed that nitrous oxide, which is inert in the lower atmosphere, will come apart when it reaches the stratosphere and that some of what is created then are the ozone-eating oxides of nitrogen. In fact, this indirect destruction of ozone happens naturally. Sunlight forms stratospheric ozone out of oxygen, and nitrous oxide, released naturally at the earth's surface, travels to the stratosphere and leads to the destruction of ozone there. The result is a balance of processes, which yields a fairly constant shield of ozone. Could mankind be threatening that natural balance by adding significantly to nature's production of nitrous oxide? "Is the big system changing?" McElroy says he asked himself.

Nitrogen is the principal source of nutrition on the earth. Bacteria living in soil and in certain plants make nitrogen available for consumption or "fix" it by breaking a powerful chemical bond. Fixed nitrogen is processed through the biosphere in a grand cycle. At some points in the cycle, some nitrogen returns to the air, part of it in the form of nitrous oxide. Human beings increase the earth's supply of fixed nitrogen by burning fossil fuels and producing chemical fertilizers that contain fixed nitrogen. This enters the great natural cycle, and some of it also becomes airborne nitrous oxide. McElroy worked up some calculations, which persuaded him that mankind's contributions of fixed nitrogen rivaled nature's. He figured that humanity must be increasing the release of nitrous oxide to the atmosphere and that the consequences for stratospheric ozone could be serious.

Tradition requires that a scientist with such a theory submit it to a scholarly journal and allow his peers to mull over it. Instead, McElroy first aired his nitrogen theory before Congress—an act of hubris that rapidly stirred up a fair amount of press, including some warnings about the "ozone-fertilizer threat." As McElroy remembers the sequence of events, he then received a letter, "a very tough letter," from the widely respected chemist Harold Johnston. "He picked off all the soft parts of our theory. It was the sort of letter that required a quick response."

The main objection to McElroy's theory lay with the oceans. A group headed by a well-known and prestigious German atmospheric chemist named Christian Junge had looked into the question of natural sources for nitrous oxide and had concluded that the oceans, not the land, supplied most of that substance to the atmosphere. If the Germans were right, then McElroy's theory was bankrupt. McElroy explains, "If the oceans controlled nitrous oxide, mankind would have a very hard time perturbing the natural system. Junge's idea undercut the thought that you could disturb the nitrogen cycle in any serious way. We wrote a paper strongly critical of their conclusions, using their own data, challenging the great man."

McElroy's team did a great deal of experimental work; they categorized global sources of fixed nitrogen and attempted to assign numbers to those sources. As it turned out, after making additional measurements, other scientists settled the dispute in McElroy's favor: in the current era at least, the land and not the ocean dominates the release of nitrous oxide to the atmosphere. Moreover, measurements have shown that nitrous oxide has been increasing in the atmosphere. Some scientists still grumble about the forum McElroy chose for presenting his theory, and some also remember that initially he overstated the threat from fertilizer. "A number of people had to clean up the lack of credibility he left behind on that one," says one of McElroy's colleagues. The fact remains, however, that McElroy was right.

It's impossible to measure the ultimate practical significance of McElroy's nitrous oxide work. At the very least, though, his theory has served as a fresh reminder of the interconnectedness of things, in this instance of the elaborate natural edifice that connects the nutrition of the planet to the maintenance of an ozone layer. McElroy speaks frequently and eloquently to this point. He likes to say, for instance, "The atmosphere is the air shared by the entire living system, inhaled and exhaled on a planetary scale, and we are doing things to it which are easily detectable but the effects of which are very hard to predict." McElroy at his best entices you to marvel at the web of nature and to imagine all the natural sciences as one. An atmospheric chemist from a group that is often in rivalry with McElroy's admits, "More than anybody else, I think, he has popularized the importance of biological processes interacting with the atmosphere."

McElroy remembers the debates over nitrous oxide fondly, of course, like a veteran recalling an old campaign. "We went way out on a limb on nitrous oxide. We were talking about things we really didn't understand. We were simplifying things we had no right to. There was always the possibility that some guy in the audience would stand up and say, 'Yes, that's very nice, but you forgot about this and this, and I'm very sorry, but as you can clearly see, everything you just said is crap.' I was very nervous giving those talks."

But he also admits he enjoyed it. "My instinct is to think about it today and talk about it yesterday," he says. "That's where I get a lot of my fun. By the time it's reviewed and published, most of the fun is gone. To me, the exciting task is to take on something you don't fully understand and to talk about it in front of an audience, and the better the audience, the more people out there who know more than we do, the more fun it is."

Success in science often implies the gradual assumption of a corporate state of being. A successful scientist often ends up with a lot of people working for him, and the time he has for doing science himself dwindles accordingly. McElroy still dreams up theories and plans for research, but these days, he says, he does most of his thinking in between times, while riding on crowded commuter trains or doing chores at home. He's often on the phone, usually talking scientific politics; he gives speeches; he teaches; he does a lot of writing.

McElroy spends a great deal of his time proselytizing for something called the Global Habitability Program, an incipient scheme to involve all the nations of the earth in a grand exploration of the globe's ecology. He participates directly but sporadically, meanwhile, in several of the team's projects. Mainly, he sits in on discussions of work in progress. The sessions, one young scientist allows, can be intimidating, but most of the team appear to like them that way. "The best thing that can happen," says one member of the group, "is a spirited discussion where a new idea gets challenged and survives. The second best thing is that the idea gets shot down."

One focus these days is carbon dioxide, the subject of what McElroy calls "one of our current favorite games." Carbon dioxide, a so-called greenhouse gas, has been on the rise in the earth's atmosphere since the onset of the Industrial Revolution. If the trend continues, many scientists now believe, it will bring on global warming and, someday, result in vast changes in climate and sea levels. It's something a few of McElroy's team are looking at.

There's the issue of tropospheric ozone, which some of the group have begun to study. In the stratosphere, ozone is beneficent, but it's nasty stuff when mixed with the air of the troposphere, the air that creatures breathe. Ozone is a constituent of urban smog, with a corrosive effect on the lungs, and it also seems to have a direct and deleterious effect on the growth of plants. The issue is clearly an important one, and McElroy's team is after it.

Some of the team are working on a very complicated computer program that attempts to mimic the behavior of substances in the planet's air. And there's the expedition to the Amazon. To be able to prophesy changes in the air, atmospheric chemists must define the sources of a number of trace gases, such as methane, carbon dioxide, and nitrous oxide. It's long been suspected that the Amazon Basin, among other tropical areas, produces significant amounts of such chemicals, but no one up to now has studied closely the chemistry of the basin's air. McElroy's team has set out to do so. Their work so far indicates that the Amazon Basin is indeed an important, global source of several important trace gases.

They also have a number of other, smaller projects. McElroy's theory on the origin of life, for instance. He plans to give that idea to his newest apprentice, once the young man has settled the fight that McElroy would like to start, with the formidable Russian, over Venusian water vapor.

Going about things in his own pugnacious way, McElroy has made some enemies, committed one or two public blunders, and produced a substantial body of notable work. He can also claim one achievement that is certain to endure. "He's made significant contributions to his students," says senior atmospheric researcher Steve Schneider. "Yung, Wofsy, those guys are good. If they're coming out that well trained, McElroy must be doing something right."

Yuk Yung, now an associate professor of planetary science at California Institute of Technology, says, "I cannot think of a more exciting way of doing science than the way in which he does it, and I feel very fortunate to have had him for a teacher."

Steve Wofsy, who is a permanent associate professor of atmospheric chemistry at Harvard, went to work for McElroy about twelve years ago. He came to McElroy's office uninvited, and they had what is remembered as a rather nasty exchange on some scientific issue. "I was brash to say the least," Wofsy recalls. McElroy liked him immediately. Wofsy recently won a McIlwane Award; he still works with McElroy. "There are two things he does very, very well," Wofsy says. "He thinks of good ideas, and he makes them sound exciting."

In the fall of 1982, McElroy and his team set out to teach basic atmospheric science to a nonscientific group of Harvard undergraduates. Several of the team pitched in, and McElroy did the lecturing. At the end of the course, they gave the students an exam that contained a lot of chemistry. Knowing that many in the class had come to it quite innocent of science, one of the team predicted that many of the students would flunk. The class scored an average grade of 84 out of a possible 100. Two of the students switched their majors to the natural sciences.

On a morning late in the fall of 1982, McElroy stands at the bottom of a sort of amphitheater, looking up at rows of seated, sleepy-looking Harvard undergraduates. He's about to wake them up. He's getting ready to explain to them the Coriolis force—it causes airborne objects to turn clockwise in the northern hemisphere and counterclockwise in the southern. The effect results from the rotation of the earth. Wofsy and another of the team's scientists are assembling a rotating apparatus. It looks like a seesaw, one that doesn't go up and down but turns. There's a seat at either end and a wastebasket in the middle, at the pivot point. "I want two good basketball players of roughly the same size," McElroy announces to the class.

Two substantial-looking fellows oblige, taking seats opposite each other on the apparatus. Wofsy hands a basketball to one of them, and as if attempting to jump-start a car, he pushes them around.

The rotating youths try to toss the basketball into the wastebasket. It seems such an easy toss. Again and again, they miss. The ball flies off to the right, far wide of the mark.

McElroy thanks them, sends them back to their seats. "Just think what an interesting game pro basketball would be if you could get Boston Garden to rotate," he says to the class. "So Newton's apple didn't fall straight down but a little to the east," he tells them, adding reassuringly, "but not far enough to miss his head."

The class laughs. McElroy owns their attention now. He holds it undiminished for an hour. He tells them why hurricanes are savage, why the southern oceans do not boil or the northern ones freeze solid, why it rains often in the tropics, why the earth has deserts, why the northeastern United States is "damn cold" in the winter while Florida is mild, why the winds exist, and why there's cause for worry about the accumulation of carbon dioxide in the air. "So," he says, when the hour is exhausted, "now you know as much as the practicing meteorologist. At least on a large scale."

Applause from the students follows—not universal but vigorous applause.

11
BARBARA McCLINTOCK

THE OVERLOOKED GENIUS OF GENETICS

by Evelyn Fox Keller

Barbara McClintock's office is tucked away in the far end of a large laboratory adjacent to a building named for her in 1977. It is notable for its simplicity and its profusion of papers. An inlet from the Long Island Sound comes to within a stone's throw of her window.

For more than forty years, McClintock has lived and worked at Cold Spring Harbor. There, spring after spring, she planted her corn, judiciously fertilizing the budding kernels according to a carefully worked out plan of genetic crosses, watched the plants grow over the summer, and spent the long, quiet winters analyzing the results.

Barbara McClintock is known to generations of biology students for her contributions to classical genetics, but when the day of molecular biology arrived, her work seemed less relevant. Now, in her eighties, McClintock emerges from a bygone era as the heroine of a major upheaval in contemporary biological thought.

From the earliest days of classical genetics, genes were thought to be simple units, laid out in a fixed linear array: the entire weight of genetic orthodoxy has depended on the stability of these fixed structures. But since the late 1960s, with the discovery of movable genetic elements in bacteria, geneticists have been obliged to reexamine some of their most basic presuppositions. Sequences of DNA can spontaneously move or transpose from one chromosomal site, even from one chromosome, to another.

News about jumping genes first began to attract serious attention in the mid-1970s. At the time, they were thought to be relatively rare occurrences, confined to one or two organisms. But today Melvin Green, at the University of California at Davis, says, "They are everywhere, in bacteria, yeast, the fruit fly *Drosophila*, and plants. Perhaps even in mice and men." More and more biologists have begun to ask,

What role do they play in the organization of the cell? No one yet knows the answer, but it is known that movable elements can turn genes on and off and that they can cause massive mutations and gene rearrangements. For this reason they are suspected of playing a role in cancer, in the development of a fertilized egg into a mature organism, and possibly even in evolution.

McClintock is the one biologist who studied transposition for decades before anyone else believed it to be possible. She saw that the implications of transposition were more radical than many biologists have yet dared to think.

Now, after decades of seclusion, McClintock finds herself thrust into the limelight. Her thirty-year-old discoveries of genetic instability in corn have become today's fashion in biological concepts. She is besieged by invitations to lecture and by requests for interviews, for advice, and for seeds of her corn stocks. Offers of honorary degrees and awards abound, capped in 1983 by the Nobel Prize. But McClintock does not welcome this flood of attention. Her friends and colleagues feel that she is just getting the recognition she has so long deserved, but what she wants above all is to preserve the independence she has forged out of years of obscurity.

She comes to her office door dressed in sport shirt and slacks, standard attire since her days as a Cornell graduate student. At Cornell, not seeing how to work in the cornfields in the voluminous skirts typical of the 1920s, she hired a tailor to make trousers and shorts. McClintock wears her hair straight and closely cropped. She is little more than five feet tall, but her physical resilience belies her age. Her aura says no nonsense, and it is not hard to see why some biologists claim to be intimidated by her. Friendly and hospitable, she is also quick and penetrating, demanding the same clarity of her visitors that she does of herself.

At the center of her office is a slate chemistry table; papers are stacked everywhere. She spends a lot of time trying to tie up the work she has been doing for the past forty years. "I knew I shouldn't be publishing it then, because I knew that no one would listen to me, so I just kept working. Now I've got all this stuff, these experiments, to write up." She makes daily plans about what she has to accomplish. "I look ahead not in terms of years but in terms of months."

She may not be happy about all the attention she is getting (especially since she sees much of it a result of fashion rather than of real understanding), but she cannot help but be pleased to see that so much of today's research resonates with her own early work. It suggests the convergence of two worlds, the meeting of classical and molecular genetics. She is pleased and very much excited: "It's going to be marvelous. We're going to have a completely new understanding of the relationship of DNA, the cell, and the organism as a whole."

Current research on gene transposition leans heavily on the new technology of recombinant DNA, a technology that permits a precise probing of the actual sequences of DNA along the chromosome. But McClintock's discoveries were made prior to the acceptance of DNA as the genetic material and well before Watson and Crick worked out the structure of the DNA molecule in 1953. Her research relied exclusively on the techniques of classical cytogenetics in which organisms with particular genetic markers, the genes' expressed features, are crossed or mated and the traits of the resulting new organisms studied carefully. Gross physical characteristics can be examined with the naked eye, while changes in the appearance of the chromosomes are studied through the microscope.

In the early 1940s, McClintock was studying mutations in corn plants. These plants, she found, had undergone some kind of chromosomal modification that led to repeated rounds of chromosome breakage and fusion. This cycle proved to be a rich and fruitful source of new genetic variation. The mutations produced could be seen in the changes in color and texture of the kernels and leaves of the growing corn plant. During the winter of 1944–45, she observed a pattern of pigmentation on a few kernels that was unlike anything she had seen before. The spots, in this case, were not random. Rather, they were distributed in an arrangement that indicated a kind of genetic instability under some form of regulation. Each kernel of corn exhibited its own characteristic frequency of "mutation," which could be seen in the size and number of its spots. Occasionally, however, McClintock observed adjacent sectors of tissue in which the frequency of mutations and the resulting number of spots had changed: in one sector it had increased, while in the other it had decreased.

From the start she was convinced that behind these curious patterns lay a clue to the most difficult problem biology has always had to contend with: the relation between genetics and development. Something had happened during the plant's development that affected its genetic properties. The term "determination event"—a term she had picked up from embryology—stuck in her mind. It refers to an event early in development that affects a plant's later development.

For two years she worked in the dark, "letting the material tell me where to go." Finally, in 1947, she could begin to draw the contours of a system of regulation and control of certain structural genes (genes directly responsible for the observed traits—in this case, the production of a pigment) that is mediated by what she called two

controlling elements. The first of these, adjacent to a structural gene,
might be said to turn that gene on and off at a rate that is in turn
controlled by a second element, generally at some distance from the
first, perhaps even on another chromosome. But the location of these
controlling elements is not fixed. Indeed, they jump around. Their
effectiveness—and their eventual discovery—depended on their
ability to move. Just when she thought she had determined their
positions, she found that among the progeny were plants in which
the same elements resided in new places—next to new structural
genes on the same chromosome or sometimes even on different chromosomes. Here were genetic elements that could not only move
from one site to another but could extend their control to a number of
different structural genes. The original gene was no longer subject
to mutation, but a new gene was.

Perhaps most important of all, the time and frequency of such
transpositions of one or both controlling elements appeared to be
coordinated with respect to the developmental cycle of the plant and
kernel—responding, as it were, to signals from the organism as a
whole. With such changes occurring in the genetic constitution of
individual cells, the problem of genetic uniformity—so long the
stumbling block to a synthesis of genetics and development—might
be resolved. McClintock was confident that she had found a mechanism for generating actual diversity in the developing tissue of the
organism.

She devoted another three years to checking and double-checking
all of the intricate experimental details that went into her argument.
A ninety-page unpublished manuscript, written in 1949, summarizes
the results pertaining to just the first system of controlling elements
she had identified. Before she was willing to publish, she sought to
eliminate every conceivable possibility of error. Her fastidiousness
was matched by her private certainty that there was no error.

In 1951, she made her conclusions public at the Cold Spring
Harbor Symposium, an annual event that attracts biologists from
around the world. Her presentation was met with stony silence. "No
one understood it," she says, and she began to feel ignored. However,
Stanford geneticist Allan Campbell, then a graduate student attending
the symposium, sensed in the audience a communal awe and admiration for her. Campbell acknowledges that most people felt it was very
difficult to understand her theories and fit them into what was known.
"McClintock's theory is becoming like Einstein's theory of relativity,"
he says. "Everyone admires it, but few can say they understand it."
He thinks it was her own misunderstanding if she saw the silent
response as rejection.

Her next attempts got no louder a response. Ten years later, when François Jacob and Jacques Monod made biological headlines with their discovery of a system of regulation and control in the bacterium *Escherichia coli* (for which they were awarded a 1965 Nobel Prize), she tried once again. What people had earlier found difficult to follow, they now found impossible.

In the interim, molecular biology had come to full flower; its emphasis was on the simple and readily analyzable *E. coli*. By contrast, corn genetics required a language of classical genetics with which fewer and fewer biologists were familiar. While McClintock's own work became ever more complicated, the mood in biology was of growing impatience with the complexity of higher organisms. Furthermore, and perhaps especially important, Monod and Jacob's system lacked the most radical and potentially transforming feature of McClintock's: transposition. They had found that the synthesis of specific enzymes in *E. coli* could be turned off and on by certain regulating genes. While the discovery of Monod and Jacob did call for a kind of feedback, it maintained the fundamental inviolability of DNA. By contrast, McClintock's analysis depended on the notion that the arrangement of the DNA was itself subject to the influence of cellular and extracellular processes. In 1960, no one was ready to consider this possibility. Biologists were certain that the normal arrangement of DNA was fixed.

Despite the fact that she felt ignored, McClintock continued her work. Her confidence was unshakable. "If you know you are on the right track, if you have this inner knowledge, then nobody can turn you off . . . regardless of what they say." She admits that she was at first disturbed by the lack of response, but once she got over her initial disappointment, she bided her time and listened. In fact, she says, "It was a great opportunity not to be listened to, but to listen." So much was going on. From time to time, she would try again. As late as the mid-1960s, she tried to disarm an audience at Brookhaven by pointing out, "We have transduction and transformation—what's wrong with transposition?" Just a few years later, the word transposition began to creep into the vocabulary of molecular biologists.

Today's growing interest in her work was first triggered by the discovery in the late 1960s of transposable elements in bacteria; researchers quickly connected it with similar phenomena in McClintock's older work on corn. Throughout the 1970s, more and more instances of mobile, or transposable, genetic elements accumulated—not only in bacteria but in higher organisms, as well. The subject of the 1980 Cold Spring Harbor Symposium was "Movable Genetic Elements." While she was not on the program, her name loomed large throughout the week-long discussion. Perhaps the hall-mark of this discussion was the evidence of new respect for what might be learned from higher organisms and the number of biologists who over the last decade have returned to the study of such classical and complex organisms as maize and *Drosophila*.

The work McClintock began in the 1940s is serving as something of a bridge between two worlds—the worlds of classical and molecular genetics. Today several researchers, including Nina Fedoroff, at the Carnegie Institution of Washington, Frances and Ben Burr, at Brookhaven National Laboratory, and Heinz Saedler and Peter Starlinger, in Germany, compete in the effort to bring the newest molecular technology to bear on McClintock's system, trying to understand just how movable genes work. Many remain skeptical of McClintock's interpretation of the developmental function of trans-position, and no one is quite sure what the marriage of modern and classical technique will produce. But the odds are good that it will produce something major. Barbara McClintock has been right too many times.

The corn geneticist Marcus Rhoades, McClintock's old colleague from the early 1930s, has often wondered how it was that she could see so much more than the rest of them. He once remarked, "I've known a lot of famous scientists. But the only one I thought really was a genius was McClintock. By God, she's good—there is no ques-tion about that." McClintock has always had the respect of classical geneticists. What is new is that a lot more molecular biologists have begun to concur. Matthew Meselson, at Harvard University, recently speculated that history will "record her as the pioneer of new and very much more subtle and complex genetic theories that are as yet only dimly understood." He may be right.

12

CHARLES DARWIN

AN INTERVIEW
AT DOWN HOUSE

by Roger Bingham

You hear the cane first: the rhythmic click, click of an iron tip biting into gravel. The sound comes from a copse of trees away from the house, across sloping lawns and the brilliant colors of the flower beds. It is a perfect English day. The clicks draw closer. A white-haired terrier darts into sight, then checks as a voice calls, "Polly! Heel!" As the dog runs back, her owner appears, swinging his cane and walking with a slow, steady gait. Charles Darwin, the foremost scientist of the age, is taking his regular, midday constitutional around the Sandwalk.

He notices his visitor and comes across the lawn. He is an arresting figure in long black cloak and black slouch hat that contrasts sharply with the white of his untrimmed beard. He is tall, but he carries himself with a stoop. His handshake is vigorous and welcoming, his manner courtly and deferential, belying his acute shyness. For forty years, Down House in the Kentish countryside has been his retreat. Guests, other than family and an intimate circle of scientists, have been a rarity.

Darwin leads the way past the sundial to the veranda behind the ivy-trellised house and sits in a wicker chair. There is a certain propriety in his posture: long legs crossed, one wrist gripped by the other hand in his lap. With his hat removed and the bald head and furrowed brow exposed, his appearance is sage, even patriarchal. And yet, when the light catches his face in a certain way, the deep-set, bluish-gray eyes are so overshadowed by heavy brow ridges and bushy eyebrows that the apelike caricature beloved of cartoonists springs easily to mind.

At seventy-three, Charles Darwin is an enigma. The public knows him as author of the outrageous notion of apes in the human family

129

tree; the man who transferred God's workload to a process called natural selection; the man who in his own lifetime has caused a revolution in biology. The public also knows Darwin as the adventurer who sailed around the world in his twenties only to lapse into a life of chronic illness; as a virtual recluse who will not leave the citadel of Down to defend his own theories; as the elusive general whose lieutenants, like Professor Huxley, fight at the front line and eat bishops for breakfast.

And yet here he sits—an engaging man, modest to a fault, wearing his learning lightly. He is a most unlikely revolutionary.

It is a bit disconcerting to look out from the veranda, across this garden at Down House, knowing that its creatures are feeding and breeding, surviving and dying, and to sit in the company of the man who has explained it all. Surely there must be a *sign* of this man's special standing with Mother Nature. If he raised his arm, perhaps a squirrel or two would acknowledge. It is, of course, a momentary folly, and the story that Darwin begins to tell underlines the flaw in such an attitude. You realize, as he talks, that his greatness lies in his almost childlike sense of wonder at the natural world.

"I remember a day very much like this at Moor Park," Darwin says, referring to his home before he moved to Down. "I was wrestling with my big book—the one that I later abstracted into *The Origin of Species*—and feeling very despondent. It seemed to me that my mind had become just a machine for grinding a large number of facts into theories; and my stomach had got into a horrid state. The weather was quite delicious, though, and I strolled a little, then fell asleep on the grass. I awoke with a chorus of birds singing around me, squirrels running up trees, and some woodpeckers laughing. It was as pleasant and rural a scene as ever I saw." Darwin laughs, triumphantly slaps his knee, and continues, "And I did not care *one penny* how any of the beasts or birds had been formed!"

His mellow laughter is infectious, and for a moment, eyes twinkling, he is the very picture of benevolence. But there is also mischief. The gleeful irreverence of the schoolboy has emerged. Suddenly, it becomes possible to reconcile the venerable sage of Down with the picture his children, now grown, paint. They tell of an affectionate father romping on his hands and knees with them while the story of life on earth, an unfinished manuscript, lay temporarily abandoned in the study. One can imagine the young boy at Shrewsbury School, helping his brother Erasmus do chemistry experiments in their makeshift home laboratory. For this, Darwin earned the nickname Gas and a public rebuke from his headmaster for wasting time. And it is possible to understand why Darwin's father accused him of caring for nothing but hunting, dogs, and ratcatching and warned him that he was in danger of becoming a disgrace to his family.

Mention of his school days brings a slight chill to Darwin's mood. "I was considered a very ordinary boy," he says, shifting in his chair, "rather below the common standard in intellect." Darwin's modesty has charm, but sometimes it seems excessive. You almost wish he would forget himself and brag a little. How many other men, after all, have rewritten Genesis? But it is not to be. Pressed for the ingredients of eminence, he lists his talents dispassionately, counting them on his fingers. (He uses his hands a great deal in conversation.) "Foremost," he enumerates, "a love of science. Unbounded patience. And I think I might make claim to some small talent for observation and inventiveness. Common sense, of course."

Darwin attributes his success to simple habits. "I have always been methodical," Darwin says. "Five years of sailing about the world in the cramped quarters of the *Beagle* enforced the habits of a lifetime. Perhaps my success lies in simple economies of time and thought—and doggedness. I have always said, to quote the novelist, 'It's dogged as does it.' And I have one other golden rule: count the minutes. Which reminds me," he says, standing up, "luncheon awaits us."

He leads the way through the drawing room, stops by his wife Emma's piano near the window, and points to a pot of worms next to a pile of sheet music, Mozart on top. Darwin produces a whistle and blows a short sharp blast. The worms are unimpressed. Now he moves to the keyboard and strikes several base notes. The worms retreat. "It is my only musical talent," he says with a smile. "I have no ear—and yet some ability to move worms." With a furtive glance, he gestures toward the dining room. "I think," he says, "my wife would prefer that I kept the worms in the hothouse."

Although his father, grandfather, and uncle were physicians, young Charles was not destined to uphold the tradition. He abandoned his medical studies at Edinburgh University after being sickened by the spectacle of surgery without anesthesia. Charles's father, despairing that his son might enter a life of idle sportsmanship, steered the young man toward Cambridge and a career in the church. "It seems ludicrous that I once intended to be a clergyman," Darwin now admits, although at the time, he says, "I did not in the least doubt the strict and literal truth of every word in the Bible."

Young Darwin found his clerical studies at Cambridge boring. He preferred being with his fellow undergraduates and spent much time hunting, drinking, and playing cards. He became friends with the professor of botany, the Reverend John Stevens Henslow. He picked up some geology from Professor Adam Sedgwick. And he became a collector of beetles. "All I have learnt of any value," he says, "has been self-taught."

Darwin's memories of the time evoke the picture of an enthusiastic young naturalist plunging headlong into mud in search of a specimen, popping a live beetle into his mouth to free his hand for another specimen, tapping rocks with his geological hammer. Darwin delighted in natural surroundings. But he also enjoyed the methodical side of collecting. He has always kept meticulous tallies—of birds shot, beetles and barnacles identified, and later of backgammon games by the thousand with Emma.

On December 27, 1831, Darwin's life took a fateful turn. "The most important event in my life," he calls it. "It determined my whole career." H.M.S. *Beagle* set sail from Devonport, England, on a 40,000-mile surveying voyage that would last almost five years. On board, as unpaid naturalist, was Darwin, only twenty-two years old. The young man eagerly trekked into the wet jungles of South America and across the barren rocks of the Galapagos Islands—looking, collecting specimens, taking notes, and, in his mind, trying to make sense of it all.

Darwin returned to England in 1836 and, three years later, married his first cousin, Emma Wedgwood, granddaughter of the well-known pottery maker. In 1842, they moved to Down House, named for the village of Down, and started a family. By then he had published his journal of the voyage with great success. He had been a secretary of the Geological Society. His new theory on the formation of coral reefs was in press. He was becoming a respected scientist. With surprising ease, he exchanged the life of a seafaring adventurer for the quiet English countryside. Darwin has not left England since.

After luncheon, Darwin leads the way to his study. It is very much a workplace. Every surface is cluttered: a microscope here, rocks and reagents there, plant germination experiments in another corner. Shelves of books fill one wall. Tacked above the fireplace are scribbled notes. The center of the study is dominated by a long, low table, piled with manuscripts, ink pots, and plants. Polly's basket sits by the sofa. When he is writing—or, as now, talking with a visitor—Darwin sits in an armchair mounted on casters. He has a board across the arms for a desk. Everything is suited to his convenience, even Darwin's practice of tearing thick books into segments to make reading easier.

The clutter and seeming carelessness, however, exist within a daily routine that has not varied in forty years. Darwin rises early and takes a turn or two around the Sandwalk before breakfasting at 7:45. From 8:00 until 9:30, which he considers his best time, Darwin works. Then he passes an hour in the drawing room reading his mail or listening to Emma read a novel before another bout of work. At noon, he walks again, then takes luncheon before reading the newspaper, writing letters, and retiring to his bedroom to smoke a cigarette, a habit he picked up from the gauchos in South America. At 4:00 he walks again, then works for another hour. At 6:00, another rest and a cigarette before dinner. Then, his great delight, backgammon with Emma, some reading, and listening to Emma play piano. He is in bed by 10:30. "My routine is essential to my well-being," Darwin insists, referring to the chronic catalog of ailments that have plagued him ever since the voyage. "I dislike surprises; they knock me up so."

This afternoon, however, comes a surprise that delights him. His publisher has sent word that his latest book is an unexpected success. "*Formation of Vegetable Mould Through the Action of Worms* is not a title calculated to inspire interest," Darwin says.

As he talks, Darwin gets up from his chair and, slippers shuffling, goes into the hall. You hear the sound of a lid on a jar, then a couple of hearty sniffs, and Darwin reappears rubbing his nostrils. "I've been trying to cut down," he says sheepishly, "but I find snuff such a pleasant stimulant during my work periods. When they were younger, the children used to tease me about it quite outrageously."

Memories of his children seem to bring back mixed emotions. "Children are one's greatest happiness but often a still greater misery." There is a sadness in the man's face, no doubt a memory of the three of his ten children who died—Mary as an infant, Charles at the age of two, and his favorite, Annie, at ten. Annie's death, in particular, was a severe blow. Close friends say that it was the final straw in Darwin's fading belief in a personal God. "A man of science," he says, "ought to have no children . . . perhaps not a wife. For then there would be nothing in this wide world worth caring for, and a man might work away like a Trojan."

For more than twenty years after the *Beagle* voyage, Darwin labored on his theory of evolution. He had written a thirty-five-page sketch of it six years after returning to England but was not ready to publish. Two years later, he expanded it to 230 pages. Still Darwin withheld publication, instead spending more years amassing more data. In 1856, his good friend Charles Lyell, the great geologist, came across a paper by Alfred Russel Wallace, a young British naturalist who was independently arriving at ideas resembling Darwin's. Lyell warned Darwin that if he did not publish soon, Wallace might soon steal his thunder. Darwin stepped up his pace but was still far from publishing when the rural tranquillity of Down House was rudely shattered one June morning in 1858. Darwin's mail included an envelope from Ternate, one of the Spice Islands between New Guinea and Borneo. Foreign mail was a commonplace at Down; over the years, Darwin had assembled what was almost a research organization of corresponding scientists to answer his incessant questions on species. But this letter was a shock.

It contained a crisply written, 4,000-word manuscript entitled "On the Tendency of Varieties to Depart Indefinitely from the Original Type." The author was Wallace. His paper, even down to the phrasing, might as well have been extracted from Darwin's unpublished words of sixteen years earlier.

"The life of wild animals is a struggle for existence," Wallace wrote. "Those which are best adapted to obtain a regular supply of food and to defend themselves against the attacks of their enemies and the vicissitudes of the seasons must necessarily obtain and preserve a superiority in population." Wallace said that what applied to individuals also applied to varieties. "The superior variety would then alone remain . . . this new, improved, and populous race might itself, in the course of time, give rise to new varieties . . . here then we have progression and continued divergence."

Wallace had sent his paper to Darwin, asking that if it had any merit, it be forwarded to Lyell.

Now, more than twenty years later, Darwin is still discomfited by the memory of that June morning. "I told Lyell that if Wallace had read my sketch of 1842 he could not have made a better abstract," Darwin recalls. "All my originality seemed smashed—and after twenty years of marshaling evidence." A less honorable man might simply have "misplaced" Wallace's manuscript and rushed his own into print. Instead, Darwin placed the matter in the hands of Lyell and Joseph Hooker, a botanist friend.

"This delicate situation," as Darwin describes it, was resolved by a joint presentation of both men's writings at a meeting of the prestigious Linnaean Society the following month. Darwin's name preceded Wallace's and has ever since.

Stirred into action, Darwin abandoned his *magnum opus* and reduced it to what he considered a mere abstract, a 490-page tome entitled *On the Origin of Species by Means of Natural Selection, or the Preservation of Favoured Races in the Struggle for Life*. Sixteen months later, on November 24, 1859, it was published in an edition of 1,250 copies, and it sold out the same day.

The furor it caused was no surprise. "I warned Darwin," T. H. Huxley recalls, "that he was in store for a great deal of abuse and misrepresentation and told him that I was sharpening up my beak and claws in readiness." In the hope of avoiding confrontation, Darwin omitted mention of man in the book, except for one cryptic reference: "In the distant future . . . light will be thrown on the origin of man and his history." Today he explains his initial reluctance: "That man must come under the same law was unavoidable. But I was inadequately prepared to sustain the argument. To have neglected the passing reference would, I believe, have been dishonorable; to have said more would have cast doubt on the remainder of the work."

The critics pounced, anyway, and the famous debate between Huxley and Samuel Wilberforce, the Bishop of Oxford, came the next year at the British Association meeting. As usual, Darwin stayed away, cosseting his delicate health. Today Darwin recalls the debate with pleasure: "Huxley attacking a live bishop, by Jove! I would as soon have died as tried to answer him in such an assembly."

In recent years the debate has quieted. Virtually all scientists now accept evolution. And though Darwin wrote a more explicit work on human evolution, *The Descent of Man*, even the church now concedes that one can be both a Christian and a Darwinist. The years of debate have clearly defused the issue. Darwin has even produced a book on the evolution of behavior, *The Expression of the Emotions in Man and Animals*. Darwin does not shrink from suggesting that man's mind as well as his body is subject to evolutionary forces. Wallace, however, refuses to join him, asserting instead that human intelligence is the gift of a divine creator. "I am dreadfully disappointed," Darwin says. "He has murdered our child."

It is an uncharacteristic overstatement. Darwin's child, after a long gestation and a traumatic birth, has come of age. And the father has lived to see the world agree with the eloquent passage that concludes *The Origin of Species:*

> There is grandeur in this view of life, with its several powers having been originally breathed into a few forms, or into one; and that, whilst this planet has gone cycling on according to the fixed laws of gravity, from so simple a beginning endless forms most beautiful and most wonderful have been, and are being, evolved.

*   *   *

The author of "The Origin of Species," who was variously described as "the Newton of biology" and "the most dangerous man in England," was laid to rest—one week after his death at the age of 73—in the north east corner of the nave of Westminster Abbey, appropriately close to Newton's own monument.

It might be presumed that the elaborate ceremonial was evidence of some ecclesiastical accommodation for Mr. Darwin's intellectual legacy as well as his bodily remains: belated forgiveness to the corpse for earlier heresies of the corpus. More likely, some have said, it was a response forced by the weight of public opinion: the Philosopher was held in affectionate regard and profound reverence by his countrymen.

And yet, as the more thoughtful of his mourners will surely have reflected, for the author of a theory that denied a special relationship between Man and Creator to be granted permanent residence in this house of God is a circumstance not without irony.

It is tempting to speculate whether, if he had followed his youthful intent to become a clergyman, Darwin would have secured so exalted a resting place. Instead, he was granted virtual canonisation as an unbeliever in the abbey: a saint to scientists.

The preceding visit with the celebrated naturalist, set shortly before his death more than a hundred years ago, is confected from historical fact. The quotations are from Darwin's writings, adapted with dramatic license to a more conversational manner.

13

ROBERT WILSON

LORD OF THE RINGS

by Philip J. Hilts

In 1977, the frontier of physics was to be found in a curious laboratory near Weston, Illinois. But a visitor one spring morning might be forgiven thoughts of a different frontier. The occasion was an early-morning horseback ride. The laboratory director, Robert Wilson, wore his baggy jeans Western style, hanging well below his center of gravity. His black boots had pointed toes and whorls of fancy stitching. He rode his horse as comfortably as if he were relaxing against a fence, back as straight as a rod.

Ahead was an odd geographical feature, an object clearly made by man. It was a long earthen mound, stretching off to the left and right, curving out of view. The whole mound cannot be discerned from horseback, but maps of the area show it curving around for four miles, making a complete circle. The clearest sense of its size comes from photographs of Illinois taken from a satellite about three hundred miles in space. The spreading towns and suburbs of the region appear as ragged blotches. Against this background emerges one sharp and seemingly perfect circle. It is the only feature on earth of such size and regularity, and it stands out against the Midwestern landscape like a dandelion in short grass.

This great circular mound on the Illinois prairie lies on top of an immense piece of machinery—possibly the largest machine of any kind on earth—the Fermi National Laboratory's giant accelerator, built to smash together the infinitesimally small and most elementary particles of nature. Robert Rathbun Wilson was the machine's chief builder and its director from the laboratory's beginnings in 1967 until 1978.

The machine Wilson built is one of the monuments of Big Science, a monument that the future may find a fitting symbol of our technological culture—as the great pyramids, the gardens of Versailles, and the great cathedrals of Europe are symbols of the cultures that produced them. It represents the highest aspirations of physics—to discover what the world is made of and by what conjury it is made to appear as a solid world—and includes aspirations of culture and art. It is a machine that was built to do more than simply function.

Robert Wilson, far more than most physicists, is aware of the aesthetic dimensions of science. The giant particle accelerator might have been built without him, but it would have been an entirely different and drabber machine. Before Wilson, the machines of physics were a chaos of wires, tubes, and metal bars. But the main body of the Fermilab machine, which runs through the four-mile tunnel under the mound, is painted in bright red, blue, and yellow, the wires and other paraphernalia are neatly hidden, and the key parts of the machine were designed to be straight and trim.

At one moment during Wilson's morning ride at Fermilab, he trotted his horse not far from the tall ring of earth under which the machine was working. He looked over and gauged the height of the mound, or the "berm" as physicists call it.

Since the machine was buried twenty feet underground, it seemed unnecessary to have another ten feet of earth heaped on top of it. "Does that absorb extra radiation from the machine?"

"No," Wilson replied. "Mostly we just put it there to accentuate the ring. When we were building it, we looked out and saw that the ring just wasn't very visible. I was really disappointed. You could see where the cooling ponds were to be but not the ring itself. So when we dug the cooling ponds, I had them pile the dirt up here."

The history of powerful machines that accelerate particles is short enough that Robert Wilson was born before any such device existed. He was born in Frontier, Wyoming, and for years before he had any interest in physics or its trappings, Robert Wilson was a cowboy. In high school, he dreamed of becoming a rancher.

Wilson still seems in some way more cowboy than professor. His posture seems oddly rigid. But even in his late sixties, when Wilson climbs on a horse, it is like watching the gears and levers of a machine that are awkward at rest become all at once coordinated and smooth when working.

Wilson's education in physics and machine building began in his adolescent years on the ranch. Working there in the summertime, he absorbed some of the cowhand's sense of self-sufficiency—he learned enough about the behavior of horses, weather, and machines to feel comfortable and productive in the open spaces of Wyoming. Yet there were parts of ranch life Wilson loathed: the strain of mowing and raking hay, the hot sun, the lurching mower he rode under a cloud of mosquitoes.

"But thank God," says Wilson, "every so often it would rain. You couldn't put up hay. So you would take the chance to go up the mountains on horseback. You would ride for strays or push the cattle from one place to another." One summer when he was sixteen or seventeen years old, he did no haying at all, but stayed by himself in the mountains tending cattle. He was alone and in charge of the world.

That summer Wilson read Sinclair Lewis's *Arrowsmith*, a romantic novel that follows the struggle of one scientific researcher. "That romantic idealization of a man dedicated to research made a deep impression upon me," Wilson says. "Lewis portrays in his novel a young and devoted medical scientist who, working long hours in solitude, finally experiences the ultimate exaltation that comes to any creative person. I often led a very solitary life in Wyoming, and for some reason it was natural for me to relate to Lewis's hero. I felt I had something in common with Arrowsmith on his research frontier."

Against the advice of his father, Wilson left home for the University of California at Berkeley. He studied electrical engineering, philosophy, and then physics at the radiation laboratory run by Ernest O. Lawrence. Lawrence had just built his first tiny model of the cyclotron—the predecessor of nearly all the great accelerators operating now. Essentially, the cyclotron was designed to move particles with increasing velocity along a spiral path.

There was no glamour in physics during the 1930s, not even a living wage for a novice researcher. "No one in my family had even heard of a physicist," Wilson says. "I always had to explain that I wasn't a druggist." But there was a certain spirit developing among those willing to spend their lives in Lawrence's lab. While Wilson remembers Ernest Lawrence in a number of moods and poses, he cannot remember Lawrence ever walking: "Even if he was going only a few feet, or across the room, he raced. And he expected everyone else to run all the time, too." They not only ran but worked absurd hours and built their equipment from scratch. "Nearly everything was secondhand or had been scrounged from some factory or dump yard," Wilson recalls. "The electronic equipment was obtained by taking discarded radios apart. Most of the mechanical parts were handmade in the small shop, and usually the physicists themselves turned out the parts on an old lathe."

While Wilson was at Berkeley, Lawrence constantly dreamed and planned a newer, bigger version of his cyclotron. Three versions had been built before Wilson arrived, and he was assigned to work on one with a diameter of little more than two feet. By the time Wilson left Berkeley, at age twenty-five, he was working with a cyclotron that had a magnet large enough for all twenty-seven radiation laboratory researchers to stand inside its arch. With each larger machine, particles could be made to run faster and made to hit the target with greater energy. At each new level of energy, more information could be pried out of the hard, closed shell of the atomic nucleus. When the machine was producing particles with an energy of 80,000 electron volts, Lawrence was talking about making a million volts. When the million-volt mark was reached, Lawrence had already been fund raising on the basis of 25-million-volt particles. Soon, he raised the number to 100 million. By the late 1950s, particles were coming out of other circular accelerators at 1 billion volts.

For the past forty years, the foremost occupation of physicists has been to read, like a star map, the arcs and angles and trajectories that emerge from the accelerator's flash of energy. From this, the elementary structure of matter may be deduced. The method is indirect, but it is the only way to see the skeleton of the universe—that frame of particles that underlies and supports the flesh of all appearance.

There is a belief in physics that discovery is a young man's game, and when Wilson was fifty years old and director of Cornell's physics lab, he began to complain to his wife. He was not doing much physics anymore, he said, and he did not want just to roost as a lab director. He thought of taking up sculpting full time. But as his thoughts were pushing him that way, in the mid-1960s, he received an invitation to a conference in Frascati, near Rome. Among the things to be discussed were plans for a new 200-billion-volt accelerator that would be more than three times bigger than anything then built; these were the first plans for the machine that would become Fermilab.

At lunch during the conference, an important accidental meeting occurred. Wilson sat at a table with the designers of the new machine, and when asked what he thought, he said he did not like the way the designs were presented; they lacked verve. He also said the design was probably a poor one. He had no way to back up his statements, and lunch ended bitterly.

Wilson left Italy for Paris, where he hoped to play squash with a friend and join the drawing sessions at the Grande Chaumière. He soon found himself looking at a beautiful naked model but drawing pictures of accelerators. He was upset at what he had said in Rome and began to think about the machine. "Wherever I went that week," Wilson said, "the bistros or sidewalk cafés, I sat and made designs of accelerators."

When he had been in Paris years before, in 1954, he had visited a number of cathedrals and wrote later:

> As a builder of accelerators, I could thrill to what appeared to me to be a medieval physicist responding to a very challenging physical problem. I saw the similarity between the cathedral and the accelerator. The one structure was intended to reach a soaring height in space; the other is intended to reach a comparable height in energy.

When Wilson returned home after the Italian conference, he formally challenged the plans for the 200-billion-volt accelerator as unnecessarily complicated and expensive. After a futile debate with a group of physicists meeting in New York, Wilson wanted to drop the matter. But politics were conspiring oddly. President Johnson eventually intervened after months of bitter regional fighting over the lab's proposed construction site. Congress had decided upon a reduced budget: and an offer of directorship was made to Wilson. In redesigning the machine, Wilson made the outrageous claim that the accelerator could be built for so much less than the $250 million budget that he could afford to add several expensive experimental facilities not in the plans. He made the outrage worse when he said the thing would be finished in five years, several years ahead of other, competing estimates. After a year of work, Wilson revised his estimate of when the machine would be completed. Not five but four years, he announced.

The job before him at what was locally called Coon Hollow, near Batavia, Illinois, was to construct the greatest machine of physics. In rhetorical iron and grammatical wires, it would end the questions of one era in physics and begin the interrogation of the next era.

To keep Wilson's promises, risks had to be taken. Wilson thought if a machine worked as soon as it was turned on, with no scrambling and reworking, then the machine was overdesigned, and thus overexpensive. An earlier design had 500 magnets producing a 200-billion-volt beam of particles; Wilson had the magnets mass-produced in a risky manner so he could afford to buy 1,000 of them and could make a 400-billion-volt beam.

Some said that the future of high-energy physics in America was doubtful after a decade of political infighting, with a government then unwilling to spend enough money to make a proper laboratory. Wilson used both humor and drama to urge along his colleagues under an impossible budget and an absurd deadline. An architect once brought him a set of plans knowing they were not exactly what Wilson had requested. Wilson bellowed. He took the drawings and tore them up as the architect looked on. He threw the shreds on the floor. He jumped on them. He gesticulated madly before throwing the man out of his office.

Wilson began buoyantly, and the work went deceptively well. He wrote of the design process, recalling his experience with cathedrals:

> I am sure that both the designers of cathedrals and the designers of accelerators proceeded almost entirely on educated intuition, guided by aesthetics. I find out a little here, by a calculation, and a little there; then I draw those parts of the design on paper. After that, I just freely and intuitively draw in smooth connecting lines, lines that cover my ignorance of detail. I keep drawing, correcting here and there by calculations, until it appears the accelerator might work. When the parts and forms have essentially the same relationship that parts of a sculpture should have to the whole, then I am satisfied.

By 1971, the main-ring magnets were in the tunnel and were connected to the power supply. The computer and its control equipment were ready. Protons had been accelerated in a linear machine, pushed into a small booster accelerator, and fed into the main ring. They raced around the full four miles for a few turns. This was less than four years after Wilson had walked into a vacant rented room, set up some folding chairs before a blank blackboard, and chalked a circle on it.

But the elation ended abruptly. The Fermilab tunnel had been built during the winter, when the ground and its moisture were frozen, and the heat and humidity of the following July created a rainstorm inside the tunnel, above the magnets. The water should not have caused a failure. But magnets began to explode—thousands of volts shot through their insulation and crashed to the ground, burning up the magnetic coils. They exploded one at a time. Each one had to be cut from the 1,000-magnet train, pulled out, repaired, and laboriously placed back in the main-ring train. Each blown magnet cost a day of labor and brought more doubts and bewilderment.

Later, invisible cracks in the fiberglas insulation of the magnets were discovered. In a dry tunnel, this would have caused no trouble; in a wet tunnel, water worked down through the cracks in the magnets' insulation to the high-voltage coils. The power jumped from coil to water to ground and blew up the magnet.

It was impossible for the Fermilab technicians to tell how many of the magnets had these cracks. They simply had to turn the magnets on each day and wait to see if one would blow. After a blown magnet was replaced, the machine would again be turned on. The physicists waited to see if another would go. Day by day, magnet by magnet, the physicists watched the new machine come apart. The number of blown magnets reached twenty, then fifty, and the number still went up, a day at a time. One hundred magnets blew; 150, 200 magnets burst their bindings.

Over these months, Robert Wilson aged ungracefully. Frantic suggestions were made to him about how to get the lab out of this growing disaster. He refused to listen. He said he had to wait; the whole staff had to wait. The work at each stage was monstrously time-consuming. At one point, the chief engineer, Hank Hinterberger, informed Wilson that one problem alone—checking each of the thousand vacuum pumps for leaks—would require about two and a half months of labor by Hinterberger's staff. "Okay, you've got two weeks," snapped Wilson.

The entire population of the Fermilab site was ordered from its regular work and into the crisis. But there was no sign of relief. Two hundred and fifty magnets, 300 magnets blew, and the number continued to rise. Wilson's decisions appeared to many to be wild and loose. The whole project seemed to lose its moorings. As physicist Robert March reported a staff member's remark: "We thought Wilson was done for. Either he would quit or have a heart attack, or one of us would go berserk and shoot him."

Professional accelerator builders at Berkeley and in Europe became a little gleeful, and there were jokes about cowboys and accelerators. Fermilab's crisis continued for nearly a year. More than 350 of the magnets exploded before the drier winter and the end of the ordeal. Then physicists tried to produce a beam of protons in the machine.

Physicist Drasko Jovanovich, who was among those coaxing up the beam in the control room, wrote the weary entries in the log book for the night of January 21, 1972. The book looked like the log from a foundering ship:

> 8:30 Troubles   Troubles
>   Beam doesn't go all the
>   way out.
>   Tune splitter had
>   bumps on it—being
>   worked on.
>
> 9:00 Nav- [word bro-
>   ken]   Wiped out.
>   Hangup—numbers
>   wrong.
>   transmission system
>   down. . . .

At 10:00 P.M., Jovanovich reports, Robert Wilson walked into the control room. The room was dim, the scopes and digital counters flickered. Wilson produced a small book from his pocket and read aloud from it a ballad in ancient French, stanza after stanza, his arm motioning and his voice echoing down the hall. It was "The Song of Roland," a ballad sung to French soldiers since ancient times to give them courage as they marched to battle:

> *Let no shameful songs be sung in our despite!*
> *The pagans are wrong, Christians are in the right!*
> *And well he knew not one would flinch or flee . . .*

"We didn't understand the ancient French," says Jovanovich, who listened to the ballad, "but we understood very well the occasion." Work in the control room went on through the night and the next day. Then there was a break in the mood. The beam appeared in the main ring; it was sustained, and the energy of the shooting protons grew.

Wilson left Fermilab during this period to testify before Congress about what was happening to the project. He spoke about the comrades at the machine. "Last night they were making final adjustments. Their blood was up. I could feel that those 200-billion-electron-volt protons were in our grasp at last—and then another magnet exploded. . . . I have complete confidence in my colleagues; they are a skillful, an utterly determined, if a small group, and they will make it; if not today, they will make it tomorrow; if not tomorrow, the next day. . . ." At this point, the Congressional Record is interrupted. There are brackets, and a note. "NOTE: 200 Billion Electron Volts were reached at 1:08 P.M.; central standard time, March 1, 1972." In March of the following year, Fermilab achieved 400 billion volts; in May of 1976, 500 billion volts. During years when the overrun alone in a defense contract could amount to more than a billion dollars, Fermilab was built under the budgeted $250 million. Actually, $243 million were spent, and $7 million were returned to the government.

There are some physicists who say that without Fermilab and without Robert Wilson's successful schedule and budget for the machine, accelerators around the world would not have reached such high energies for another two or three decades. And when those energies finally came, they would not have been in American machines but in European or Soviet ones. After Ernest Lawrence, Robert Wilson has been the chief figure in physics, always ready to build a newer, bigger machine—even when it seemed impossible, even at the expense of current experiments.

Particle physics of the twentieth century is like, in at least one respect, the boom in astronomy in the seventeenth century. In that time, just after the invention of telescopes, there was a race to create newer and bigger telescopes, because each larger size practically guaranteed new discoveries, new depths of vision. Each new telescope was soon superseded by another, and so astronomy advanced in leapfrog fashion. It has been the same with particle accelerators from the time of Ernest Lawrence to the time of Robert Wilson.

14
HERBERT SIMON

BOUNDLESS RATIONALITY

by Patrick Tierney

Most children suspect that adults are illogical; Herbert Simon built a career around this childhood insight. He grew up in Milwaukee as the youngest member of a German Jewish family with a tradition of loud arguments. His grandmother was a particularly talented provocateur, and she often needed Herbert, who was a good listener, to referee who-did-what-to-whom. By the time he was twelve, he knew that even well-intentioned adults see the same thing in remarkably different ways—and that no amount of persuasion can budge the antagonists. "You do not change people's opinions," he noted in his autobiography, "by defeating them with logic."

Fifty years later, in 1978, Simon received the Nobel Prize in economics for his theory of "bounded rationality," a polite way of describing how people muddle through in a world of baffling complexity. Bounded rationality challenges the central core of twentieth-century economic theory by claiming that human behavior can't be logically defined. And, disconcertingly enough, Simon writes computer programs to prove it. His work is gradually changing the way businesses are run and thinking is understood.

The concept of neat behavioral rules understandably appeals to scientists, but Simon considers it nonsense. Formal logic, with its aloof, closed world of interlocking laws, has no explanation for irrational behavior.

Ironically, many people see Simon himself as a kind of computer, a machine man endowed with limitless logic and boundless rationality. "He has no idiosyncrasies, and he's ruthless in resisting distractions to his work," says Alan Perlis, head of Yale's computer science department. "Herbert Simon is the most rational human being I have ever met."

"I'm somewhat amused when people accuse me of being rational or logical," Simon says. "In my description of human thinking and human problem solving, there's relatively little room for deductive logic"—reasoning from the general to the specific. For the most part, he says, people use examples from the world around them to reach broad conclusions. When dealing with human beings, he adds, "the word *logic* is a slippery word, anyway."

That's because what's logical isn't always sensible. Sometimes people make silly mistakes. Other times they unconsciously create shortcuts—in activities as different as shopping and playing games— that the lumbering approaches of formal logic would take years to figure out.

As a political science undergraduate at the University of Chicago during the Depression, Simon studied Milwaukee's recreation department, which was trying, unsuccessfully, to serve two masters. One was the city council; it was in charge of building playgrounds. The other was the school board; it hired leaders to run playground games. The city council seemed bent on turning Milwaukee into a seamless reach of asphalt playing surface surrounded by a few trees—the council was also responsible for planting trees—while the school board apparently wanted to spend all available funds to hire an army of recreation leaders. Their fiscal battle would have made good copy for a war correspondent. How, Simon puzzled, could two rational groups, both of which had the same goal of providing good recreation, quarrel over priorities?

In his doctoral dissertation, he reached a conclusion. "Rationality does not determine behavior," he wrote, arguing that behavior is governed by two factors. The first is humanity's perverse tendency to let feelings overcome logic. The other is the human tendency to take shortcuts that violate formal logic. The reason for both, Simon said, is that individuals can process only so much information. The Swedish Academy cited this academic work, published in 1947 as *Administrative Behavior*, for dramatically advancing the understanding of business economics and organizational research. Yet Simon recalls that his Ph.D. panel was unimpressed. It all seemed so obvious. Everyone knows that the tidy organization chart, with its godlike administrators and clean lines of authority, is an ephemeral ideal sabotaged by incompetence, indifference, and in-house rivalries. Why write a book about it?

Yet Simon's argument was quite provocative. It jolted both Freudian psychiatrists, who attributed behavior to an undefinable subconscious that they declined to explain, and economists, who constructed airtight systems describing individuals without individuality. Simon saw the individual, with all his apparent quirks, as the key to group behavior. Simon got his information by visiting real cities, talking to real administrators, and riding in real police squad cars.

Simon went to Carnegie-Mellon University in Pittsburgh in 1949 to help found the Graduate School of Industrial Administration. There he and his colleagues conducted landmark behavioral studies on executives. Among their findings was that people and classic economic assumptions are at odds.

"The mainstream model used by economists, mathematicians, and statisticians says a person acts rationally if he applies a consistent set of values—economists call it a utility function—over a vast array of choices in order to pick the best possible one," explains Simon in his office, burrowed among books, files, and mounds of papers. A case in point: Simon had twenty-three executives at a large firm read a 10,000-word history of a hypothetical company and then identify the company's most crucial problem. Sales executives said it was in sales. Managers saw it as production. Accountants saw it as a bookkeeping problem.

Moreover, making the "best" decision quickly is impossible if there are more than half a dozen alternatives, because over a minute or two individuals can remember only five to seven facts at a time. The analytical capabilities that classic business theory credits to executives are wildly unrealistic.

"Classic models of rationality assume we're supermen living in an imaginary simple world," maintains Simon, looking decidedly down-to-earth in an old blue sweater vest. "Bounded rationality looks at the psychological limits in human beings—the way we simplify in the face of complexity."

People simplify by inventing rules of thumb to find solutions that are good enough, if not perfect. Simon calls this "satisficing." In Simon's model, most businessmen do *not* constantly strive to squeeze out the last dollar of profit. They merely try to maintain a decent return on investment and a fair share of the market.

Satisficing explains why a hurried executive with a hundred ties to choose from grabs the first one that seems to match his suit; he doesn't carefully, logically examine every one. It also explains why corporations don't rush to seize new opportunities during times of normal profits. Simon terms this kind of accommodation "subjective rationality" because it makes sense in the press of time, even if the executive isn't perfectly dressed and companies don't capture every possible percentage point of market share.

Critics say Simon's theory contributes little, if anything, to economic forecasting or national policy. Even Simon's supporters think of bounded rationality as a different perspective on economics rather than a set of rules with great predictive power. "Bounded rationality clearly says something powerful about human behavior," wrote political scientist Lawrence Mohr of the University of Michigan in a 1982 book, *Explaining Administrative Behavior.* "Not so clear, however, is just what it says about which behavior."

Still, Simon's Nobel recognition came at a time when economists faced—and still face—intractable problems with an embarrassingly cloudy crystal ball. From "investment confidence" to "inflationary psychology," the economy depends on people's thoughts and feelings. And people, including economists, prove unpredictable. What rational model could take into account the policy shifts of successive political administrations? Economic ideologies, whether Keynesian or supply side, keep breaking down, and leaders invent makeshift rules that roughly approximate their goals. They satisfice, though no one is totally satisfied.

"I don't think we'll get an understanding of government policy," Simon says, "unless we're willing to make more direct, behavioral studies of human beings than economists are accustomed to making. They're always keeping people at arm's length, looking at them through the wrong end of the telescope. Economists love using gross aggregates like 'American per capita income.' Well, your 'capita income' isn't my 'capita income.' National quarterly statistics about this, that, and the other don't tell us how people make up their minds."

Wassily Leontief, another Nobel Prize-winning economist, agrees. He scrutinized forty-four papers published in a recent two-year period on "rational expectations"—the theory that businesses respond rationally to government decisions. Only two of the papers included any direct observation of businessmen. "There's nothing wrong with the mathematics here," Leontief says as he holds up a paper bulging with equations. "But it's absolutely irrelevant. There are no *facts.*"

Simon's insistence on observable facts influenced a bestseller, In *Search of Excellence: Lessons from America's Best-Run Companies.* Thomas Peters and Robert Waterman of the Stanford business school, the authors, point out that traditional management philosophy is hobbled by a "rational bent that views askance the very sources of innovation in the excellent companies." Most well-run companies, they say, thumb their noses at such rigidity. Digital Equipment and Emerson Electric, for example, pass up the economies of scale claimed for huge plants, choosing instead small factories where executives don't short-circuit under information overloads. The 3M Co. rejects inflexible departmental divisions to "allow some chaos in return for quick action and regular experimentation." Wang Labs, skirting elaborate market tests, fires off barrages of new products that get quick consumer feedback. Such companies tap the creative potential of their unpredictable employees and customers. "What our rational economist friends tell us ought not to be possible, the excellent companies do routinely," Peters and Waterman conclude.

In Search of Excellence marks the first attempt to sell Simon's idea to American managers. It's hardly a blueprint, however. A blueprint for bounded rationality would have to have built-in allowances for invention, surprise, mistakes—all unpredictable. Simon's point, in fact, is that sweeping economic models are of little use to individual firms, which must constantly find new ways to defeat the inertia that creeps into most bureaucracies. One way is to promote people who travel unconventional career paths. Another is to retrain workers continuously for different jobs. Yet another is to create hierarchies that are flexible and horizontal, to keep down the number of layers.

But all of this is simply another way of saying, "Expect the unexpected." Until now, well-run companies have stumbled serendipitously onto innovative techniques—like the executive grabbing for a tie. "Satisficing is the best description I've come across for how good executives make decisions," says Gerald Meyers, former chairman of American Motors and a former student of Simon's. "Yet I can't think of a single decision I've made better because I knew that."

Oddly, Simon's vision of business is identified more with mathematical analysis and superrational MBAs than with bounded rationality. "Economists don't quite know what to do with bounded rationality," says Stanford economist Lee Bach, former dean of Carnegie-Mellon's industrial administration program. "Simon also contributed to a whole movement which substitutes precise mathematical analysis and computer programs for things like inventory control. Now that's the rational side of Simon. So people who only know his work in math and computers think he's superrational; people who only know his work in psychology think he's irrational. That's why he's so darn hard to understand."

In January 1956, Herbert Simon walked into a classroom at Carnegie-Mellon and announced to his waiting graduate students: "Over Christmas, Allen Newell and I invented a thinking machine." Foreheads furrowed.

"We sort of knew what he meant by thinking," recalls Edward Feigenbaum, one of the students and now head of the computer science department at Stanford. "But what did he mean by machine?"

What Simon and his collaborators—Newell, then a graduate student at Carnegie-Mellon, and J. C. Shaw, a senior programmer at the Rand Corporation—had done was to create not a machine but a breakthrough computer program. It was capable of finding new proofs for the abstruse theorems from the *Principia Mathematica,* Whitehead and Russell's classic exploration of the logic that underlies mathematics, so its creators called it the Logic Theorist.

The program ran on Rand's Johnniac, a monstrous dinosaur ancestor to today's mainframe computers. Computers were then viewed as mere number crunchers, outsized electronic analogs of mechanical calculators. No one believed a computer could process nonnumerical symbols, much less think like a human, as Simon and his coworkers wanted to show. "We wish to understand how a mathematician, for example, is able to prove a theorem even though he does not know when he starts, how, or if, he is going to succeed," they wrote.

They supplied the Logic Theorist with five given statements, or axioms, of symbolic logic and instructed it to prove a theorem—a mathematical conclusion—by building a logic path back to the axioms. In other words, it reasoned backward, just as people often do and just as Whitehead and Russell had initially done. Only afterward did the two mathematician-philosophers build their elegant proofs that moved deductively from axiom to theorem.

"The Logic Theorist gave the first justification to the claim that artificial intelligence was a science," Pamela McCorduck wrote in 1979 in *Machines Who Think.* The term artificial intelligence, coined by John McCarthy of Dartmouth in 1952, denoted computers capable of solving real-world problems. McCarthy used the mathematics of formal logic to mimic thought, but it proved impossibly cumbersome because it forced the computer to consider the effect of every decision en route to a solution. Using this brute-force method, as researchers call it, a computer 100 times faster than those of the early 1950s would have needed 10^{120} years—longer than the universe is expected to exist—to finish a chess game. Simon says he and his cocreators avoided this cul-de-sac "because we borrowed what we already knew about human problem solving and tried to embed that in our early programs."

The Logic Theorist relied on simple rules of thumb to solve difficult intellectual problems. It didn't waste time looking for every possible combination of answers, for example. Similarly, Simon and Newell, in earlier chess-playing programs, had focused the computer's attention on the center of the board, where most of the action is. Simon and his colleagues, in other words, taught computers to simplify in the face of complexity, to set priorities and pursue them as people do. Today, artificial intelligence researchers refer to this as a heuristic approach. To logicians, it's not strictly logical.

It also can discover new proofs. The Logic Theorist, for instance, found an improved proof for theorem 2.85 of the *Principia,* delighting Lord Russell. But when the Logic Theorist was named a co-author in a paper submitted to the *Journal of Symbolic Logic,* the editor's dander rose. "He should have been amused," Simon says. "The point was that computers could do things humans call intelligent."

Others did get the point. "Almost everything people are doing in artificial intelligence today is built around a few powerful ideas Simon had in the 1950s," says Marvin Minsky, cofounder of the artificial intelligence lab at Massachusetts Institute of Technology. Feigenbaum, Simon's former student, has taken the heuristic approach the farthest. He and his Stanford colleagues dominate commercial applications of artificial intelligence programs that aid in diagnosing illnesses, prospecting for minerals, analyzing chemicals, and drilling for oil.

"Artificial intelligence has always had two goals," says Feigenbaum. "One is to build intelligent machines. The other is to use computers as models for human thought. I'm more interested in intelligent machines, while Herb Simon is more interested in human thought."

Psychologists seeking to understand cognition—the process by which people perceive and "know"—recognized the importance of the Logic Theorist, too. "At Harvard and MIT, I became disillusioned with [B. F.] Skinner's stimulus-response method," says Carnegie-Mellon psychologist John Hayes. "I worked with children and found they were much more interested in problem solving than in rewards and punishments. But for Skinner, man was simply a stimulus-response mechanism. I remember he once stood up at a conference and said good psychologists don't talk about thinking or the mind. Well, Simon and Newell really turned psychology around. Today psychologists all over the country are looking at complex, cognitive tasks. Looking at people as problem solvers rather than stimulus-response mechanisms has been very fruitful, particularly in education."

Although researchers in artificial intelligence and cognitive psychology have brought problem solving into the language of scientific discussion, they've yet to approach man's biggest problems—love and hatred. "You can't solve everything at once," Simon says cheerfully. "That's another aspect of bounded rationality."

An intriguing duality surfaces in Simon's personality. He seems diffident, even shy, when he begins talking. Something of the Midwestern boy lingers, along with wide vowels, from growing up in

Milwaukee. But once a discussion gets underway, a tough competitor emerges. He sits up straight. The gestures stiffen. He looks like a military commander marshaling his arguments. "If he weren't my father, I'd be intimidated by Herbert Simon," his daughter Katherine once said. Beneath the surface simmers a formidable temper.

Simon wins most of his arguments at Carnegie-Mellon, where he sits on the board of trustees and teaches both psychology and computer science. He moves freely between departments but is no tourist. Whenever he travels, he speaks the language of that discipline, whether of Newtonian mechanics, chemistry, technological innovation, scientific causality, business economics, cognitive psychology, or artificial intelligence. "I know of no one who has written so many good, technical papers in so many fields," says Allen Newell, who's been Simon's computer science partner at Carnegie-Mellon.

"Simon is unique because every field he's in claims him as their own," says James Morgan, an economics professor from the University of Michigan. "He's able to bring balance to the warring factions of hard and soft science because he knows both. He's a real Renaissance man."

Appropriately, one of Simon's latest interests is "The Bacon Program," a computer simulation that rediscovers natural laws, which he's doing in association with Patrick Langley, a researcher at Carnegie's Robotics Institute. It's named for Sir Francis Bacon, the eclectic Elizabethan genius whose inductive methods Simon admires. Bacon, the Renaissance man of England, may be a good simulation for Herbert Simon, for if Sir Francis was accused of writing "On . . . Everything," the same holds true for Simon.

But what can he do for an encore at age sixty-six? Like Bacon, he's really a missionary who wants to heighten man's intelligence, an unlikely calling for someone who's spent his life debunking rationality. Simon puts limits on rationality in the name of higher reason. After all, the so-called rational model of human behavior, where everybody "maximizes" his "utility function," is a good definition for selfishness. It's also a paradox. Not everyone in society can simultaneously maximize their personal equations—humanly or mathematically. Simon worries about that.

"If I had to pick the most serious problem, it would be the amazing ability of the human species to turn any game they play into a zero-sum game. Namely, 'I win—you lose.' The only way we know we're better off is by comparing our lives with somebody else's. How could most Americans ever think of themselves as anything but deliriously rich—except by comparing themselves to other Americans who are even more deliriously rich?"

He gestures at the paper clutter that threatens to engulf his office. "My agenda keeps getting longer and longer," he says. "I'm not a very planful person, as you can see from this room. Usually, there are a number of research problems on the stack. I work on them as I get an opportunity to. Some get solved. Some don't."

Please Shut the Gate

Coombe Mill
Experimental
Station

15

JAMES LOVELOCK

INVENTOR AT LARGE

by Roger Bingham

In the English county of Cornwall, a narrow road wends through ancestral countryside. Scattered farms and a patchwork quilt of fields are stitched together by tall hedgerows. Along the road a wooden gate bears a neat blue-and-white sign: Coombe Mill Experimental Station. In the shopping center of science, dominated by the supermarkets and conglomerates of government institutions and university laboratories, Coombe Mill is a corner store. The proprietor is Jim Lovelock—more properly, Professor James Lovelock, F.R.S.—freelance inventor, independent scientist, iconoclast.

Beyond the gate, in front of a rambling white farmhouse, stands a statue representing Gaia, Greek goddess of the earth. The door of the house opens, and Lovelock emerges, a small, sprightly man with boyish features (he is in his mid-sixties but looks years younger) and a shock of long, wavy gray hair. He warns off Kristofferson, the peacock, and grins: "I bet you don't know many scientists who have to shoo peacocks out of their laboratory."

The Coombe Mill laboratory is a room perhaps the size of a double garage at one end of the house. It is crammed with electronic components: a sophisticated bench-top computer, various oscilloscopes, readout and monitoring equipment, a gas chromatograph. In one corner stands Lovelock's latest device, a detector ordered by the National Oceanic and Atmospheric Administration (NOAA), custom-made by Lovelock to measure perfluorocarbon in the atmosphere. It is a prototype for instruments that NOAA tested in the fall of 1983 by releasing a quantity of perfluorocarbon tracer into the atmosphere and following it across half the North American continent; by measuring concentrations of the tracer, scientists can analyze atmospheric currents. A similar detector is designed to measure ocean currents.

Lovelock's inventions have always functioned for him as a form of barter. Before he became independent, they allowed him to wander across interdisciplinary boundaries, solving problems. Whenever something intricate needed to be measured, Lovelock could find the way to do it. He holds a degree in chemistry, as well as doctorates in medicine and biophysics. He has worked in cryobiology, freezing hamsters stiff as a board and resuscitating them. He has acted as a consultant to NASA, winning three certificates of recognition for his contributions to the space program, and has developed a scheme for detecting life on other planets. His inventions are myriad, ranging from a tiny thumb gauge for measuring a diver's blood pressure underwater, to the prototype wax pencil, to a method for freezing bull sperm, to the series of detection instruments now widely used for everything from analyzing atmospheric components to sensing the presence of explosives.

Since 1963, his hardware has served to buy Lovelock his freedom, permitting him to realize his "ultimate objective . . . to work like the artist or novelist . . . to do scientific creative work without any constraints."

Lovelock calls the thread that has held his work together during the free-lance years "the quest for Gaia," and the results of his search have been summarized in his book *Gaia: A New Look at Life on Earth*. Essentially, Lovelock conceives of the earth's living matter (biota), air, oceans, and land surface as a single organism, a finely tuned homeostatic system of feedback loops that has, as he puts it, "the capacity to keep our planet a fit place for life." Life does not exist simply because material conditions happened to favor it, he argues; rather, life alters the conditions to ensure its survival and works actively to maintain them.

According to the Gaia hypothesis, the atmosphere is manipulated and modulated on a day-to-day basis from the surface of the earth. The manipulator is life itself, from the vast production of methane by bacteria, to the cycling of essential minerals like iodine from marine algae, to the land. "The atmosphere is not merely a biological product," Lovelock writes, "but more probably a biological construction: not living, but like a cat's fur, a bird's feathers, or the paper of a wasp's nest, an extension of a living system designed to maintain a chosen environment." The Gaian version of planetary democracy is a kind of ecological Gettysburg address: government of the biosphere, by the biosphere, for the biosphere.

It is an appealing prospect, this myth for our times, a fine, holistic vision of Mother Earth succoring her teeming brood with the aid of cybernetics. It is pastoral philosophy, the wisdom of the landsman: look after the earth, and the earth will look after you. It could even be argued, as it is by some of Lovelock's critics, that too much reliance on Gaia's capacity to regulate and heal herself leads to complacency and a kindergarten ethic: pollute the environment, and Mommy (Gaia) with her feedback loops will clean up the mess.

Gaia sounds too mystical for some tastes, too self-evident for others. When he first began describing the idea in the 1960s, Lovelock recalls, his fellow scientists were resistant. "The looks of blank amazement were wondrous to behold. . . . But those same people who objected then now talk of 'biogeochemical cycles.' They're saying much the same things as I."

Some of Lovelock's peers rate him a genius; most simply do not know what to make of him. Those who have encountered him at scientific gatherings invariably describe him as modest and retiring, painfully shy. He is soft-spoken and prone to attacks of what his principal collaborator, Lynn Margulis of Boston University, calls "seminaritis, where he talks quieter and quieter, doesn't project, doesn't explain himself." To a large extent, Margulis says, Lovelock is a recluse, a solitary who distances himself from the madding crowd as an act of self-preservation. Hence the idyllic isolation of Coombe Mill and Lovelock's "Limit of Social Interaction": he prefers to be in the company of no more than four people.

In such a setting, the shyness will often vanish, and Lovelock takes on a different character: the mischievous extremist. Spurred on by his wife, Helen, his conversation peppered with mild expletives, he is quite likely to profess himself an elitist and dismiss the appellation "people's" associated with anything. Tribalism is his pet hate; education runs a close second. He recalls his own school days with venom. "I loathed ever second I was there. . . . On a lovely summer day, to be trapped in a bloody schoolroom, reading daft books on stupid subjects—real Dullsville stuff—when I could have been out in the country going for a walk or at the library teaching myself. . . ."

Lovelock detested being taught *at* and has no patience with academic convention. To this day, he has a cavalier disregard for ivory-tower scholarship with its traditional baggage of elaborated references and convoluted footnotes.

And yet if he comes across a scientific report that he considers sloppy or inaccurate, he fumes. A recent article produced a typical tirade. "It's arrant rubbish! They haven't even done their homework. It's so bad it's shocking." I pointed out that one of the authors had considerable standing. "I don't give a damn. He's right out of his field. It's as daft as that business about viruses from space. Equally childish nonscience."

As a teenager, Lovelock dealt with "No Trespassing" signs on footpaths he considered public rights-of-way by concocting an explosive charge and blowing them out of the ground. In the mid-1950s, as a senior researcher at the National Institute for Medical Research, outside London, his style was essentially the same, if a little muted. At the time, he had devised a diathermy tank for rewarming frozen hamsters. NIMR's rather bizarre cryobiological work had been popularized in a play written by a former employee, with Lovelock as scientific adviser. For publicity, a photograph was taken showing Lovelock peering into a scaled-up version of the tank, large enough to accommodate one of the actors, who looked to be frozen in a state of suspended animation. Lovelock pinned the photograph to the wall of his office.

Shortly afterward, a team of Russian surgeons visited NIMR. Lovelock took them on a tour, putting a frozen hamster through its paces in the diathermy apparatus. The delegation retired to Lovelock's office and saw the photograph. "Of course, they wanted to know about it," Lovelock recalls, "and like a fool I said, 'Well, naturally we've carried the research on to humans.'" The Russians clamored for details. "I'm terribly sorry," Lovelock deadpanned, "but that's classified." Ever since, he says, he has had a vision: "Somewhere in Siberia there's a giant mound of corpses and this surgeon saying: 'But I saw it with my own eyes!' I've never dared to accept an invitation to Russia. I know they'd send me straight to Siberia. 'Okay,' they'd say, 'now you warm them up!'"

Lovelock was already a loner as a child. Science was a salvation for him, one he came to at the precociously early age of four when his father gave him a Christmas present of batteries, a collection of wires, a bell, light bulbs, and other oddments. After his much-despised schooling, he went via a firm of scientific contract consultants and evening classes at London University to study chemistry at Manchester University.

After graduating, he went to the Medical Research Council and began wartime research on the transmission and control of infection by aerial bactericides. From there he moved to the Common Cold Research Unit before joining the famous NIMR cryobiology group in 1951. His major contribution there was explaining the physical processes of cell damage during freezing and why neutral solutes, like glycerol, offered protection. Lovelock spent a year at Harvard on a Rockefeller fellowship—selling armfuls of his rare blood type at fifty dollars a pint to keep the family in food—before returning to NIMR and a collaboration with Tony James and Nobel Laureate Archer Martin, inventors of gas liquid partition chromatography.

After twenty years at NIMR, however, he was ready to strike out alone.

By the mid-1960s, Lovelock was in the United States at NASA's Jet Propulsion Laboratory, consulting on analytical hardware for the Mars mission. Because of his biomedical background, he was drawn into the debates of the bioscience team, which was designing life-detection experiments. Lovelock found the prevailing approach too geocentric for his taste. It posed the question "Is there life as we know it?" based on contemporary microbiology. Lovelock advocated instead a scheme that turned on analyses of planetary atmospheres. The presence of life on a planet, he argued, should profoundly affect the atmospheric profile, producing departures from the expected inorganic steady-state equilibrium.

With a JPL colleague, Dian Hitchcock, Lovelock tested his idea on the earth's atmosphere and found it to have "an astonishing and unexpected degree of contrivance," as he put it. For example, given sunlight and the oxygen concentration of the atmosphere, the amount of methane in equilibrium after oxygen and methane have reacted to form carbon dioxide and water should be less than one part in 10^{36}. Instead, the figure is one in 10^6. A discrepancy approaching thirty orders of magnitude takes a great deal of explaining: it requires the introduction into the atmosphere of perhaps two billion tons of methane annually.

The story is the same for other gases. Earth has "too much" nitrogen—the chemically stable form is the nitrate ion, so nitrogen and oxygen should have reacted together and gone into solution in the oceans—and "too much" ammonia, nitrous oxide, carbon monoxide, and hydrogen. Moreover, computer models of earth's atmosphere in the absence of life suggest that, almost predictably, its composition should be somewhere between those of its nearest neighbors, Mars and Venus. So why is the earth's atmosphere chemically and thermodynamically out of kilter? According to Lovelock and Hitchcock, the presence of life itself somehow drove the atmosphere into disequilibrium and then maintained it for billions of years. They reasoned that finding similar disequilibria in the atmosphere of other planets would be suggestive, though not proof, of life.

The conventional geochemical wisdom of the time still held that life—all forms, not merely humankind—adapted to rather than affected the environment. Our atmosphere, for example, was thought to be the result of planetary outgassing, the release of gases from within the planet as the earth formed. Subsequent abiological reactions, according to this theory, brought it to its present state.

There were some notable exceptions to the conventional view:

G. Evelyn Hutchinson of Yale had suggested a decade earlier that both oxygen and methane production were principally biogenic, life-mediated processes. But the extent of life's influence on other bio-spheric cycles, the production and transport of other gases and minerals—in essence, the biggest recycling business on earth—was neither fully appreciated nor widely accepted.

By the time Lovelock finished his work at the Jet Propulsion Laboratory, he had caught his first glimpse of Gaia. He returned to the thatched cottage in England, determined to develop his idea.

Lovelock first presented the Gaia hypothesis to a scientific group at a meeting on the "Origins of Life" at Princeton in 1969. As Lynn Margulis recalls, "Jim gave his little piece, nobody understood him, and they ignored him. It made zero impression." Shortly afterward, she began to collaborate with Lovelock. He had already pinpointed the anomalies and disequilibria in the earth's atmosphere; she, as a microbiologist, was able to suggest the life processes that might ex-plain them. In a series of papers, they developed the analogy of the atmosphere as circulatory system of the biosphere: Gaia's lifeblood is made up of gases and minerals that move in a continuous cycle, maintaining the earth's temperature, physical makeup, oxidation-reduction state, and acidity in the optimum condition for the support of life.

They raised a series of intriguing questions. We know, for example, from the fossil record that the climate has never been completely unfavorable for life during its existence on earth. The oceans have never boiled or frozen. Even during the Ice Age, the temperature fall was relatively minor, and the glaciations did not encroach beyond the 45-degree parallels of latitude, leaving 70 percent of the earth's surface free of ice and able to support a flourishing biota. And yet if the sun has been following the normal course for a main sequence star, its energy output should have increased greatly from its genesis until the present. On that reckoning, if we are now at the peak of energy output, the earth "should" have been frozen for much of the time that life has existed. It wasn't. Why not?

Even well-documented fluctuations in solar output have failed to produce the predicted result. An increase in solar output should lead to heating, water evaporation, and haziness, increasing absorption of radiation and further temperature rise. The cycle repeats until the surface of the planet resembles Venus. On the other hand, a fluctua-tion that lowers temperatures leads to an increase in snow and ice cover, changing the earth's albedo (essentially a measure of its reflec-tivity; the darker the surface, the more heat it retains) and reflecting more sunlight back into space. The temperature falls still further until the downward spiral produces an ice-ball planet. Both catastrophes have been avoided. How? Why has our climate remained so constant?

Another riddle: why is the sea salty? The answer seems obvious. Rain and rivers constantly wash dissolved salts into the sea; the sea surface evaporates, cycling rain back onto the land but leaving the nonvolatile salts in solution. As time goes by, the sea gets saltier. We know the concentration of salt in the sea—about 3.4 percent—and we know how much salt runs in each year. We can also calculate the amount of salt from another source, the upwelling rock that forms at mid-ocean ridges during sea-floor spreading. So it should be possible by simple division to estimate the age of the oceans, the length of time they theoretically should have existed in order to reach present salinity levels. The answer turns out to be 60 million years, which is obviously wrong; life forms very similar to those of today—that is, requiring water of the same general composition—have existed in the oceans for hundreds of millions of years. The question now becomes, if the sea has existed all those years, why is it not much saltier?

There is something else to consider. With the exception of a few rare adaptations like brine shrimp, living cells cannot tolerate a salinity in excess of 6 percent: the cells simply disintegrate. How remarkable, then, that for aeons the salinity of the oceans has remained within the narrow limits essential to the preservation of life. A coincidence? Not according to Lovelock. "Since life began," he says, "the salinity of the oceans has been under biological control."

Lovelock's book and his papers with Margulis abound with similar examples of biospheric cycles interpreted according to the Gaian hypothesis. They argue that our anthropocentrism has led us largely to ignore the powerful effect, sustained over billions of years, of microorganisms—the bacteria, algae, protozoa—on regulatory cycles. And they stress the importance of bringing together scientists from previously unallied disciplines to understand the complex entity they call Gaia.

All this raises a tantalizing question about the relationship between man and the hypothetical Gaia. It is Lovelock's conviction that Gaia should be seen as a complex system with an impressive track record for maintaining homeostasis and a suitable environment for life to flourish. Yet man, in evolutionary terms the newest kid on the block, seems to have developed an unparalleled capacity for blighting Gaia's feedback loops, instead of acting, to use René Dubos's analogy, as steward to life on earth.

Research detailing human impact on the earth's surface and atmosphere is widespread. Some scientists argue, for example, that the use of fossil fuels has led to an increase in carbon dioxide concentrations, which may produce a "greenhouse effect" and the raising of global temperatures. In the same way, agricultural methods such as deforestation could conceivably alter the earth's albedo, lowering temperatures. It is impossible to predict how the balance of power between man and Gaia might shift, but, Lovelock argues, it is essential to understand the Gaian system and avoid fatal damage to her vital organs.

A summer school held at the University of Santa Clara, California, and at NASA's Ames Research Center went some way to doing precisely that—as the organizers put it, "to enhance the development of a community of scholars to pursue interdisciplinary research toward an understanding of the influence of the biota on the atmosphere and sediments." According to Kenneth Nealson of Scripps Institution of Oceanography, "It was possibly the first like it that's ever been given. People who had worked only in geochemistry their whole lives came face to face with biologists studying the same thing."

Topics under discussion revealed how much greater acceptance there is of biogenic influences than twenty years ago. Lecturers talked of the role of bacteria in the formation of mineral deposits, for example, and in the destruction of stonework that used to be attributed to abiological reactions and simple weathering. Nealson is certain of one thing: "What we're seeing is organisms making a living, finding a niche for themselves. And anybody who thinks all of this stuff we see on the surface of the earth is strictly abiological just doesn't have a wide enough vision."

For Lynn Margulis, probably Gaia's most outspoken advocate in the United States, the ultimate goal would be the evaluation of a full-fledged science of Gaia. "The baby is born," she says. "Now it's a question of teaching it to walk." If it does, Jim Lovelock, cloistered in the calm of the English countryside, will be a proud father.

16
BIRGIT ZIPSER

THE BIOLOGIST AND THE MUD LEECH

by Garrett Epps

On Birgit Zipser's bulletin board is a postcard a friend sent her, an Edward Gorey drawing that mocks a Victorian children's alphabet. A small girl is wading in a pond. In the water nearby, something small, dark, and dangerous is streaking toward her. "F is for FANNY sucked dry by a leech," reads the characteristically macabre Gorey caption.

Zipser's laboratory, an elegant, sunny converted boathouse on the edge of Long Island Sound, is home to 4,000 mud leeches, *Hemopis marmorata*. Zipser, a brain biologist, studies electrical links between nerve cells. She has devoted eight years to these tiny animals. An average morning at her lab, which is part of the Cold Spring Harbor complex headed by molecular biologist James D. Watson, finds Zipser at her dissecting table, carving out a leech's nervous system with microsurgical instruments designed for use on the eye. In a translucent paper cup, the next victim swims, its flickering darkness catching the eye like a tiny shadow that has escaped its body.

Zipser's leeches are not the bloodsuckers of tropical romance and medieval medicine. Still, many people are turned off by the idea of working with leeches. Not all are laymen. Zipser and others feel there has been a bias in the scientific community against neurological research on ignoble animals like the leech, animals that, lacking backbones, are farther "down" the evolutionary scale than mice and cats.

To Zipser, however, the leech is useful, interesting, and in its way, beautiful. She is a tiny, graceful woman with a sharp nose and gentle eyes. When she speaks, she stares into the distance with an air of remote repose. Often she clasps her hands, palms outward, in front of her mouth while she searches for the right word or phrase. Part of the delay simply reflects the effort of phrasing her thoughts in English, instead of her native German. Part reflects her thoughtful, sometimes cautious personality. When they do emerge, her sentences have the ring of careful thought. "Even an ugly thing like the leech is beautiful to me, because I know how each muscle operates," she says. "It's like a beautiful little machine or a computer. My son keeps asking me if he can use my leeches for fish bait, and I won't let him."

Others, too, began to see the beauty of the leech when Zipser and her then collaborator, molecular biologist Ronald McKay, published in Britain's prestigious journal *Nature* in 1981. They described how they used the leech's simplicity to help shed light on the mystery of neural specificity—the baffling and complex puzzle of how nerve cells tell each other where they are and what they do.

Somehow, during the early development of the nervous system, each nerve cell, or neuron, knows how to connect with dozens or hundreds of other nerve cells by means of long nerve fibers called axons. Some of these cells are nearby; others are located half a body away. When the connections are complete, the nervous system is wired like a television set full of printed circuits. If anything disrupts the hooking-up process or breaks the connections once they are made, it is usually not possible to restore the connection. That is why most forms of mental retardation and brain damage are incurable.

Zipser is trying to understand how the neurons interact to form connections. But she knows the medical applications are far down the road, a journey of a thousand miles that begins with the two and a half inches of the mud leech.

The leech is useful for neurological research because its nervous system is extremely simply. A leech has rudimentary "brains" in the head and the tail, as well as in the ganglia, or groups of neurons, extending in a straight line between head and tail at regular intervals along its body. All told, a leech has 10,000 neurons. The human brain by contrast has 10 billion.

Unlike human neurons, furthermore, each leech neuron is large enough to be studied through a small dissecting microscope. And the leech's behavior patterns are simple—swimming, eating, mating, and responding to light, pressure, and pain. So it is relatively easy to identify which neurons govern which kinds of behavior.

Zipser was attracted to the leech after working on cats and African electric fish. "I wanted to see the neurons I was working on," she explains. Cat and fish neurons, like human neurons, are tiny. In 1974, while she was a postdoctoral fellow at Albert Einstein Medical College in New York City, she came to Cold Spring Harbor for a summer course in leech physiology taught by Stanford neurobiologist John

Nicholls. Since then, Zipser has done original research on the work-
ings of the leech nervous system, studying the neurons that govern
sexual behavior and observing the side effects of enkephalins, or
natural opiates, on various sets of neurons. She is not interested in
any specific effect in the leech but rather in the way networks of
neurons interact and communicate.

Zipser is unraveling part of the leech's nervous system by enlisting
the immunological system, the powerful array of defenses by which
an organism fights invading bacteria and viruses. When molecules of
foreign protein invade an animal, its immune system fights the in-
vaders by creating antibodies, specialized proteins that seek out and
destroy the enemy. These foreign proteins, or antigens, cause the
body to produce custom-designed antibodies. So sophisticated are
these antibodies that they seek out the protein they are designed to
fight—and only that protein.

In theory, then, antibodies offer a chance to devise a chemical
detection system far more precise than any synthetic chemical human
researchers produce, especially since antibodies can detect their
antigens even in dead tissue.

To get dependable supplies of antibodies, Zipser applies a newly
perfected technique that uses cancer cells to manufacture so-called
monoclonal antibodies, antibodies that are all identical. She does this
by grinding up a leech nervous system and injecting it into a laboratory
mouse. After a few weeks, the mouse forms antibodies to the foreign
leech proteins and concentrates them in its spleen. The scientist then
removes the spleen, fuses spleen cells with cancer cells, and retrieves
hundreds of viable monoclonal antibodies.

Initially, Zipser had no idea what any given antibody could show
them about neural connections, but she applied her knowledge of
leech physiology to screen these antibodies. She dosed leech nerve
cord tissue with specific antibodies, stained it with fluorescent material, then looked at the stain traces to see which neurons the
antibodies attacked.

Next, Zipser decided which stained tissues were worth studying in
detail. Of the 475 antibodies produced in the first series of fusions of
spleen cells and cancer cells, about forty attacked a small number of
neurons. Some of these fit into networks that Zipser understands.
Others were wild cards, neurons that do not fit the present knowledge
of the nervous system but which were lit up by the same antibody.
These share some chemical similarity with the neurons whose functions are known. The similarities, Zipser reasons, may be recognition
signals in the chemical language of neural specificity.

"Extrapolation from our initial sample makes it possible that every cell has one or more chemical markers shared by only small subsets of neurons," Zipser and McKay wrote in their original *Nature* article. The situation seems analogous to a color-coded electric cable containing many wires, where each wire (neuron) has its own unique color (molecule) to facilitate proper recognition and connection at terminals.

But Zipser and another neurobiologist recently constructed a more revealing metaphor. It is as if, they say, the brain researcher were a political scientist who has been trying to study a mysterious meeting of parliament. Unfortunately, she can only watch it through thick, fogged glass that shuts out all sound and makes it impossible to see the delegates' faces clearly. Sporadically, decisions emerge from the parliament, but the researcher can neither hear the debates nor reconstruct the voting patterns.

Now, however, the political scientist has fashioned a microphone (dosing leech tissue with antibodies and staining it) that lets her address the delegates and a phrase book (tracing neural reactions to specific antibodies) that contains a list of nouns and a single sentence to plug them into: "Will all —— please stand up?"

The political scientist can begin by asking the question randomly (dosing tissue with antibodies) and noting which delegates stand up (which neurons react). Some questions will produce no response. ("Will all tables please stand up?") Some produce so much response they will be useless or redundant. ("Will all those awake please stand up?") But a few will produce tantalizing suggestive pictures. ("All those named Jones? All those on the appropriations committee? All those wearing green shoes?")

The scientist does not know the significance of her questions. But she can carefully note who responds to each and begin to theorize about links between the groups. Some questions will help her devise a conventional political analysis (the appropriations committee). Some may suggest a more complex sociology (the Jones family). Some may be meaningful in subtle ways (green shoes might indicate nonconformists of different parties).

Like the mysterious phrase book, Zipser says, the monoclonal antibodies are an incomplete but important new tool for decoding the parliament, the complicated neural connections and specificities, of the brain.

John Nicholls, the Stanford neurobiologist who uses the leech for neurological research, believes that Zipser's work is "a significant advance toward unraveling the nervous system. Here what one is doing," Nicholls says, "is labeling not just the sensory cells—that would be quite an advance—but the cells that respond to noxious stimulation."

Nicholls is currently looking at leech nerve connections to see how they form synapses. Zipser's research using monoclonal antibodies will be helpful to him, he says. "Their work gives you a handle on the biochemistry of the individual cells."

Another who is impressed with Zipser is James D. Watson, Nobel Prize winner, author of *The Double Helix*, and head of the Cold Spring Harbor facility. "The thing which has amazed me is the large number [of antibodies produced] without apparent overlaps," he comments. "It looks to me like you might have thousands of specificities."

If so, each neuron would be chemically linked to hundreds of other sets of neurons for reasons we can only guess at. Zipser is more cautious when it comes to numbers. "It could be that a given neuron carries different labels," she notes. "One could specify that it's a sensory neuron, another what network it's linked into—for example, that it's a sex neuron—and another could show which ganglion it occurs in."

Zipser first presented the findings at the European Neuroscience Meeting in September 1980 in Brighton, England. "Two kinds of people came up to me afterwards," she remarks with a faint smile. "There were people who were interested in monoclonal antibodies, and there were people who had been doing invertebrate research for a long time. They were terribly pleased to see everybody converging on the leech."

Zipser is also pleased that her findings may help dignify the leech as a research tool. She recalls questions about it from Senator William Proxmire, whose position on the Senate Appropriations Committee has allowed him to set himself up as a gadfly of government-funded research. Proxmire caught wind of an earlier project of Zipser's on leech sexual behavior and asked some caustic questions about it at a budget hearing.

"It turns out that it's a pretty interesting study," reflects Robert Mills, the Appropriations Committee staff member who alerted Proxmire to the project. To Mills, the inquiry was minor. But for Zipser the episode was a cause for deep anxiety. She feared that she might lose her funding.

"I grew up in a society where people were hungry, people were starving, people were scared," she recalls. She was born Birgit Ostermann in Oldenburg, Germany, near the North Sea coast of Lower Saxony. It was 1943. Her father was an aerial-reconnaissance photo interpreter for the German military, and her mother ran the family drugstore. She dimly remembers the Allied bombing, but most of her memories are of war's bitter aftermath—of a society shattered by fascism, war, and defeat, struggling to rebuild. "I go

back to Germany, and there are all these signs—Keep Off the Grass,"
she says. "When I grew up, it was like a creative playground. There
were no signs. It was rubble. Instead of blocks, I played with bricks."

While still in secondary school, she decided that the devastation
around her had been matched by inner devastation—that she would
have to leave. "In our history class, we ended in 1929," she recalls.
"It wasn't just a political vacuum; it was a cultural vacuum." A shy
child, she clashed with authoritarian teachers and daydreamed of a
time when she would speak to a roomful of people and command
their attention.

"I hated Germany violently," she says. "People were afraid of their
neighbors and dressed very carefully so they would not talk about
them. . . . Germany was such a formal culture." It was also, she felt,
one that doomed women to an inferior role. Women worked; Zipser's
mother, who had run the family drugstore, eventually took over her
second husband's thriving wholesale meat business, as well. But the
higher ranks of the professions seemed to be largely closed to them.
"It was much more difficult for a woman in Germany to become a
scientist," she says.

"One of the ideas I had was that I wouldn't get married until I was
thirty-five, because in Germany husbands destroyed their wives'
careers." But at twenty-one, on a trip to England, she met David
Zipser, an American molecular biologist six years her senior. He
changed that idea, and they were married in January 1965.

Zipser finished college and graduate school in the United States.
Her dissertation was on the mormyrid, an African fish that uses weak
spurts of electric current for communication and navigation. "It was
really very nerve-racking working with them," she says. "They were
susceptible to something called ich, and they would die." They were
also adept at forcing their way out of the covered fish tanks at night;
she would find them dead on the floor in the morning. "And whenever they had a rainy season in Africa, I couldn't get any more fish,"
she says.

Her postdoctoral work was on cats and mice. Then she decided to
shift to invertebrates and went to work as assistant professor of
physiology at Downstate Medical Center in Brooklyn. "At Downstate,
there was no one who was interested in the leech," she says. "So I
just went into a room and closed the door and did my work."

A certain solitude has always been part of the scientific enterprise
for Zipser. "I'm self-motivating," she says. "That's probably my only
good feature." In 1978, she came to Cold Spring Harbor, the only
full-time neurobiologist on a faculty dominated by molecular biologists who study the actions of DNA and other substances within the
individual cell.

David was already working there. With their two children, Karl and Nina, they moved into a house a few miles from the lab's waterfront campus. Zipser began to use monoclonal antibody techniques in her leech research. There was some skepticism about the project at the lab and in the scientific community, she says. "So I just sort of did it on the side—in the evenings. When it began to work, I started doing it full time."

Zipser cautiously discusses the implications of any breakthrough in understanding neural specificity. Medical science might be able to apply such new knowledge to rearrange the wiring of the brain. "I'm not convinced that all synaptic connections are made and not broken again," she says. "Neurons have the ability to recognize other neurons throughout life."

A cure for brain defects might be enough to keep even William Proxmire happy, she thinks. But her part in that effort will consist of hacking away at leeches and other squishy, icky beasts.

"I'm much more interested in basic science than in medical speculation," she says. "All these great solutions are going to fall out of it. We are going to unravel the chemistry of the brain. But one can't do science pursuing some grand scheme. One has to focus on a little thing."

17

JOHN WHEELER

MESSENGER AT THE GATES OF TIME

by Dennis Overbye

In the distance beyond a wall of picture windows five stories above the University of Texas campus, hills break like a green wave on the edge of Austin. Abraham Lincoln, Albert Einstein, and Niels Bohr stare down from a corner of an enormous, yet cluttered, book-lined office.

A cartoon on the blackboard shows a giant, coat-sleeved hand juggling five mysteriously decorated balls. The hand belongs to John Archibald Wheeler, the physicist who helped invent the theory of nuclear fission, contributed heavily to the design of the atomic and hydrogen bombs, and pointed Richard Feynman on the way to a Nobel Prize for quantum electrodynamics. At present, he is the physics community's resident impresario of black holes and other grand contingencies of nature. Wheeler's latest venture takes him deep into the philosophical roots of physics with an eye toward the apocalypse of gravitational collapse. Between visits from students and colleagues and the preparation of tomorrow's final exam, Wheeler fusses over the cartoon—redrawing the thumb and contemplating the arrangement of the balls, which represent the fundamental laws of physics.

"Let's see," he says, frowning, "have I left out any clues?" The drawing dramatizes Wheeler's unique position at the center of ideas in the world of physics—a dexterous juggler who sifts and weighs the provisory concepts of physical law, hunting for what he calls "the glittering central mechanism of the universe." He punches the air with a clenched fist. "The goal is to understand the plan of creation, period."

Physically, Wheeler is unassuming: a rather short, conservative man, immaculately dressed like the Princeton gentleman that he is in a sport coat, tie, and button-down shirt. His solemn face turns cherubic when he smiles or laughs. But this reserved, almost deferential demeanor masks an audacious adventurer, a poet-physicist for whom metaphor is as important a tool as calculus. In his early seventies, his ideas are considered boldly speculative by scientists half his age. Wheeler prides himself for always being at the frontier of new thought. "I'm afraid I'm like Daniel Boone," he says. "Whenever anyone moved within a mile of him, he felt crowded and moved on." So Wheeler moves on.

The oldest child in a peripatetic family of librarians, Wheeler as a youth was fascinated by things mechanical. He remembers at an early age converting brass light switches into pistols that shot rubber bands. He graduated to carving machines out of wood, guns, locks, and even a working calculator complete with gears and buttons. His special mania is for anything that goes bang. When he was ten, Wheeler blew off part of his finger with a dynamite cap. Once he broke up a faculty tea at Princeton, where he taught for most of his career, by setting off a string of firecrackers on the windowsill. Today he keeps Roman candles and firecrackers in a chest on his desk, ready for special occasions. "What good is a discovery if you can't celebrate it with firecrackers?" he asks with a chuckle.

Wheeler's father was head of the Enoch Pratt Free Library in Baltimore when Wheeler entered Johns Hopkins University to study electrical engineering. After a frustrating summer spent rewinding electrical motors in a silver mine in Mexico, he opted for a field in which progress was more permanent and switched to theoretical physics, emerging with his doctorate in 1933 at the early age of twenty-one.

A year later, he was on a boat to Denmark. At that time, the world capital of physics was Copenhagen, where the legendary Niels Bohr presided over a small research institute. Bohr was the leader and guiding philosophical light in the development of quantum theory, which had revolutionized science. The uncertainty principle, a cornerstone of that revolution, placed fundamental limits on what could be known about nature. For example, it is impossible—even in theory—to determine simultaneously both the position and momentum of an electron. Measuring one quantity destroys the capability to measure the other, leading to severe paradoxes of nature. In Copenhagen, these and other puzzles were pondered in ceaseless bull sessions, lectures, lunches, and quiet walks in the woods.

"You can talk about people like Buddha, Jesus, Moses, Confucius, but the thing that really convinced me that such people existed were the conversations with Bohr," recalls Wheeler. Bohr did most of the talking; listening to him was like watching a one-man tennis game as he argued back and forth with himself to arrive at some conclusion. He operated according to the dialectical notion that without paradox there is no hope of progress, a belief he deeply instilled in Wheeler. "A great truth," according to Bohr, "is a truth whose opposite is also a great truth." According to some people, Wheeler's emulation of Bohr is so complete that it even extends to his mannerisms. They were friends and collaborators until Bohr's death in 1962. Wheeler broke down when he read to his Princeton class an announcement of Bohr's death.

Wheeler was not as close to Albert Einstein, whom he used to call on during his long tenure at Princeton, which began in 1938. Einstein was then at the Institute for Advanced Study in Princeton. "All comparisons are odious," admits Wheeler, "but as much as I admire Einstein, I think Bohr was the greater human being. The biggest thing Einstein did for people was to communicate the feeling that you could hope to understand the universe. I would regard Einstein as declaring the goal we should work toward and Bohr as providing the method and style."

In 1939, Bohr visited the United States. Bohr brought the news that German scientists had managed to split uranium atoms by bombarding them with neutrons. It was the first word in this country that nuclear fission had been achieved. Student and mentor immediately set to work on the historic paper that laid the theoretical basis for nuclear fission—and the atomic bomb.

During the war, Wheeler advised Du Pont de Nemours and Company on plutonium production for the Manhattan Project. Afterward he served on the U.S. Reactor Safeguard Committee. He remembers warning a joint meeting of the American and British committees on the danger of sabotage by a clever, trusted individual, someone "animated by some crazy ideology." Sitting across the table was a member of the British committee, Klaus Fuchs, whom Wheeler calls "the greatest spy of all time." Within months of Wheeler's warning, Fuchs was in prison for exporting the secret of the atomic bomb to the Soviets.

In Berlin for the 1979 Einstein centennial, Wheeler noticed Fuchs's name on the list of dignitaries and arranged a meeting. "I just wanted to have an adventure," he explains, "to get a look at him. I was careful to have a notebook in one hand and a cup of coffee in the other so I wouldn't have to shake hands."

In 1950, Wheeler was dragged back to the United States from a sabbatical in Paris to help Edward Teller and others develop the hydrogen bomb. "If I had been living in the United States, I might not have done it," he says. "But in Europe after the war, things were different. Bohr himself had said to me, 'Do you imagine for one minute that Europe would be free if it were not for the American atomic bomb?' " He organized an outpost of Los Alamos at Princeton under the name of Project Matterhorn and commuted once a month by train to New Mexico.

The payoff came on Eniwetok atoll in the South Pacific in 1952 where the first hydrogen bomb was tested. Wheeler was there. The only concerns he will admit to are wondering, after his group had done all the theoretical calculations, if it would work.

For many years, Wheeler has played a behind-the-scenes role as adviser to defense policy makers. Following the 1957 launch of *Sputnik,* he helped to organize the then secret and select Project 137 of scientific advisers to the Defense Department, which later became the highly publicized Jason Group. Wheeler gained notoriety on the Princeton campus for his advocacy of home fallout shelters, and anti-war radicals tagged him "Veeler." It was a harsh and excessive characterization of the gentle man—a man who considers the phrase "a defender of civilization" the ultimate accolade.

Wheeler and his wife of nearly fifty years, Janette, begin each day by reading aloud to each other over breakfast, sampling a variety of books. Tall, silver-haired, and outgoing, Janette describes herself as "an ERA-type person." They met at a Unitarian youth gathering in Baltimore when Wheeler was a graduate student and became engaged after their fourth date. They married three days after Wheeler's return from Copenhagen in 1935. The family includes three children and eight grandchildren. In summer, the entire clan, as many as sixteen strong, gathers at the Wheelers' elegant summer home in Maine. There his favorite vacation pastime is shooting sand-filled beer cans out of a five-inch-diameter Spanish-American War cannon into a bay near Boothbay Harbor.

His Austin house is equipped with an indoor swimming pool in which Wheeler swims a quarter of a mile every day. Among his other activities he numbers collecting unusual rocks, as well as ideas. "I like to see what are the furthest limits of any field of thought. What's the strangest thing that's been found in psychology? What's the most exotic language? One doesn't feel he's made the richness of the world his own until he's been in touch with all these strangenesses."

This lust for strangeness almost killed him once. While at a conference at Lake Como in Italy in 1977, he went mountain climbing alone to find a geyser that the Latin writer Pliny had described as "a river of milk" pouring out a hole in the mountainside. He fell, cracked his head, and was rescued by some Dutch hikers who heard him moaning in the brush.

Nearly all of Wheeler's scientific life is recorded in a set of bound notebooks that serve as a scientific diary and dialogue with himself. He started keeping them during the war years, and many remain classified. The current volume, along with a dictionary or thesaurus, is never very far away from him. Wheeler has pasted programs from Einstein centennial celebrations, letters, and other documents in among the lecture notes, descriptions of his travels, conversations with other scientists and his publishers, memos to himself, reflections, equations, speculations, and even thoughts about these interviews, all recorded in his flowing hand with a black fountain pen.

One 1971 entry is particularly revealing of Wheeler's character: "The word is now the sword. In the Middle Ages no man was a man who could not wield a sword. Today a man is not a man who cannot project thought with power."

In 1976, after thirty-eight years at Princeton, Wheeler was faced, in four years, with mandatory retirement from teaching. He accepted a position at the University of Texas where a more flexible policy gave him a new lease on the teaching life he considers so vital. Today he enjoys something of a celebrity status on the Texas campus. In addition to heading the Center for Theoretical Physics there, he continues to teach both graduate and undergraduate courses.

"It means everything to me to have students I can discuss issues with," Wheeler explains. "The student has an uncommitted mind; if you can't sell him something, there's something wrong with the idea. You have to keep trying your case." Many of Wheeler's former students, like Nobelist Feynman, are among the top rank of today's physicists; two have gone on to the presidencies of a university and a technical institute.

The black hole trail began for Wheeler in 1952 when he received permission to teach a Princeton graduate course on general relativity. According to Einstein's theory, gravity is just geometry; space is warped by the presence of matter or energy, just as a mattress sags under a heavy body. The greater the local concentration of mass, the tighter the curvature of space around it.

In the 1920s and 1930s, atronomers began to speculate about what happened to stars when their thermonuclear fires ran out of fuel and gravity crushed them inward. A star the size of our sun would shrink to a white dwarf, about as big as the earth, while gravity could hammer heavier stars into a solid ball of neutrons weighing billions of tons per teaspoonful—a giant atomic nucleus twenty miles in diameter. Just before the war, J. Robert Oppenheimer—who later directed the atom bomb project—and his graduate student Hartland Snyder calculated that a really massive star could crash through even this neutron-star stage, contracting to such a density that space would be warped around it like a black fist; neither light nor anything else would ever be able to leave the star. The remains of the star would be squeezed to an infinitely dense point, crushing itself out of existence; space would be infinitely curved. Then, as Wheeler likes to say, "smoke pours out of the computer." The result is a cosmic dead end called a singularity, where general relativity, space, time, and even the laws of physics break down. (It seems highly appropriate that the September 1939 issue of *Physical Review* that carried Oppenheimer's and Snyder's paper on gravitational collapse also had Wheeler and Bohr's paper on the mechanism of nuclear fission.)

Wheeler realized that if one takes general relativity seriously, this gravitational catastrophe is a real possibility. He spent the next twenty years of his life theoretically verifying and filling in the details, first through his own efforts, then through his students at Princeton and everybody else he could urge onto the problem. In fact, in 1967, it was Wheeler who christened this strange creation of nature with the name black hole.

To Wheeler a black hole is only a rehearsal for the ultimate cataclysm that he believes will ring down the curtain of creation at the end of the universe. In this so-called big crunch, the bell tolls for us all. Today he refers to black holes as "gates of time." It is not the blackness of their surface that interests him; it is the utter oblivion at their center. "There is no 'after' after the big crunch, just as there is no 'before' before the big bang," he stresses; therefore, "space and time are not fundamental categories of nature." In fact, time dies.

As a star or the universe contracts to microscopic dimensions, even geometry has to pay its dues to the uncertainty principle; destinies become probabilities. One consequence, says Wheeler, is that space is like an ocean. Viewed from far above, it looks smooth and flat, but the closer you look, the rougher and more violent it looks. The illusion of continuity disappears completely over distances shorter than 10^{-33} centimeters, a hundred million billion times smaller than a proton; space looks like "foam," full of tiny tunnels called "wormholes" connecting and disconnecting random points. "But no geometry will ever reveal the physics going on at these small distances," he explains.

If the universe contracts according to the laws of black-hole physics, there is a chance, says Wheeler—or so it appeared in a view explored by Wheeler in early 1970—that a new universe could emerge with a different geometry. The big crunch would turn into another big bang. The result would be an oscillating universe, an endless cycle of cosmic expansion and contraction. The changing of the universe from shape to shape takes place on a stage that Wheeler calls superspace, an abstract infinite-dimensional space in which each point corresponds to an entire configuration or geometry of the universe. "Superspace is not some poetic fancy," insists Wheeler. "It is the dynamic arena of general relativity." According to this modern mathematical formulation of the Einstein theory, the universe as it evolves traces a "leaf of history"—Wheeler's term for a two-dimensional plane—from the big bang to the big crunch. Does another "leaf," another universe, take off at that point?

Wheeler once thought it did; now further mathematical analysis convinces him the answer is no: no cycles, no universe after universe, no world without end. Superspace does lay out an infinite ensemble of *conceivable* worlds; there is room for universes that live only five minutes before collapsing, universes in which all stars are red, or blue, or in which there are no stars at all. Most of these, Wheeler notes, are "stillborn," they contain no life. The question is— Is life possible in any of these alternatives? Other cosmologists, notably Robert Dicke and Brandon Carter, have suggested that our own universe is uniquely tuned to produce life, the way a plant exists to grow a flower. We might be, in effect, the crown of creation. By this admittedly self-centered logic, known as the anthropic principle, the universe is the way it is because we are here, having somehow selected it from the superuniverse of possibilities. Einstein wondered whether God had any choice in the creation of the world; so does Wheeler. Any universe without life, he suggests, is a meaningless one; an impossible concept.

Wheeler's present position has evolved to embrace a new concept he terms "observer participancy." He now believes that "unless the blind dice of mutation and natural selection lead to life and consciousness and observership at some point down the road, the universe could not have come into being in the first place." This position, which is quite different from Dicke's and Carter's, has developed as the range of Wheeler's thinking has expanded from superspace and black holes to the concept of what he terms an observer-dependent, participatory universe. Since 1973, Wheeler has advocated the view that the plan of creation is intimately related to the quantum uncertainty principle. "In some strange sense, the quantum principle tells us that we are dealing with a participatory universe," he concludes. "Without observer participancy, there is no physics."

His favorite metaphor for the quantum principle is a game of twenty questions he played once at a faculty party. When it was his turn to guess, his fellow players tricked him by not making up a word, but instead let his questions gradually define the word "cloud," which he correctly guessed. "I thought that the word existed before I named it, just as we think the electron is there before we measure it," recollects the theorist, "but my questions had a part in bringing the word into being, just as our measurements have a part in bringing into being the position *or* the velocity of the electron."

Wheeler wonders if this principle could be a prescription for building the laws of physics out of the primordial nothing—a command to create, to counterpose against the black hole's urge to destroy: "The gates of time tell us that physics must be built from a foundation of no physics."

"Wheeler's philosophy of science is much more radically relativistic than Einstein's," explains physicist Freeman Dyson of the Institute for Advanced Study. "Wheeler would make all physical law relative to observers. He has us creating physical laws by our existence. In principle, if the role of observers in the universe is as essential as he imagines, life may even create physical laws by conscious decision. This is a radical departure from the objective reality in which Einstein believed so firmly," says Dyson.

Boiled down, Wheeler's new intellectual adventure is summarized by these succinct words of his: "Of all strange features of the universe, none are stranger than these: time is transcended, laws are mutable, and observer participancy matters."

Most physicists believe that Wheeler, with his theories of "genesis and observership," has probably gone too far this time. But Wheeler, ever so gently, contends that most of his critics are too busy working on today's problems to worry about tomorrow's.

To some, such audacious speculations seem to mesh with the efforts of a few physicists to explain alleged parapsychological phenomena like ESP or telekinesis. "They thought they had a friend," grumbles Wheeler. Some people may have been surprised or even shocked when the usually reserved physicist used a symposium on physics and consciousness two years ago to attack parapsychology. Wheeler regards ESP as self-delusion or worse and strongly resents seeing quantum theory, which is radical enough already, getting tangled up with what he considers the occult. "The best way to find oneself outside the ranks of science is to find oneself inside the ranks of mysticism," he complains.

These days Wheeler's chief priority is trying to understand how individual acts of observership can be stirred together to produce genesis. He and some of his students are investigating whether the quantum principle can be derived from some deeper, more fundamental idea using information theory. He wonders if nature can be thought of as a giant, self-organizing computer. But as Wheeler emphasizes, it is still barely more than an idea for an idea.

"If there's one thing in physics I feel more responsible for than any other, it's this perception of how everything fits together. I like to think of myself as having a sense of judgment. I'm willing to go anywhere, talk to anybody, ask any question that will make headway. I confess to being an optimist about things, especially about someday being able to understand how things are put together. So many young people are forced to specialize in one line or another that a younger person can't afford to try and cover this waterfront—only an old fogey who can afford to make a fool of himself," he says, laughing.

"If I don't, who will?"

This Participatory Universe

No elementary phenomenon is a phenomenon until it is a registered or "observed" phenomenon. That is the central revolutionary lesson of quantum theory—no less revolutionary for quantum theory being the solid guiding principle of all of modern physics, no less solid for our not having yet fathomed that theory's deep and secret underpinnings. The universe does not exist "out there," independent of us. We are inescapably involved in bringing about that which appears to be happening. We are not only observers. We are participators. In some strange sense this is a *participatory universe*.

The past is theory. It has no existence except in the records of the present. We are participators, at the *microscopic* level, in making that past as well as the present and the future.

The universe came into being in a big bang, before which, Einstein's theory instructs us, there was no before. Not only particles and fields of force had to come into being at the big bang, but the laws of physics themselves, and this by a process as higgledy-piggledy as genetic mutation or the second law of thermodynamics.

But how did the universe come into being? Was it through some strange, far-off process beyond hope of analysis? Or is the mechanism that came into play one which all the time shows itself?

Are elementary quantum phenomena, those untouchable, indivisible acts of creation, indeed the building material of all that is? Beyond particles, beyond fields of force, beyond geometry, beyond space and time themselves, is the ultimate constituent the still more ethereal act of observer participancy? For Dr. Samuel Johnson the stone was real enough when he kicked it. The subsequent discovery that the matter in that rock is made of positive and negative electric charges and more than 99.99 percent empty space does not diminish the pain that it inflicts on one's toe. If the stone is someday revealed to be altogether emptiness, "reality" will be none the worse for the finding.

Are billions upon billions of acts of observer participancy the foundation of everything? We are about as far as we can be today from knowing enough about the deeper machinery of the universe to answer this question. Increasing knowledge about detail has brought an increasing ignorance about plan. The very fact that we can ask such a strange question shows how uncertain we are about the deeper foundations of the quantum and its ultimate implication.

Recent decades have taught us that physics is a magic window. It shows us the illusion that lies behind reality— and the reality that lies behind illusion. Its scope is immensely greater than we once realized. We are no longer satisfied with insights only into particles, or fields of force, or geometry, or even space and time. Today we demand of physics some understanding of existence itself.

John Archibald Wheeler

18

TUZO WILSON

EARTHQUAKES, VOLCANOES, AND VISIONS

by Roger Bingham

That the continents move—that hugh chunks of crust are split apart and driven thousands of miles and others are swallowed whole, that the very bedrock of the earth's surface is a series of rafts floating hither and yon at the mercy of unseen currents—is a staggering idea, perhaps the most important insight since the discovery that the earth is round. As recently as the 1960s, a scientist who publicly espoused such ideas was putting his career at risk. But the theory of continental drift, more accurately known in its modern version as global plate tectonics, has revolutionized and revitalized the earth sciences and is now widely accepted.

When the German scientist Alfred Wegener first proposed the theory of continental drift early in this century, he met with resounding skepticism. It remained for a new generation of explorers, dreamers, and synthesizers to establish the credibility of Wegener's ideas. Prominent among these has been the Canadian scientist John Tuzo Wilson, one of the principal theoreticians of the new synthesis and for twenty years probably its most outspoken advocate.

This latter-day Wegener is a tall, solidly built man—more granite than limestone—with an easy smile and eyes that twinkle. Now in his seventies, Tuzo Wilson could reasonably be described as the Grand Old Man of geophysics. He was there at the birth of the discipline as a student at the University of Toronto, where he later taught for many years, and served a few years back as the first non-American president of the American Geophysical Union, which altered its rules to accommodate his election. His energy is formidable; since 1974, he has been director of Toronto's respected Ontario Science Centre, popularizing science as he popularized the modern drift theory.

The consequences of the drift-tectonics theory are far-reaching. It offers explanations of earthquakes and volcanoes, long-term climatic change, the distribution of precious gems, minerals, oil and coal, even the geographical spread of plants and animals. It tells us that Boston was once in the tropics and that Los Angeles is en route to San Francisco. It is a powerful tool for understanding the planet.

Essentially, the theory views the earth as a mobile jigsaw puzzle. The planet's outer shell is broken into a mosaic of rigid plates about sixty miles thick that "float" on a plastic, semisolid lower layer like the cracked shell of a soft-boiled egg. The plates consist primarily of oceanic crust; the continents are in effect passengers riding the rafts of the plates.

The motion of the plates is ponderous, averaging perhaps a few inches per year. Where the plates bump and grind against each other in their global slow dancing, the effects are dramatic, producing earthquakes. Draw a line joining the earth's areas of seismic activity, and the boundaries of the plates clearly emerge. California's San Andreas Fault, for example, marks one boundary where the Pacific plate is sliding northwest past the North American plate. The movement is not smooth: as the giant slabs push past each other, friction builds up, and they lock. Along the fault, strain develops, and the snagged boundary rock snaps and shifts, jumping as much as thirty feet in an overpowering tremor.

Where two plates pull away from each other at rift zones such as the mid-ocean ridges, new material wells up from beneath to fill the gap, hardens, and becomes part of the plates. Where two plates collide, one overrides, and the other is thrust down into the earth's interior at sites marked by the deep ocean trenches. Plates are thus born at the rift zones and destroyed at the trenches as they sink back into the earth. These sinking zones have another dramatic marker, the chains of volcanoes that sprout above the dying plate, such as in the Cascade Range of North America where Mount St. Helens lies.

It is an encompassing, overwhelming picture. There are gaps in the theory, awkward pieces as yet unexplained. There is no agreement about what forces drive the plates: the major stumbling block in Wegener's time, too. But the parts fit together remarkably well. It is puzzling that the scientific community was so resistant to continental drift and allowed it to languish in an intellectual backwater for almost half a century. In the Soviet Union, resistance with ideological overtones continues today. Many Russian geophysicists, increasingly isolated from Western science, still oppose plate tectonics as an unproven, foreign idea.

Wilson's role in the resurrection of the theory was pivotal. As well as supplying major creative insights, his facility for seeing the grand design amidst a welter of details enabled him to synthesize the mounting data into a product that scientists were eventually willing to buy. Wilson has always been part scientist, part salesman, and his unusual talents were certainly used to the fullest during the years that continental drift made a comeback. It was perhaps the most productive period of a distinguished career.

Born in 1908 to a Scottish engineer and a Canadian Huguenot, Wilson attended schools in Ottawa, then entered the University of Toronto to study physics. During the summer vacations, he did geological field studies and prospecting as an assistant to Noel Odell, an Englishman who had been on the 1924 Everest expedition with George Mallory. Wilson recalls life in the wilderness as "an elemental existence" and tells of chasing caribou, catching ducks by hand, and killing fish with the paddle of a canoe. He credits Odell with fostering his interest in geology—so effectively, in fact, that he applied to switch from physics to geology at the end of his first year at the university.

By a lucky coincidence, Toronto's classical physicist Lachlan Gilchrist had been toying with the idea of training a student in both disciplines, "and I became the guinea pig," Wilson recalls, "the first student in Canada to take an undergraduate course in geophysics." The experience, he believes, was crucial and gave him a unique perspective, unlike the pure geologists who had no feel for physics or the pure physicists who had no sense of the earth's complexity.

Wilson made good use of his unique training. Although he was in his fifties by the time the drift renaissance began, well past the usual age of maximum scientific creativity, Wilson became a central figure.

Among other contributions, Wilson was one of the first to focus attention on the fact that many major faults in the earth's crust have a definite beginning and end. He saw that these transform faults, as he called them, link sections of rift zones or trenches or interconnect the two, as California's San Andreas Fault helps link the East Pacific rift zone in the Gulf of California to the Juan de Fuca rift zone off the coast of Oregon. Thus, transform faults mark the edges of two crustal blocks, and their existence, as Wilson was the first to see, implies that the earth's surface is divided up into blocks or plates. The insight cleared the way for the rigorous formulation of plate tectonics theory. If he had done nothing else, it would have made his name in geophysics. "It's not an exaggeration to say that he has had some of the most imaginative and progressive ideas in geophysics in the past twenty years," says William A. Nierenberg, director of Scripps Institution of Oceanography.

In person, Wilson exudes a courtly charm reminiscent of a nineteenth-century gentleman. But beneath the urbane exterior lies a risk taker and an adventurer in ideas. According to Dave Strangway, head of the geology department at Toronto, "Tuzo was always the center of activity. He would blow into the place, things would go like crazy, then he'd blow out again, and things would slow down. When Tuzo was around, there was always something dynamic going on." It was his style to get ideas into circulation. If they were wrong, by the same token, he would simply admit it graciously and move on.

Wilson has always been more concerned with global concepts than decimal places. He admits, "I'm no good at fiddling with details" and acknowledges that other scientists have criticized him for it. "They say, what's this Wilson fellow guessing again for when he hasn't been out doing the oceanographic work? A great many people don't want to take a chance on imagining anything—and that leaves quite an opportunity for someone who's willing to gamble."

During a period when science has become increasingly specialized, with disciplines spawning subdisciplines and their tribes of attendant experts, Wilson has remained what his University of Toronto colleague George Garland calls "a whole earth man." In that sense, Wilson's career is an echo of Wegener's. Until his early death on the Greenland ice cap, Wegener had been something of an explorer; he had mastered meteorology and astronomy before he came to geophysics and had an unparalleled talent for synthesizing information.

Wegener presented the earliest versions of his continental-drift hypothesis in Germany in 1912. The conventional view of the earth at the time held that it was still cooling and contracting from its original molten state. Mountain ranges were thought to have been pushed up in much the same way as wrinkles form in the skin of a drying, shrinking apple. All surface movements were vertical; the earth was seen as too rigid to allow for horizontal displacements. Ancient, transoceanic land bridges, long since sunken, were said to explain the occurrence of identical plant and animal fossils on continents widely separated by ocean.

Wegener's hypothesis represented a radically different interpretation that directly challenged the flaws in the received wisdom. Mountains, he said, are found in narrow, curvilinear belts; if the shrinking apple analogy were accurate, they should be evenly distributed across the surface of the earth. Nor could he accept the notion of continents or land bridges sinking into the ocean floor. The principle of isostasy (which holds that the continents float in hydrodynamic equilibrium on a layer of denser material) would be violated. Continents were insufficiently dense to sink into the floors.

So why were fossils of small reptiles like *Mesosaurus*, for example, found only in Brazil and South Africa? Wegener dismissed land bridges. The prospect of crews of *Mesosaurus* putting to sea like primordial owls and pussycats in a flotilla of pea-green boats seemed unrealistic. For Wegener, movement of the continents was the obvious answer. Quite simply, there must have been a time when Africa was just down the road from Brazil, an easy swim for *Mesosaurus*. The geological evidence—the continuity of distinctive rock formations in continents now widely separated—forced the same conclusion.

Pulling together his strands of evidence from geological formations, the fossil record, and ancient climates, Wegener produced the well-known reconstruction of Pangaea, his massive protocontinent, surrounded by the universal ocean, Panthalassa. The map was crude, but it bears a clear resemblance to modern versions.

Although the hypothesis produced a mixed reaction initially, it soon fell into disfavor. The eminent Cambridge physicist Sir Harold Jeffreys demolished Wegener's proposed driving mechanism. The notion of continents of solid rock moving through ocean floors of solid rock in a rigid earth was, Jeffreys said, impossible. Jeffreys was not alone.

And then, in the 1950s and early 1960s, new investigative techniques led to a spate of discoveries that transformed the stagnating earth sciences and revived interest in continental drift. Essentially, the investigations focused on two areas: the nature of the ocean floors and the magnetism of ancient rocks.

When rocks cool and harden, the iron particles they contain become magnetized in alignment with the earth's prevailing magnetic field. The direction is locked in, so that the rocks become a kind of fossilized compass. Scientists examining ancient rock from India, for example, discovered that its average magnetic inclination 150 million years ago was about 30 degrees south; by 25 million years ago, it had flipped to 15 degrees north.

One interpretation clearly jibes with continental drift: India moved north from below the equator. But there was another possibility. If the North Pole itself had wandered, the magnetic field would change, imprinting different magnetic values on stationary rocks. Teams in America and England examined the polar-wandering theory by looking at the paleomagnetism of rocks in their respective countries and plotting the movement of the pole. The resulting curves began at the same point, had the same shape, but veered away from each other. The only way to superimpose them, the teams discovered, was to close the Atlantic and reorientate Europe and North America—just as Wegener suggested.

Drift seemed to be back in business, a suggestion that was confirmed by the oceanographic studies. Virtually nothing was known of the ocean floor, except for the existence of a submarine mountain range running along the axis of the Atlantic (the mid-Atlantic ridge). But in the 1950s, a team at Lamont-Doherty Geological Observatory, working with ocean floor echo soundings, produced a series of startling results. The mid-Atlantic ridge, they discovered, was not unique: it was part of a 40,000-mile-long system of ridges that circle the globe like the stitching on a baseball. The simplest way to spot ridges was to look for earthquakes. They also found the crest of the mid-Atlantic ridge was notched by a valley, apparently a rift.

About the same time, the British geophysicist Sir Edward Bullard devised a method for measuring the rate of heat flow from the earth's interior. It was far greater at the ocean ridges than elsewhere on the continents or ocean floor.

The man who pulled all these observations into a coherent picture was the late Harry Hess of Princeton. In a seminal paper circulated in 1960 and titled "History of Ocean Basins" (but tentative enough for Hess to describe it as "an essay in geopoetry"), he proposed that the mid-ocean ridges were outlets for molten rock upwelling from the mantle to form new ocean crust. According to Hess, convection cells in the mantle forced the material up, as if on a conveyor belt, to "patch" the growing rent in the crust. The new ocean floor spreads symmetrically on both sides of the ridges, creeping slowly toward the deep ocean trenches where it is destroyed. The process takes about 200 million years and explains why no ocean-floor rock older than that has ever been found: it is constantly being swept to one side, into the trash can of the ocean trenches.

It is at this point that Tuzo Wilson entered the picture. For most of his career, Wilson was a nondrifter. He had dismissed the drift theory in 1959 as "without a cause or a physical theory." And yet, in the space of a few years, Wilson developed some of the fundamental evidence supporting drift, wrote a key paper that prompted the formulation of plate tectonics theory, and became, as Garland puts it, "the evangelist of drift." Why the about-face? Wilson thinks he was swayed by the paleomagnetic evidence and Hess's work.

Wilson attacked the problem of drift by looking at the distribution of ocean islands in the Atlantic. If the continents had drifted, he reasoned, there must be some evidence of passage in their wake— some kind of footprint. And if Hess's ideas were correct, volcanic islands, driven up through the crust near the mid-ocean ridges, would have been carried progressively farther away from the ridges by the conveyer belt of drift. Wilson produced a compendious survey of the islands, which supported his thesis: the farther an island was from the mid-Atlantic ridge, the greater its age.

By a similar kind of reasoning, Wilson suggested a mechanism for the formation of the Hawaiian Islands, the compelling but still controversial idea of hot spots within the earth. The conventional explanation of island chains was that they were formed by "leakage" from a large fault in the crust; all the islands in a chain were thought to be of the same vintage. Wilson disagreed. He argued that the Hawaiian Islands had been punched up in sequence, like rivets, through the Pacific plate as it moved over a hot spot.

Another crucial bit of evidence came from a paleomagnetic study published a year earlier by Cambridge research student Fred Vine and his supervisor Drummond Matthews. Looking through magnetic recordings made near ocean ridges by research ships, they tried to explain a curious pattern: linear ribbons of apparently different intensity paralleling the ridges like the stripes of a zebra. In effect, Vine and Matthews discovered a magnetic tape recording of the history of sea-floor spreading, equivalent to Tuzo Wilson's surface history based on ocean islands.

For an as yet unexplained reason, the earth's magnetic field periodically reverses itself. There have been 171 reversals in the past 76 million years. Each reversal showed up on the recording as a different stripe. As molten rock oozes up from the mantle at mid-ocean ridges and cools, it becomes magnetized in the direction of the earth's field and spreads symmetrically to either side of the ridge to form a stripe of a given polarity. The variation in the stripes' polarity, as they moved away from the ridges, confirmed Hess's theory and supplied a method for calibrating the rate of spread, rather like counting tree rings.

By a lucky coincidence, the University of Cambridge (the home base of Vine, Matthews, and Dan McKenzie, who was shortly to become a major theorist of plate tectonics) was host in 1965 to Tuzo Wilson and Harry Hess. Both men saw the importance of the Vine-Matthews hypothesis, and it was during this period that Wilson had his greatest insight—the identification of an entirely new class of faults—transform faults, whose discovery presaged the modern plate tectonics theory.

Within two years of Wilson's idea, McKenzie and Bob Parker at Cambridge and, independently, Jason Morgan at Princeton took Wilson's germinal concept of crustal blocks and developed it into a full-blown, theoretical formulation involving the movement of rigid plates.

Now, two decades later, it seems inconceivable that Wilson and the other proponents of drift could have met with opposition to their work. In fact, Wilson recalls spending a great deal of his time spreading the word, communicating the latest findings to his scientific peers. What now seems blindingly obvious still needed a champion in the sixties, and it was Wilson, more than anyone else, who filled the role.

Since then, his grand ideas have continued to bear fruit, as a report in the March 7, 1980, issue of *Science* showed. The article reviewed progress in explaining some of the geologically peculiar features of North America: rock formations that seemed not to fit with the rest of the continent.

In 1968, Wilson had made yet another well-educated guess and concluded that part of Florida came from Africa, coastal New England and Newfoundland from Europe, and sections of Nevada, British Columbia, and Alaska from Asia. It now turns out that his insight was remarkably, if not entirely, accurate. Other workers had the same ideas, but, typically, Wilson was the only one prepared to risk his name on a clear statement.

The western coastal blocks are now thought to be islands that were added to the North American continent. On the East Coast, a block now named Avalon apparently did not become a part of North America until about 300 million years ago. And as for Florida, it seems that North America may have borrowed it from North Africa when Pangaea began to break up.

Ask Wilson about his prediction and he shrugs modestly. "It wasn't just a guess. I did follow up the evidence—but I didn't hesitate to put it down once it seeemed clear. Perhaps that's the difference: I take a shot at it."

In March, 1980, a range of mountains in the Antarctic was named for Wilson. Appropriately, the Wilson Mountains lie just north of a range named for another great explorer, Alfred Wegener.

19

MARK PTASHNE

MOLECULAR MISSION

by Philip J. Hilts

The building that houses the Harvard Biological Laboratories on Divinity Avenue is ringed in stone with specimens of the science. Grasshoppers, horses, wasps, and other creatures in colorful menagerie are engraved on the doors. There have been complaints of rivers of ants, Pharaoh ants, leaking into the building and trickling up to all five floors of the lab. The open windows invite a number of winged subjects for study. But the biologists seem uninterested. Their concern is with biological matters several orders of magnitude smaller. Genes, chiefly. DNA.

Among those most concerned about these matters is Mark Ptashne, who is past chairman of the Department of Biochemistry and Molecular Biology at Harvard and who until recently occupied a lab in the Divinity Avenue building. Ptashne is in his mid-forties. Still, he dresses like a student. His summer uniform comprises a pair of frayed blue-jean shorts, a dark T-shirt, and sandals. He wears long sideburns and glasses with black aviator frames.

He is a musician, a fine amateur violinist. He has been a political activist, first a leftist and then, in defense of DNA work, an establishmentarian. He was a participant, as a member of the faculty's liberal caucus, in the Harvard student strikes and the architect of a parliamentary maneuver that put the Harvard faculty firmly on record as opposing the Vietnam War.

But what Ptashne cares about, and what he has spent seventeen years of his life pursuing, almost obsessively, is a tiny creature that exists on the border between life and the lifeless. It is called lambda, and it is a virus.

He has a certain kind of love for this creature, and it started when he became infatuated by a puzzle in biology. When James Watson and Francis Crick wrote their two-page classical paper announcing the structure of DNA in 1953, they sparked an explosion in the biological sciences that is on the scale of the Newtonian or Einsteinian revolutions in physics. But after their work and elaborations and corrections upon it, there stood in biology another large question, which focused on the control of genes and DNA. It went like this: Every cell in the body contains the same set of about 50,000 genes, so why do the genes in a heart cell make proteins for muscle contraction but fail to make insulin, adrenaline, brain peptides, and so on? The heart cell has the genes to do these things—so what turns off the appropriate genes? How does this switch work?

Within a year or two of the Watson and Crick paper, two French biologists, François Jacob and Jacques Monod, began to set out a theory to explain this odd state of affairs. Most DNA messages, they said, must be turned off most of the time. Only those signals useful to each specialized cell are allowed to be active in that cell. There must be some substance within each cell—and unique to each variety of cell—that shuts off, or represses, the other genes.

The idea of the repressor, almost from the first time he heard it, haunted Ptashne. "This problem had certain earmarks, certain aspects which don't normally exist in biology," he says. "It affected me deeply and aesthetically. It was a beautiful, formal problem: either the theory was correct, or it was not. If not, there were clear alternatives. Biology rarely presents you with a problem that neatly."

The repressor could be one of several types of chemical substances. It might act directly on the DNA itself or on any number of other sites in the cell machinery between the gene and the products made from its instructions. But whatever it was and however it worked, the repressor was a new and extremely important principle of life. When Jacob and Monod published their repressor theory, it was a challenge to molecular biologists to find out if the repressor was real, to isolate it, and to discover how it worked.

The lambda virus was the creature in which Ptashne hoped to find and describe the repressor. Lambda, on its own, can do nothing. It has no cell walls, no activity within, no organized cellular machinery. Lambda and other viruses are so simple each appears to be nothing more than a little string of DNA in a protein jacket, bent on making endless copies of itself.

Lambda belongs to a class of viruses that can enter and destroy bacteria and so are called bacteria eaters or bacteriophages. Lambda attaches itself by its tail to the outer surface of a bacterium. The head of the virus is packed with DNA; its tail is a hollow tube, and through it the DNA is quickly shot into the bacterium. The viral shell hangs like an empty cicada husk on tree bark, while its DNA enters and commandeers the machinery of the bacterial cell. The new DNA orders copies made of itself, complete with its lost hull and tail. The copying goes on until finally, about forty-five minutes later, a hundred to a thousand of the viruses are produced. Then the bacterium bursts, and a new crop of viruses begins to float out toward other bacterial skins, where they may attach themselves and begin the process again.

But this whole cycle can be repressed. The virus may attach to the bacterium and inject its DNA as usual, but instead of taking over and immediately duplicating itself, the lambda DNA can instead become a "sleeper" set of genes. It becomes integrated into the bacterium's normal DNA, its potentially lethal genes dutifully reproduced and passed on to all the progeny of the bacterium. Then, generations later, triggered by the intrusion of ultraviolet light or a carcinogenic chemical into the bacterium, lambda genes may come to life again and start producing new viruses, which burst the body of their host to get free.

It is this stunning ability to turn off its normal life cycle, remain inactive, and then later spring to life that Mark Ptashne studied from 1965 until now, looking first for the repressor that could hold lambda genes dormant and later for the minute details of how this molecular switch works.

When Mark Ptashne stood taking his doctoral exam before Nobelist Salvador Luria and other professors of biology, Luria asked him, now that he had finished his experimental work on *E. coli* for the doctorate, what would he do next? He was not interested in what he had been doing, Ptashne said. His doctoral work had only been something to do until he could attempt to isolate the repressor.

His answer "created much mirth and merriment," and with some justification, Ptashne now says. It was 1965, and the problem of the repressor had been a principal question since the structure of DNA had been worked out. Jacob and Monod had made specific predictions about the repressor in 1961, and leading biologists of the world had worked on the problem more or less constantly ever since. All had failed.

Biologist Nancy Hopkins, now a full professor at MIT, was in 1965 an undergraduate student taking courses from Matthew Meselson, James Watson, and teaching assistant Mark Ptashne. "I remember that even within the first two lectures it was clear to me, with no experience, that the repressor was *the* problem. I asked Mark, if he was such a smart guy, why wasn't he working on the repressor? He laughed and said it was hard." She also asked the eminent Watson. He said that there was no chemical test, no assay, for it, and so he couldn't do it. And there were Jacob and Monod, who had created the theory of the repressor. Their failure to find it was a source of great disappointment and tension.

Ptashne, though, had more ambition than even the usual ferocious twenty-five-year-old, and more physical energy. He also had a streak of boldness. He could not resist the situation, though he wondered from time to time what a huge crater it would make in his life if the enterprise failed. But the thing about boldness is that it ignores consequences. When physicist Sidney Coleman met Ptashne, he says, "he impressed me, impressed everyone, as being a very hard-driving individual. Ambitious. Extremely energetic. Anyone who stood between Mark and what he wanted would soon have a Mark-sized hole in him."

The first time he went skiing, a friend recalls, Ptashne spent a little while on the learner slopes. But soon he slid over to the top of an advanced run, one that had dangers for experienced skiers, and he announced to his friends that he was going down. No, they said. "Yes, I am," he said, "and furthermore, if I kill myself when I go down, it will be your fault for not helping." His friends dragged along and tried to keep him from the worst injuries by placing themselves at the most difficult spots in the run. But soon Ptashne came flying down toward them. "His feet were three feet apart, and his poles were tucked under his arms—he was in a racer's schuss! We screamed, 'Fall, Mark, fall!' " But Ptashne shot past with a look of mixed elation and terror. Out of control, he finally drove straight into a curve and a great snowbank. His injuries, luckily, were not permanent.

Ptashne began work on the repressor in 1965, after he had been accepted into Harvard's prestigious Society of Fellows and earned himself his own laboratory on the fourth floor of the Harvard Biological Laboratories. On the third floor was Walter Gilbert, a physicist who had recently switched to biology and who had also decided to search for the repressor.

Gilbert was an experienced scientist with a sharpness of mind and toughness of manner that engendered tales. Ptashne was the louder, shorter, younger man. He had come into science chiefly because of the repressor. He admired Gilbert and thought of working with him. "But I felt right from the beginning that Wally was much too strong a personality to survive under. My personality was sufficiently egotistical that it would have to survive independently."

So they began to compete in the search but by different methods and on different genetic systems. Both worked with the common and best understood of bacteria, the *Escherichia coli*, which reproduces very quickly—a generation passes every twenty minutes—and can be grown simply in tubes or dishes filled with a nutritious broth of fundamental chemicals.

Gilbert chose to work with the system of *E. coli* that involves metabolism of lactose, or milk sugar. *E. coli* has the ability to live off many varieties of food, one of which is lactose. When lactose is absent from its environs, however, *E. coli* does not need its sugar-cleaving enzyme and so shuts down the gene that makes it. Gilbert sought the repressor that could do this.

Ptashne worked with the bacteriophage lambda, focusing on its ability to remain dormant in the *E. coli* cells for extended periods. According to the theories of Jacob and Monod, the lambda would behave this way because it produced a repressor that turned off the cell's genes. This is what Ptashne set out to examine.

The chief difficulty of the experiments was that there are no more than about a hundred molecules of repressor in each cell—amid hundreds of thousands of other molecules. In addition, no one was entirely sure what the repressor was made of or how it worked. Then, too, the whole idea of a simple repressor could be wrong. To do any experiment at all required making a series of assumptions, just to know what sort of test to use for the unknown substance.

Ptashne had some ideas to start with, but his initial trials failed. He turned to a second and a third variation. And a fourth. Months were lost with nothing but dead cells and dirty glassware as a result. By his own count, over the first year of work he tried some thirteen ways of making the repressor separate itself from chemical confusion in the cells. They failed completely. Gilbert's experiments were not going well, either. Lab workers who recall that period say the competition between the two became sharp.

Ptashne was working nights and weekends. Dinners with friends were cut off early so he could return to the lab. If he scheduled even an hour or two off, he worried about it for days beforehand. The tension appeared in a variety of physical symptoms, as well. At one point, he went to a doctor, who said he was simply exhausted and that he could either see a psychiatrist and start taking pills or take a couple of weeks in bed. "I think I asked for the pills," Ptashne says.

It was nearly eighteen months after he started that Ptashne began work on "hysterical scheme number 14." This time the idea was to get lambda-carrying *E. coli* to stop making everything except the repressor. To do this, he first had to irradiate the lambda-infected bacteria with ultraviolet light. He assumed this would damage the genes so they could not be copied into RNA, the DNA-like substance that carries the genetic code to the ribosomes, where DNA instructions are translated into proteins. It would not, however, seriously debilitate the ribosomal machinery itself. So fresh, undamaged lambda DNA injected into the bacteria should synthesize proteins as usual.

When fresh lambda entered the cell, it would encounter repressor molecules, which hadn't been destroyed, and the virus would settle into the dormant state in which it makes nothing but repressor. In fact, he could introduce ten or twenty fresh lambdas to produce more and more repressor until the repressor molecule existed in large quantities within the cell.

In theory.

Ptashne soon found that even under heavy radiation, some bacterial DNA continued to work, producing other protein molecules, so that repressor proteins were still only a fraction of the total.

The pervasive uncertainty in biology is apparent in the daily lab work: a biologist, working alone at a benchful of flasks, filters, pipettes, and other simple implements, may do the same experiment a dozen or two dozen times before it works. He will likely never know precisely why it did not work so many times before it finally did. Failure may come because of dirty glassware, an improper temperature, a bit too much of one chemical, or for no discernible reason.

Reflecting on this period, Ptashne says, "I think the most important experience you have as an experimental scientist is realizing the extent to which you can be fooled, the extent to which your impulses and aspirations lead you to believe things which have nothing to do with the way things actually work. . . . I have notebooks full of crackpot experiments, theory upon theory, wonderful constructs . . . I had done everything right, and now from x, y must follow. But then y doesn't follow at all. I'd find it enormously amusing that the world could conspire to make something fit so beautifully with your constructs, which just happen to be wrong. . . . You find out that no matter how much you want something to be true, no matter how much you're just sure it must be true—the scientist learns that what he thinks could well be completely false."

Ptashne's schemes grew more elaborate to accommodate obstacles. Because other proteins were still being made in the damaged cells, allowing repressor to be only a small percentage of the total, his extracts were not pure enough simply to filter out the repressor.

So he devised a further refinement. He irradiated *E. coli* as before but this time divided the bacteria into two batches. To one batch he added the fresh lambda phage and amino acids containing radioactive tritium. Because amino acids make up proteins, when the phage began to manufacture its repressor protein, these radioactive amino acids would be incorporated into it, as well into other proteins still being made in the cell.

For comparison, to his second batch he fed a different type of radioactive amino acids and a fresh phage that was damaged so that it could not make repressor. Thus only bacterial proteins, all of which were also produced in the other batch, would be labeled with these amino acids. Because the two types of radioactive particles emit different amounts of energy, a protein such as repressor, produced only in one of the batches and thus labeled with only one of the types, should be discernible.

He mixed the two cultures, extracted the proteins from the combined batches, spread them out on a chromatographic column, which separates proteins from one another by weight, and put them in a radiation counter. As the hours went by, he could see the tiny difference become visible as the clicks counted thousands of radioactive particles. Eventually, a bump, then a sharp, tritium-labeled spike rose above the haze of background counts. It was the repressor.

"I think this could only be embarrassing if it's seen as some great heroic event," says Ptashne. "But when you are doing something like that, the only way to keep yourself going and take all nature's blows is to build for yourself a Faustian conflict. Every day you get up in the morning, and you are shaking with rage, and you must go and fling down the doors of science. There is an enormously inflated sense of self-importance and historical moment. It may be false, but for me it was necessary."

By the time he had isolated the repressor, there was disappointment waiting. Partly it was because the achievement had dribbled out over months at the end. Partly it was because Gilbert's team finished a few weeks ahead of his and was ready to send their paper into a journal when Ptashne finally had consistent, repeatable results.

"I had no sense of elation, just of relief," Ptashne said. "It is like having a headache for ten years, and suddenly it goes away. It comes back, unfortunately, the next week, if you're crazy enough to be doing experimental science."

He was, and it did. Though the product of the repressor gene had been isolated and proved to be a protein, the more important question remained: What did this repressor do? Was it just one chemical in a chain of several agents and reactions that accounted for repression? Or did it actually recognize a target on the DNA and bind there to shut down the expression of lambda genes, conforming to one of the simple, elegant alternatives that Jacob and Monod had proposed? Using his purified, radioactively labeled repressor, he began immediately to test this question.

With Nancy Hopkins's help, he prepared two batches of DNA—one of lambda and one of a nearly identical virus, phage 434, that made a different repressor and thus, presumably, had a different target, or operator, on the DNA. If each virus had an operator unique in its DNA code, as they theorized, the repressor of one would not recognize the operator of the other. He put each into a centrifuge and mixed in his lambda repressor. The repressor protein was smaller and lighter, so it should stay floating near the top of the tube. But if it bound to the long, coiled strands of DNA, the two should drop together farther down the tube. Moreover, if it bound to lambda DNA but not to the DNA of the nearly identical virus, that would prove there was a specific, identifiable site on the DNA that each repressor recognized and acted on.

The results came one morning as Nancy Hopkins was running the experiment. She took the numbers, scratched out on a sheet of graph paper, to the seminar Ptashne was attending. This time the answers came without pain or labor; the result fell out quickly. This time there was more than relief. The two began hurrying down the hallways, talking excitedly to anyone who would listen.

The question of how the repressor accomplished its task was answered: it was by recognizing and binding to a specific sequence of lambda DNA that the repressor turned the other lambda genes off.

After the initial fever, Ptashne gradually allowed the world to intervene in his life. He played a major role in the controversy over recombinant DNA. His continuing repressor work, in which he helped to create lines of "superproducing" bacteria, brought him to the attention of the many commercial gene-splicing interests that sprang up in the 1970s. He intensified his work at the violin, almost as if he were beginning a second career in it. Though he had a fine violin and planned to buy a still better one as his skill grew, he had no intention of buying a Stradivarius. But then he had a chance once to bring one home. "I played it for a week, and by the end of the third day, I could not sleep; I had visions about it. I was bewitched and seduced by the thing." He is still paying for it.

Within a year he also bought a large, old home in Cambridge and began to furnish it with objects of art. He was tidying up the world as he grew older.

He mellowed in his dealings with those who worked under him in the lab. James Watson, Ptashne's mentor in the years when the repressor work was most intense, sums up the change: "Mark was hopelessly irresponsible for other people; he is getting a sense of responsibility now. Mark is self-centered and really didn't care about others. He was interested in them—I was probably the same way—only when they were interesting."

Ptashne's harshness was the chief recurring theme in conversations about him among the students and laboratory workers in the first five years he ran a laboratory. Though he was fair and concerned, he was unable to take an amiable attitude toward students and their work. His common mode of communication was critical remarks or demands for progress on a project. For some it was a powerful stimulus; others left the lab.

By 1981, Ptashne thought the lambda repressor system had finally been fully explained. The early repressor experiments had shown that in its dormant state, virtually the only one of lambda's fifty genes working is the repressor gene. The product of this gene, the repressor, binds to the DNA in such a way that it prevents "reading" of the lambda genes, and the lambda remains dormant. But the intricacy of the system only emerged later, when it became clear that the repressor is actually misnamed: it doesn't just turn *off* genes; it also turns *on* the manufacture of its own gene. And the further intricacy: there is a repressor of the repressor. The system is a closed circle, like the M. C. Escher work "Drawing Hands," which depicts two hands on a piece of paper, each using a pencil to draw the other.

Under normal circumstances, the repressor remains in place and keeps this second repressor, called cro, silent and the virus dormant. But there are substances that can change this balance and allow cro to come out and repress the repressor. During what biologists call the SOS response, when the DNA of *E. coli* begins to be damaged by carcinogens, the cell produces an enzyme, called recA, that cleaves several kinds of repressors up and down the bacterial DNA, among them the lambda repressor, which is cut in half and rendered unable to bind as usual to the DNA. The repressor can no longer block the "start" signal. The first of the lambda genes freed, it turns out, orders manufacture of the second repressor, cro, which returns to block the first repressor's gene.

In fact, the double-repressor mechanics of the system work so that the change of state from dormant to active lambda occurs quite abruptly. It seems, says Ptashne, as if the lambda control system has evolved so that whenever the cell is in danger, the lambda genes will switch on and burst out of the host.

The molecular details look like this: the place where repressors act to shut down a gene is called a binding site, or an operator. The operator is split into three separate sites where the repressor can land. Each site has a molecular structure arranged in a way that attracts the special configuration of atoms that is the repressor molecule. Site one exerts the most attraction, and this site fills up with repressor first. The second site, on its own, exerts far less attraction, but this is one of the tricks that run the system: the molecule that binds to site one then bends over to site two, where it adds attractive power to this otherwise weak site. When these two sites are bound by repressor, this, in turn, stimulates the enzyme that transcribes the repressor gene and produces more repressor.

The lambda repressor is thus both a negative and a positive regulator: the repressors sitting on the DNA not only block a "start" signal; they are also partly responsible for making more repressor molecules and keeping the binding sites filled. When one function is disturbed—when recA cleaves the repressor and inactivates it—both functions collapse, and the system flips to its second state: the previously repressed lambda genes begin to function, and virus particles are produced.

The third of the binding sites operates in this new state. The third site is where the second repressor, cro, first attaches itself. In the case of ultraviolet radiation or the introduction of some carcinogen, repressor molecules are destroyed, leaving sites one and two open. In that event cro goes to work, but it binds first to site three, halting the making of the first repressor because it blocks the entrance to the repressor gene to the left. With no repressor being made and with site three filled by cro, one and two remain open, allowing the "reading" of the lambda genes to the right that are needed for virus growth. Soon hundreds of lambda viruses are being made within *E. coli.*

For sixteen years Ptashne closeted himself intellectually with this single problem—one passage in the life of the lambda. Then, finally, he admitted that the work was "probably" complete and he would have to move on to something else.

Unlike the achievements in the arts, which can be voluminous and accessible to the world, this intellectual achievement was more typical of science. The greatest mental effort of Ptashne, and perhaps ten people under him, had been laid out over years upon a single fine detail. The total work came down to six pages of narrative in *Nature,* published at the end of 1981.

"To whatever extent I justify my scientific life, it is that I stuck with a simple biological system, realizing that one doesn't understand it . . . driving it to the point where one really has a clear picture of how it works and why," says Ptashne. Coming back on this thought, he adds, "To a certain extent, this is a rationalization. You are never sure why you do what you do."

THE OTHER EINSTEIN

by Timothy Ferris

When Albert Einstein died, in Princeton Hospital at 1:15 on the morning of April 18, 1955, having mumbled his last words in German to a night nurse who understood no German, he left both a scientific and a philosophical legacy. His scientific legacy has endured. The fate of Einstein's philosophical legacy, rooted in his deep commitment to human values and especially to peace, remains in doubt.

Einstein's science is flourishing. Quantum physics, which Einstein helped to invent, has spread its luminescent wings until it now embraces most of physical science. The theories of relativity, regarded as the epitome of the strange when Einstein first loosed them upon the world, have become so widely accepted that today they seem almost prosaic. The equations of special relativity are employed every day by experimenters who boost the mass of subatomic particles by accelerating them to nearly the velocity of light. General relativity, a mathematically abstruse masterpiece that had, like Bach's *Well-Tempered Clavier,* been more admired than performed while its author was alive, has become enormously popular as a tool for investigating some of the most exciting mysteries of physics, from black holes to quasars.

Einstein's lifelong quest for a unified theory of physics has reawakened, too, though in a form he might hardly recognize. Theoretical physicists seeking a unified theory of particle interactions are making progress by invoking the staggering energy levels that prevailed in the first moments after the big bang. The key to how the universe works today may well be how it worked in the first moments of its creation, back when it was wrapped up in its space-time continuum as tightly as the petals of a flower in the bud. To understand the physics of such an epoch, researchers seek a common

211

ground between quantum mechanics, the physics of the very small, and general relativity, the physics of the cosmos as a whole. That quest has become one of the most pressing pursuits in science. "The questions raised by Einstein," says Abraham Pais, author of an exemplary biography, *Subtle Is the Lord . . . The Science and the Life of Albert Einstein*, "are still among those actively pursued in physics research today."

But Einstein was more than a scientist. He was also a dedicated humanitarian, who wrote as much about ethical and social issues as about science. "Knowledge and skills alone cannot lead humanity to a happy and dignified life," he asserted. "Humanity has every reason to place the proclaimers of high moral standards and values above the discoverers of objective truth. What humanity owes to personalities like Buddha, Moses, and Jesus ranks for me higher than all the achievements of the inquiring and constructive mind." Ethical leaders like Spinoza and St. Francis of Assisi shared a "cosmic religious feeling," Einstein felt. The "most important function of art and science," he argued, is "to awaken this feeling and keep it alive."

As Bertrand Russell said, "Einstein was not only a great scientist; he was a great man." But the world has paid much closer attention to Einstein's science than to his humanitarianism. The governments of the superpowers employ tens of thousands of people who know how to transform Einstein's equations into bombs, few who have studied his counsel on why the bombs should not be built. There is little new in this. Jacob Bronowski called it "trying to buy the corpse of science," and it was an old story when Archimedes was put to work defending Syracuse with the instruments of war he invented and detested. What has changed is the destructive power of the weapons. "All our lauded technological progress—our very civilization—is like the ax in the hand of the pathological criminal," Einstein wrote. That was in 1917. The technology of destruction has since increased a millionfold, but tolerance among nations has not.

One great obstacle to understanding Einstein better is that we think we already know him. His is a peerless myth—Einstein of the rumpled sweater and snowy hair, naive and absentminded yet crammed with incomprehensible wisdom, the high school dropout who failed algebra but proved to know more than the professorial stuffed shirts, the brilliant mathematician who found time to help children with their homework.

Nor is the myth entirely false. Einstein *was,* for instance, absentminded. His wife, Elsa, used to bundle him up in his overcoat and leave him in the foyer, only to find him standing there a half hour later, lost in thought. Attending a reception, Einstein busied himself scribbling equations, then stood when the speeches ended and joined in the general applause, not realizing that the guests were applauding him. But he didn't fail math; he dropped out of Munich's Luitpold Gymnasium (now the Albert Einstein Gymnasium) because he hated its authoritarian atmosphere. Nor, as John Stachel, editor of the thirty- to forty-volume Einstein papers to be published by Princeton University Press beginning in 1985, remarks, was he "born old." The young Einstein looked less like Albert Schweitzer than like Bob Dylan—incendiary dark eyes under a tangle of flyaway black hair, his head cocked back in an attitude of ad hoc assurance.

But to appreciate Einstein's qualities, we must peer behind the thunderheads of the myth. There stands an Einstein of Zenlike poise who was, first and last, pacific. Peace was the subject of hundreds of his essays, letters, and lectures. His last conversation with his old friend Otto Nathan, just a few hours before his death, concerned civil liberties. The last document he signed was a proclamation against the use of nuclear arms. The advent of nuclear weapons, he maintained, had transformed international tolerance and understanding from a desirable goal into a practical necessity. He argued that the bomb had left the world with no choice but to renounce all-out war, which he called "the savage and inhuman relic of an age of barbarism."

His pacifism drew fire from the politicians. President Truman's Undersecretary of State Sumner Welles dismissed as "impossible" Einstein's proposal for a world government. When Einstein's name appeared (without his permission, incidentally) on a letter advocating a break in U.S. relations with Franco's Spain, Rep. John Rankin of Mississippi cried out in the House, "I call upon the Department of Justice to put a stop to this man Einstein." But Einstein kept speaking out, even when close friends warned that he was getting himself into trouble. He played no significant role in the development of the atomic bomb and indeed disregarded early suggestions that his $E = mc^2$ could be employed to make weapons. But he was quick to understand that the bombs, once built, must spell the end either to total war or to the societies that wage it.

He was a stranger not only to bellicosity but to the competitiveness and materialism that Western societies so often champion in their young. In 1932, invited to name his salary at the Institute for Advanced Study, he requested only $3,000 a year, asking, "Could I live on less?" The Institute responded by paying him $15,000 a year. Einstein spent little of it. On at least one occasion he offered to pay the salary of a colleague who had been refused reappointment at the Institute, explaining that he had more money than he needed.

Awarded the 1921 Nobel Prize for physics, Einstein neglected to mention it in his diary, in letters to friends, or years later, on a form requesting a list of the honors he had received. This was not because he felt he didn't deserve the prize. Quite the contrary: when he divorced his first wife, Mileva, in 1919, he promised her as alimony the Nobel Prize money he was confident would soon come his way. It seems instead that Einstein's attitude was one of genuine selflessness. His colleague Leopold Infeld writes that Einstein was the only scientist he worked with who cared solely for the content of scientific discoveries and not at all for whether he had made them.

Indeed, many of Einstein's worst blunders came when he distrusted his own theories. For years he discounted the prediction of general relativity, since verified by observation, that the universe expands. He also rejected, for a while, relativity's prediction of the existence of gravity waves. But the theory prevailed, and physicists today are busy designing gravity-wave telescopes to look for phenomena envisioned by Einstein's theories, if not by Einstein himself.

Einstein's fame reached oceanic dimensions, but it appears to have meant nothing to him. J. B. S. Haldane's daughter fainted when she first set eyes on Einstein. So did a judge who showed up unannounced at the door of Einstein's home in Princeton (though the judge, it must be added, was drunk). Another uninvited visitor rang the doorbell and announced to Einstein's secretary, Helen Dukas, "Madam, I have come to the United States to see the World's Fair, Professor Einstein, and the Grand Canyon." When Einstein once tried to ride a New York City subway, he was mobbed by crowds and had to get off at the first stop.

Winston Churchill, who thrived on fame, wrote that "it is better to be making the news than taking it; to be an actor rather than a critic." Einstein disagreed. "Better an understanding spectator than an electrically illuminated actor," he said. At age seventy, he wrote that he thought his accomplishments had been "overvalued beyond all bounds for incomprehensible reasons. Humanity needs a few romantic idols as spots of light in the drab field of earthly existence. I have been turned into such a spot of light."

Einstein was deeply religious, though in a way sufficiently subtle to recall the dictum that if one is asked, "Do you believe in God?" the answer least likely to be understood is "Yes." Einstein's answer was that he believed in "Spinoza's God, who reveals himself in the harmony of all being." For Spinoza as for Einstein, God *is* nature. "What I see in nature," Einstein wrote, "is a magnificent structure that we can comprehend only very imperfectly, and that must fill a thinking person with a feeling of 'humility.' This is a genuinely religious feeling that has nothing to do with mysticism. . . .

"My religiosity," he added, "consists in a humble admiration of the infinitely superior spirit that reveals itself in the little that we, with our weak and transitory understanding, can comprehend of reality."

In his scientific research, he invoked the deity so frequently that Infeld joked, "Einstein uses his concept of God more often than a Catholic priest." "I want to know how God created this world," Einstein said. "I want to know his thoughts; the rest are details." Einstein felt that science could never replace God—"Knowledge of what *is* does not open the door directly to what *should be*."

As a boy, Einstein composed little hymns to God and sang them on his way to school. As an adult, when his refusal to accept the ultimate validity of quantum physics had isolated him from the scientific mainstream, he insisted on continuing, as he put it, "to sing my solitary little old song." Its theme, he wrote his friend the physicist Max Born, was that the quantum principle, with its reliance on probability rather than strict causality, "does not really bring us any closer to the secret of the 'Old One.'"

Einstein saw God as dressed in questions more than answers— "What really interests me," he told his assistant Ernst Straus, "is whether God had any choice in the creation of the world"—and his personality was imbued with a deep sense of the mysterious. "The most beautiful experience we can have is the mysterious," he said. "It is the fundamental emotion that stands at the cradle of true art and true science. Whoever does not know it is as good as dead, and his eyes are dimmed." Here may be found the wellspring of Einstein's egolessness. "The Sphinx stares at me in reproach and reminds me painfully of the Uncomprehended, blotting out the personal aspects of life," he wrote.

A solitary man, he had few if any intimate friends. "It is strange," he wrote, "to be known so universally and yet to be so lonely." Asked what might be the ideal livelihood for a working scientist, Einstein replied, "Lighthouse keeper." Yet for all his detachment and steely will, he was, by all accounts, extraordinarily warm. A democrat in practice as well as theory, he dealt in the same friendly, unpretentious way with janitors and chiefs of state, students and movie stars. He once talked for hours with a crank (a trying experience in that cranks tend to be full of answers while scientists are full of questions) because the man's family told Einstein that he could be cured of his obsession in no other way. He took pains to put people at ease; colleague Banesh Hoffman recalls that when he was introduced to Einstein in the 1940s, feeling "utterly overawed and scared," Einstein suggested that Hoffman explain his work, then added, "Please go slowly. I don't understand things quickly."

"When Einstein said that," Hoffman remembers, "all my fears left me. It was *magical*—what he said and how he said it. He treated us all as equals." Einstein's friends and associates often used the word magic when describing him. Einstein used the word when describing nature. "Direct observation of facts," he said, "has always had for me a kind of magical attraction."

Though he had every excuse to retreat into the privacy he craved, Einstein chose to immerse himself in the affairs of this world. "One must divide one's time between politics and equations," he said. He played the violin at Israel fundraisers, wrote recommendations for so many students and colleagues that university administrators eventually came to disregard them, answered most of the thousands of letters he received—and he really did help a few schoolchildren with their homework, assuring them that they shouldn't worry about their difficulties with math, as his were even greater.

Einstein was, of course, a great intuitive artist of science, but he was also inordinately persistent. "Einstein never gave up," recalls Hoffman. In his biography, Pais remarks:

> When he was on his way from special relativity to general relativity, he was almost alone in believing that you ought to generalize the notion of relativity of uniform motion to the notion of relativity of all motion. That didn't bother him. He kept thinking, kept doing, and after a period of about eight years, suddenly there was revealed to him what I would call, and I say these words with all respect, a piece of divine truth—general relativity.

Straus, Einstein's assistant from 1944 to 1948, recalls getting a glimpse of Einstein's almost manic tenacity. He and Einstein had finished writing a joint paper and were looking for a paper clip. They found one, but it was too badly bent to use, so they searched for a tool with which to straighten it. Einstein came across a box of new paper clips. Instantly, he began shaping one of them into a tool with which to repair the bent paper clip. "When I asked him what he was doing," Straus recalled, "he said, 'Once I am set on a goal, it becomes difficult to deflect me.' "

Einstein had his faults. He was not, for instance, a good family man. He forgot his children's birthdays, confided to friends that he had married "disgracefully" both times, and wound up, like Mark Twain, mothered by women who brought him his slippers and denied him his cherished cigars. He was an unexceptional mathematician, though his intuition was so powerful that he could grope his way to solving unfamiliar equations.

He had no gift for popularizing his ideas. Infeld, who collaborated with him on a nontechnical book, *The Evolution of Physics,* attributed this to his separateness. "It is not easy for Einstein to emerge from his inner isolation and to realize the way in which the ordinary man speaks and thinks," Infeld remarked. Chaim Weizmann, the chemistry professor who became a world leader of the Zionist cause, joined Einstein on an Atlantic crossing and reported, upon disembarking: "During this voyage, Einstein kept explaining his relativity theory to me again and again, and now I believe that he has fully understood it."

Nor was Einstein an especially gifted teacher. Indifferent toward rhetoric, he lectured in an almost inaudible voice, staring into the middle distance, in a style one student described as "thinking out loud." As Pais points out, nobody ever got a Ph.D. studying with Einstein.

He was as often blunt as tactful. Attending a lavish banquet at the University of Geneva honoring the 350th anniversary of its founding by Calvin, Einstein said to a patrician gentleman seated next to him, "Do you know what Calvin would have done if he were still here? . . . He would have had us all burned because of sinful gluttony."

We remember Einstein as adored, but he was also widely detested. "It is possible that Einstein was as much hated as he was loved during his lifetime," writes John Stachel. "He was hated as a Jew, a pacifist, a democrat and civil libertarian, a radical, and in later years a socialist."

For declaring that "to kill in war is not a whit better than to commit ordinary murder," and for insisting that in the nuclear age "mankind can be saved only by a supranational system," Einstein was called impractical and naive. The best reply to this charge is his own: "Is it really a sign of unpardonable naïveté," he asked, "to suggest that those in power decide among themselves that future conflicts must be settled by constitutional means rather than by the senseless sacrifice of great numbers of lives?

"The worldwide armaments race," he said, "which not only stifles scientific progress through the demands of military secrecy but serves to intensify war fears, will only be eliminated if the traditional military organization is replaced by a supranational military authority which would possess sole control of all offensive arms: a kind of world government in the interest of international security.

"Do I fear the tyranny of a world government?" he asked. "Of course I do. But I fear still more the coming of another war."

In 1945, when Einstein wrote those words, there were two or three nuclear weapons in the world. Now there are over fifty thousand of them, with a total destructive force equal to four tons of TNT for every person on earth.

A declaration against the use of nuclear arms, drafted by Bertrand Russell and signed by Einstein, put the situation this way: "There lies before us, if we choose, continual progress in happiness, knowledge, and wisdom. Shall we, instead, choose death, because we cannot forget our quarrels? We appeal, as human beings to human beings: Remember your humanity and forget the rest."

On his deathbed, Einstein refused to consider surgery for the aortal aneurysm that had brought on his collapse. "It is tasteless to prolong life artificially," he said. "I have done my share; it is time to go." His body was cremated without ceremony. The ashes were scattered at an undisclosed location so that none could make a pilgrimage to his grave.

The question of a monument has kept arising ever since. Frank Press, President Carter's science adviser and now president of the National Academy of Sciences, told the audience at an Einstein centennial celebration at Princeton in 1979 that "Einstein, were he with us today, would have been appalled that the world now spends more than $350 billion a year on arms and more than $30 billion on their research and development.

"If there is anything that the science community can do to honor the memory of Albert Einstein today," Press said, "it is to support efforts toward arms control."

But arms spending has gone up, not down. Einstein understood that real peace might be a long time coming. In 1936 he wrote a little note on the subject, on a sheet of long-lasting rag paper to be placed in a time capsule. It read:

> Dear Posterity,
>   If you have not become more just, more peaceful, and generally more rational than we are (or were)—why then, the Devil take you.
>   Having, with all respect, given utterance to this pious wish,
>   I am (or was),
>   Your,
>   *Albert Einstein*

ABOUT THE AUTHORS

Allen L. Hammond holds degrees from Stanford University and from Harvard University. He is an author, editor, and broadcaster. Hammond's publications include more than 150 articles, essays, and reviews, and he has coauthored or coedited five previous books, including *Energy and the Future*, which was published in 1973 and translated into four languages. He is the founding editor of *Science 84*, the leading popular science magazine, published by the American Association for the Advancement of Science, which has twice won the National Magazine Award for general excellence. He is also the founding editor of *Issues in Science and Technology*, a quarterly science policy journal published by the National Academies of Science and Engineering. His daily radio program, "Report on Science," is syndicated nationally by CBS.

Roger Bingham, a contributing editor of *Science 84*, has been associated with the magazine since 1980. He is also science editor of cable television's "Lifetime Network's World Report" and science editor of the California Radio Network. He has made frequent radio and television appearances as a science commentator, including PBS's "Why in the World?", National Public Radio's "Kaleidoscope," KTTV Los Angeles's "Open Line," and BBC Radio's "Science Now," and recently organized and hosted an extension lecture series on the nature of time at the University of California, Los Angeles. He was born in Lancashire, England, in 1948 and is a graduate of University College, London University. After a sabbatical year as president of the University of London Students' Union, he became a free-lance journalist and author. His novel *Wild Card*, coauthored with Raymond Hawkey, has been translated into nine languages.

Garrett Epps was born in Richmond, Virginia, in 1950. He was educated at Harvard College, where he was president of *The Harvard Crimson* in 1971 and won Harvard's David McCord Prize for artistic achievement in 1975. He received his M.A. in creative writing from Hollins College in 1975. He has served as writer and editor for *The Richmond Mercury, The Richmond Afro-American, The Virginia Churchman, The* (Fredericksburg, VA) *Free Lance–Star,* and *The Washington Post Magazine,* where he developed a specialty in science and technology journalism. His free-lance science articles have appeared in *Science 84, The New York Times Magazine,* and *Popular Computing.* He is the author of *The Shad Treatment,* which won the Lillian Smith Award for best southern novel of 1977, and of the forthcoming *Floating Island: A Novel of Washington.* He is currently senior editor of *The North Carolina Independent.* Epps and his family live in Chapel Hill, North Carolina.

Timothy Ferris is the author of two books—*The Red Limit* and *Galaxies*—and of articles that have appeared in magazines, including *Science 84, The New York Times Magazine, Esquire, GEO, Harper's, Science Digest, Reader's Digest,* and *Rolling Stone,* where he was a contributing editor for eight years. Works in progress include *SpaceShots,* an art book of extraterrestrial photographs (Pantheon, 1984); *Writing the News,* with Bruce Porter (Random House, 1985); "The Creation of the Universe," a one-hour television documentary; and a three-volume history of the concepts of space, time, and knowledge titled *Coming of Age in the Milky Way.*

Ferris has been awarded the American Association for the Advancement of Science–Westinghouse prize and the American Institute of Physics prize for writing on physics and astronomy.

Ferris produced the *Voyager* phonograph record, launched aboard twin interstellar spacecraft in 1977 and described in *Murmurs of Earth,* which he coauthored with Carl Sagan and others. His commentaries on science are heard over National Public Radio, and he is a regular contributor to *The New York Times Book Review.* For eight years professor of English at Brooklyn College of the City University of New York, he is now visiting professor at the University of Southern California.

Arthur Fisher is a native New Yorker and a graduate of the Bronx High School of Science and New York University. Since 1969, he has held the post of group editor, science and engineering at *Popular Science* magazine. Previous positions include managing editor, *Senior Science* and *Science World*; senior science editor, Harcourt, Brace; and managing editor, Dodge Books.

Fisher's articles on health and medicine, biology, physics, engineering, photography, animal behavior, and architecture have appeared in numerous periodicals, including *Science 84, Reader's Digest, The New York Times Magazine, Mosaic,* the Time-Life *Nature/Science Annual, GEO, Animal Kingdom, Science Year,* the Time-Life *Photography Annual,* and *International Wildlife.* He is coauthor of two books on technology and inventions. *Century of Wonders* and *Fire of Genius* (Doubleday), and has also written *The Healthy Heart* (Time-Life), which won the 1981 Blakeslee Award of the American Heart Association for distinguished science writing. Other awards include the Claude Bernard Award for distinguished science journalism, given by the National Society for Medical Research in 1978. Fisher is married and has one son.

Philip J. Hilts has been a reporter for *The Virginia Sentinel, The Washington Daily News,* and *The Rocky Mountain News.* He spent seven years as a free-lance writer and, since 1980, has been a reporter for *The Washington Post,* covering science, medicine, and technology. He has been a frequent contributor to *Science 84* and to *The Washington Post Sunday Magazine,* and his work has also appeared in *Reader's Digest, American Film, Omni, The Chicago Tribune Magazine,* and others. He has written three books: *Nuclear Promiscuity* (coauthored with Paul Leventhal), exploring the struggle to limit the spread of nuclear weapons; *Behavior Mod,* a survey of behavior modification theory and practice; and, most recently, *Scientific Temperaments,* a literary excursion into the creative and human side of science. His writing has been recognized by the Front Page Awards, first prize in national reporting, 1982, given by the Washington-Baltimore Newspaper Guild, and by the National Media Award, first prize in national reporting, 1983, given by the American Psychological Association; he was a nominee for the American Book Award, 1982, for *Scientific Temperaments.*

Leo Janos is a California author who was written extensively on a wide range of subjects for *Smithsonian Magazine, The New York Times, Science 84, People, Cosmopolitan, Reader's Digest,* and other publications. Janos is recipient of the U.S. Steel Foundation–American Institute of Physics Distinguished Writing Award. He is the author of *Crime of Passion,* published by Putnam in May 1983, and is currently at work on the memoirs of test pilot Chuck Yeager.

Janos was a *Time* magazine correspondent for ten years, serving as Washington correspondent, covering Congress and the White House, before being appointed Houston bureau chief during the

Apollo space flights. He was later *Time*'s entertainment correspondent on the West Coast.

Born and raised in New York, Janos did graduate study at the University of Chicago's School of Mass Communications. Before joining *Time*, he served as a correspondent for *Broadcasting* and was text editor for *America Illustrated*, the U.S. government's cultural exchange publication with the Soviet Union. He was also an executive of the Peace Corps, serving as a public affairs officer, when the new agency began. From 1964 to 1968, Janos was speechwriter, first for Vice-President Hubert H. Humphrey and then, at the White House, for President Lyndon Johnson. His other White House duties included congressional liaison for the president.

Janos is married and has three children.

William Jordan is a writer living in Long Beach, California. He has contributed to *Science 84* and other magazines and is currently at work on two books: *How to Live Happily with Vermin*, a satirical comment on the futile insistence of trying to poison the creatures that irritate us; and *Adam & Eve Through a Bug's Eye*, the *real* story of human creation as told by a fallen biologist. He holds a doctorate in entomology from the University of California at Berkeley and teaches part-time at California State University in Long Beach. When not involved in writing, he enjoys woodworking, close-up photography, hunting, fishing, gardening, and simply gazing through the window in wonder at the great freeway of human existence.

Evelyn Fox Keller, a professor of mathematics and humanities at Northeastern University, is the author of *A Feeling for the Organism: The Life and Work of Barbara McClintock*, recently published by W. H. Freeman. She is at work on a new book, *Reflections on Gender and Science*. Trained in theoretical physics and molecular biology, Professor Keller's main technical contributions have been in mathematical biology. For the past seven years, she has been working in the history, philosophy, and psychology of science. Her primary current interest is in the interrelation of ideologies of gender and of science.

Professor Keller was born and raised in New York City; she studied at Brandeis and Harvard universities. Before coming to Northeastern, she taught at NYU, SUNY at Purchase, and MIT. She is the mother of two children and currently resides in Cambridge, Massachusetts.

Tracy Kidder is a contributing editor to *The Atlantic*; a free-lance writer; a resident of Massachusetts; and an author of numerous articles for *The Atlantic, Science 84*, and two books: *The Road to Yuba City* and *The Soul of a New Machine*. For his work he has received the Sidney Hillman Foundation Award, 1978; the Pulitzer Prize in general nonfiction, 1982; the American Book Award, 1982; and the Ralph Coats Roe Medal, 1983.

Dennis Overbye was born in Seattle, Washington, raised in the Pacific Northwest, and attended college at the Massachusetts Institute of Technology. He has been a free-lance writer, a scientific photographer and solar-eclipse chaser, a part-time physicist, an editor at *Sky and Telescope*, and a staff writer at *Discover*. He is now a senior editor at *Discover* and divides his time between New York City and Woodstock, New York, where he owns a mountaintop home and about a billion gnats. He is working on a novel.

Paul Preuss is a novelist, free-lance writer, and film maker living in San Francisco. His most recent published novel is *Broken Symmetries* (Timescape/Simon & Schuster, 1983). In addition to *Science 84*, he has written for such magazines as *Travel & Leisure, Panorama, Human Behavior*, etc. His most recent film work was as writer and codirector of "Master of Light," a half-hour TV biography of Albert A. Michelson, and he has written, directed, edited, and produced numerous award-winning TV entertainment specials, documentaries, and industrial and educational films. He is a member of the Northern California Science Writers Association, the Science Fiction Writers of America, and the Motion Picture Editors Guild. He was born in 1942, son of a career air force officer, and was raised mostly in New Mexico, Hawaii, and the environs of Washington, D.C. He majored in English and drama at Yale University and graduated B.A. *cum laude* in 1966 (after a stint of film study with Jean Rouch at the Musée de l'Homme in Paris). He is married to Karen Reiser Preuss, a photographer, and has a daughter, Mona Helen, by a previous marriage.

Boyce Rensberger was born in Indianapolis in 1942. He studied marine biology and journalism at the University of Miami, graduating in 1964 with a B.S. Two years later, he earned a master's degree in behavioral science writing from Syracuse University. He was science editor of *The Detroit Free Press* for five years, a science writer for *The New York Times* for eight years, and a free-lance science writer for three years. He spent a year in Africa doing journalistic research on human evolution and wildlife conservation, an experience that led to a book, *The Cult of the Wild* (Doubleday/Anchor, 1977). As head writer, he helped create "3–2–1 Contact," a television series on science for children. He is now a senior editor of *Science 84*. He lives with his family on a small farm in Maryland where he raises cattle and eggs and works on a book that will explain the hundred greatest scientific achievements of all time.

Rudy Rucker is a free-lance writer living in Lynchburg, Virginia, with his wife and three children. His science fiction novel *Software* won the Philip K. Dick Award in 1983; and his nonfiction book *Infinity and the Mind* has been widely hailed as the best popular introduction to logic and set theory. Upcoming books by Rucker include a science fiction novel, *Master of Space and Time*, and a popular science book called *The Fourth Dimension and How to Get There*. An earlier science fiction book, *Spacetime Donuts*, includes a character loosely based on his impressions of Kurt Gödel.

John Tierney, a staff writer for *Science 84*, has been with the magazine since 1980. His articles have won the U.S. Steel Foundation–American Institute of Physics award for science writing and the Washington Monthly Journalism Award. He previously worked as a reporter for *The Washington Star* and *The Record* in Bergen County, New Jersey. He has written science, humor, and travel pieces for *Esquire*, *Playboy*, and *The Washington Post*. He graduated in 1976 from Yale University, where he enrolled with the intention of studying mathematics but ended up as an American studies major and editor of the *Yale Daily News Magazine*. He lives in Washington, D.C.

Patrick Tierney is a free-lance writer who divides his time between Pittsburgh, Pennsylvania, and Viña del Mar, Chile. Before writing for *Science 84*, he held a variety of teaching positions, including a stint of teaching English to Spanish-speaking workers at a California mine that produces much of the world's kitty litter. His work has also appeared in *Omni*, *California Magazine*, and *Pittsburgh* magazine. He was born in Lafayette, Indiana, and graduated from the University of California at Los Angeles in 1980. His hobbies include jogging and hatha yoga.

ADDITIONAL READING

Chapter 1.
Subramanyan Chandrasekhar was born in Lahore, India, on October 19, 1910, educated at the University of Madras and then at Cambridge University in England, taking degrees in both theoretical physics (1933) and astrophysics (1942). He taught at Cambridge for many years and since 1946 has been a professor at the University of Chicago. He is a naturalized American citizen.

> "Sources for History of Modern Astrophysics," a collection of interviews conducted by the American Institute of Physics, New York.

> "The Black Hole in Astrophysics: The Origin of the Concept and Its Role" by S. Chandrasekhar, *Contemporary Physics*, vol. 14, 1974.

Chapter 2.
Daniel Carleton Gajdusek was born in Yonkers, New York, on September 9, 1923. He attended college at the University of Rochester and graduated from Harvard Medical School in 1946. He interned as a pediatrician at Columbia-Presbyterian Medical Center in New York City, served his residency at Children's Hospital in Cincinnati, Ohio, and worked as the senior pediatric resident at Boston Children's Medical Center. He spent a year in Iran at Pasteur Institute, then three years based at the Walter and Eliza Hall Institute of Medical Research in Australia. Since 1958, he has worked at the National Institute of Neurological and Communicable Diseases and Stroke in Rockville, Maryland.

Kuru, Early Letters and Field Notes from the Collection of D. Carleton Gajdusek, ed. by Judith Farquhar, Raven Press, New York, 1981.

"Unconventional Viruses and the Origin and Disappearance of Kuru" by D. Carleton Gajdusek, *Science*, September 2, 1977.

Slow Transmissible Diseases of the Nervous System, vols. 1 and 2, ed. by S. B. Pruisner and W. J. Hadlow, Academic Press, New York, 1979.

Slow Virus Infections of the Central Nervous System, ed. by V. ter Meulen and M. Katz, Springer-Verlag, New York, 1977.

Chapter 3.

Sheldon Lee Glashow was born in New York City on December 5, 1932, and went to college at Cornell and graduate school at Harvard, in physics, graduating in 1959. He did research at Copenhagen University in Denmark, at the California Institute of Technology, and taught at Stanford and at the University of California at Berkeley. Since 1966, he has been on the faculty at Harvard.

Particles and Fields, readings from *Scientific American*, W. H. Freeman, San Francisco, 1980.

"Grand Unification: An Elusive Grail" by Arthur Fisher, *Mosaic*, September 1979.

"The Search for Intermediate Vector Bosons" by David Cline, Carlo Rubbia, and Simon van der Meer, *Scientific American*, March 1982.

Chapter 4.

Margaret Mead was born in Philadelphia, Pennsylvania, on December 16, 1901. She studied at DePauw University and Barnard College and did graduate work in anthropology at Columbia University, graduating in 1929. She did field work in Samoa (1925–26), in the Admiralty Islands (1928–29), in New Guinea (1931–33, 1938, 1953, 1964, 1965), and in Bali (1936–38, 1957–58). From 1926 until she died, on November 15, 1978, her research base was the American Museum of Natural History in New York City.

Margaret Mead and Samoa: The Making and Unmaking of an Anthropological Myth by Derek Freeman, Harvard University Press, Cambridge, MA, 1983.

Coming of Age in Samoa by Margaret Mead, Peter Smith, Magnolio, MA, 1928, and William Morrow, New York, 1973.

Blackberry Winter: My Early Years by Margaret Mead, William Morrow, New York, 1972.

Culture and Commitment—The New Relationships Between the Generations in the 1970s by Margaret Mead, Doubleday, Garden City, NY, 1978.

"Margaret Mead (1901–1978): In Memoriam," *American Anthropologist*, vol. 82, no. 2, June 1980.

The Rise of Anthropological Theory: A History of Theories of Culture by Marvin Harris, Harper & Row, New York, 1968.

Chapter 5.

Gerald Joseph Wasserburg was born in New Brunswick, New Jersey, on March 25, 1927. He attended college and graduate school in geology at the University of Chicago, graduating in 1954. Since that time, he has taught at the California Institute of Technology in Pasadena, California.

Geologic Time, 2nd ed., by Don L. Eicher, Foundation of Earth Sciences Series, Prentice-Hall, Englewood Cliffs, NJ, 1976.

Ages of Rocks, Planets and Stars by Henry Faul, McGraw-Hill, New York, 1966.

"Sm-Nd and Rb-Sr Chronology of Continental Crust Formation" by M. T. McCulloch and G. J. Wasserburg, *Science*, June 2, 1978.

"The Accumulation and Bulk Composition of the Moon" by G. J. Wasserburg, D. A. Papanastassiou, F. Tera, and J. C. Huneke, *Philosophical Transactions of the Royal Society of London*, A. 285, 7–22, London, 1977.

Chapter 6.

Robert Trivers was born on February 19, 1943, in Washington, D.C., and grew up in the nearby Maryland suburbs. He graduated from Harvard in 1965 and traveled to Jamaica for the first time in 1968 to study lizards. In 1972, he received his doctorate in biology from Harvard and the same year traveled to Kenya, India, and Tanzania on ethological studies. He taught at Harvard until 1978, when he moved to the University of California at Santa Cruz.

Sociobiology: The New Synthesis by Edward O. Wilson, Harvard University Press, Cambridge, MA, 1975.

On Human Nature by Edward O. Wilson, Harvard University Press, Cambridge, MA, 1978.

The Selfish Gene by Richard Dawkins, Oxford University Press, New York, 1976.

"Haplodiploidy and the Evolution of the Social Insects" by R. L. Trivers and Hope Hare, *Science*, January 23, 1976.

"The Evolution of Reciprocal Altruism" by R. L. Trivers, *Quarterly Review of Biology*, vol. 46, 1971.

"Parental Investment and Sexual Selection" by Robert L. Trivers, from *Sexual Selection and the Descent of Man*, ed. by Bernard Campbell, Aldine, Chicago, 1972.

Chapter 7.

Kurt Gödel was born in Bruenn, Czechoslovakia, on April 28, 1906. He received his doctorate from the University of Vienna in 1930 and was a member of the faculty there for five years. He also spent several years at the Institute for Advanced Study in Princeton, New Jersey, receiving a permanent appointment after he moved to the United States in 1940. He died in Princeton in January 1978.

Gödel, Escher, Bach: An Eternal Golden Braid by Douglas R. Hofstadter, Basic Books, New York, 1979.

Infinity and the Mind by Rudy Rucker, Birkhauser, Boston, 1982.

On Formally Undecidable Propositions by Kurt Gödel, Basic Books, New York, 1962.

Chapter 8.

Bernd Heinrich was born on April 19, 1940, in Germany. He went to college at the University of Maine and to graduate school at the University of California at Los Angeles, graduating in 1970. He taught for ten years at the University of California at Berkeley and since 1980 has taught at the University of Vermont.

Bumblebee Economics by Bernd Heinrich, Harvard University Press, Cambridge, MA, 1979.

"The Energetics of the Bumblebee" by Bernd Heinrich, *Scientific American*, April 1973.

In a Patch of Fireweed by Bernd Heinrich, Harvard University Press, in press.

Chapter 9.

Frank Oppenheimer was born in New York City on August 14, 1912. He attended college at the Johns Hopkins University in Baltimore and graduate school at the California Institute of Technology, receiving his degree in physics in 1939. He taught at Stanford, did research for six years at the University of California at Berkeley, then taught for two years at the University of Minnesota, until 1949. He spent ten years as a rancher, then, in 1959, was appointed to the faculty of the University of Colorado in Boulder. In 1969, he moved to San Francisco to found the Exploratorium.

Robert Oppenheimer: Letters and Recollections, ed. by Alice K. Smith and Charles Weiner, Harvard University Press, Cambridge, MA, 1980.

Lawrence and Oppenheimer by N. P. Davis, Simon & Schuster, New York, 1968.

The Physicists by D. J. Kevles, Random House, New York, 1979.

Chapter 10.

Michael McElroy was born in Belfast, Ireland, on May 18, 1939. He attended Queens University in Belfast as an undergraduate and graduate student, receiving a doctorate in applied mathematics in 1962. He did research for a year at the University of Wisconsin and then at Kit Peak National Observatory. In 1970, he moved to Harvard, where he still teaches.

The Ozone War by Lydia Dotto and Harold Schiff, Doubleday, Garden City, NY, 1978.

"The Changing Atmosphere: Its Role in Climate" by M. B. McElroy, *Proceedings of International Conference on Sun and Climate*, Toulouse, France, September 1980.

"Loss of Oxygen from Venus" by M. B. McElroy, M. J. Prather, J. M. Rodriguez, *Geophysical Research Letters*, vol. 9, no. 6, June 1982.

"Tropospheric Chemistry: A Global Perspective" by J. A. Logan, M. J. Prather, S. C. Wofsy, and M. B. McElroy, *Journal of Geophysical Research*, vol. 86, no. C8, August 20, 1981.

Chapter 11.
Barbara McClintock was born in Hartford, Connecticut, on June 16, 1902. She attended college and graduate school at Cornell, graduating in 1927. She taught at Cornell, did research at the California Institute of Technology, the University of Freiburg, and again at Cornell, and then taught for five years at the University of Missouri. Since 1941, she has done research at the Carnegie Institution's Cold Spring Harbor laboratory on Long Island.

"Transposable Genetic Elements as Agents of Gene Instability and Chromosomal Rearrangements" by Patricia Nevers and Heinz Saedler, *Nature*, July 14, 1977.

"Gene Segments on the Move" by Ben Patrusky, *Mosaic*, January 1981.

"Transposable Genetic Elements" by Stanley N. Cohen and James A. Shapiro, *Scientific American*, February 1980.

"The Control of Gene Action in Maize" by Barbara McClintock, *Brookhaven Symposia in Biology*, no. 18, 1965.

A Feeling for the Organism: The Life and Work of Barbara McClintock by Evelyn Fox Heller, W. H. Freeman, San Francisco, 1983.

Chapter 12.
Charles Robert Darwin was born in Shrewsbury, Shropshire, England, on February 12, 1809. He studied medicine at the University of Edinburgh in Scotland and the ministry at Cambridge University, graduating in 1831. That same year he embarked on the H.M.S. *Beagle* for a five-year around-the-world voyage. On his return, he worked for a while in Cambridge, then moved to London. In 1842, he left London because of ill health and spent the remainder of his life in the village of Down, in Kent, where he died on April 19, 1882.

Autobiography and Selected Letters by Charles Darwin, Dover, New York, 1958.

Darwiniana; Essays by T. H. Huxley, AMS Press, New York, 1970.

Apes, Angels, and Victorians by William Irvine, McGraw-Hill, New York, 1955.

Chapter 13.

Robert Rathbun Wilson was born in Frontier, Wyoming, on March 4, 1914. He attended college and graduate school in physics at the University of California at Berkeley, graduating in 1940. He taught at Princeton University, worked on the atom bomb project at the Los Alamos Scientific Laboratory during World War II, and taught briefly at Harvard. In 1947, he moved to Cornell, where he built accelerators and was a member of the faculty for twenty years. From 1967 to 1978 he was the founding director of the Fermi National Accelerator Laboratory. Since 1980, he has taught at Columbia University in New York City.

> *Accelerators: Machines of Nuclear Physics* by Robert R. Wilson and Raphael Littauer, Anchor Books, New York, 1960.

> *Lawrence and Oppenheimer* by Nuell P. Davis, Simon & Schuster, New York, 1969.

> *Particle Accelerators: A Brief History* by M. Stanley Livingston, Harvard University Press, Cambridge, MA, 1969.

> "The Batavia Accelerator" by R. R. Wilson, *Scientific American*, February 1974.

Chapter 14.

Herbert Alexander Simon was born in Milwaukee, Wisconsin, on June 15, 1916. He attended college and graduate school at the University of Chicago, graduating in 1943. He worked for the International City Managers Association; did research at the University of California at Berkeley; and taught for seven years at the Illinois Institute of Technology. Since 1949, he has taught at Carnegie-Mellon University in Pittsburgh.

> *Administrative Behavior* by Herbert Simon, Free Press, New York, 1947.

> *Human Problem Solving* by Allen Newell and Herbert Simon, Prentice-Hall, Englewood Cliffs, NJ, 1972.

> *Machines Who Think* by P. McCorduck, W. H. Freeman, San Francisco, 1979.

Chapter 15.

James Lovelock was born in Letchworth, England, on July 26, 1919. He received his undergraduate degree in chemistry from Manchester University in 1941 and, eight years later, a Ph.D. in medicine from the London School of Hygiene and Tropical Medicine. Beginning in

1941, he worked for twenty years for the Medical Research Council of London, with the Common Cold Research Unit between 1946 and 1951 and then, for the next four years, in cryobiology at the National Institute of Medical Research. He also spent a number of years in the United States, first at Harvard and then Yale, and returned to England in 1964 after four years of commuting between the Jet Propulsion Lab in California and Baylor College of Medicine in Houston. He has been a free-lance scientist ever since, first in Wiltshire and since 1977 at Coombe Mill.

> *Gaia, A New Look at Life on Earth* by J. E. Lovelock, Oxford University Press, Oxford, England, 1979.

> "The Quest for Gaia" by James Lovelock and Sidney Epton, *New Scientist*, February 6, 1975.

> "Spray Cans; the Threat That Never Was" by Michael Allaby and Jim Lovelock, *New Scientist*, July 17, 1980.

Chapter 16.

Birgit Zipser was born on December 6, 1943, in Oldenburg, Germany. She moved to New York in 1965, graduating from Columbia University two years later. In 1972, she received her doctorate in neurobiology from the Albert Einstein School of Medicine and continued to do research there for two more years. She taught at the Downstate Medical Center in Brooklyn until 1978, when she moved to her present position at the Cold Spring Harbor Laboratory on Long Island.

> "Monoclonal Antibodies Distinguish Identifiable Neurones in the Leech" by Birgit Zipser and Ronald McKay, *Nature*, February 12, 1981.

> "Identification of Specific Leech Neurones Immunoreactive to Enkephalin" by Birgit Zipser, *Nature*, February 28, 1980.

> "Enlisting Cancer" by Michael Shodell, *Science 80*, September/October 1980.

Chapter 17.

John Archibald Wheeler was born in Jacksonville, Florida, on July 9, 1911. He was educated at the Johns Hopkins University, receiving his degree in 1933. He did research at the University of Copenhagen; taught at the University of North Carolina; and in 1938 moved to

Princeton University. He worked on the atom bomb project at Los Alamos and other laboratories, then returned to Princeton. Since retirement from Princeton in 1976, he teaches at the University of Texas in Austin.

Some Strangeness in the Proportion: A Centennial Symposium to Celebrate the Achievements of Albert Einstein, ed. by Harry Woolf, Advanced Book Program, Addison-Wesley, Reading, MA, 1980.

Gravitation by Charles W. Misner, Kip S. Thorne, and John Archibald Wheeler, W. H. Freeman, San Francisco, CA, 1973.

Nuclear Physics in Retrospect: Proceedings of a Symposium on the 1930s, ed. by Roger Stuewer, University of Minnesota Press, Minneapolis, MN, 1979.

Magic without Magic: John Archibald Wheeler, ed. by John R. Klauder, W. H. Freeman, San Francisco, CA, 1972.

"Genesis and Observership" by John Archibald Wheeler, *Foundational Problems in the Special Sciences*, ed. by R. E. Butts and J. Hintikka, Kluwer Boston Inc., Hingham, MA, 1977.

Chapter 18.

John Tuzo Wilson was born on October 24, 1908, in Ottawa, Canada. He studied geophysics at the University of Toronto and did graduate work at the University of Cambridge and Princeton, receiving his doctorate in geology in 1936. He worked for the Geological Survey of Canada and then served for seven years in the Canadian army. He began teaching geology at the University of Toronto in 1946 and remained until 1974, when he became director of the Ontario Science Center in Toronto.

Continental Drift: The Evolution of a Concept by Ursula B. Marvin, Smithsonian Institution Press, Washington, D.C., 1973.
"The Deep Sea Drilling Project After Ten Years" by William A. Nierenberg, *American Scientist*, January/February 1978.

"Magnetic Anomalies over a Young Oceanic Ridge off Vancouver Island" by F. J. Vine and J. Tuzo Wilson, *Science*, October 22, 1965.

"A Possible Origin of the Hawaiian Islands" by J. Tuzo Wilson, *Canadian Journal of Physics*, vol. 41, 1963.

Chapter 19.

Mark Ptashne was born in Chicago, Illinois, on June 5, 1940. He attended Reed College and went to graduate school at Harvard, graduating in 1965. Since then he has taught at Harvard.

"Genetic Repressors" by Mark Ptashne and Walter Gilbert, *Scientific American*, June 1970.

"A DNA Operator-Repressor System" by Tom Maniatis and Mark Ptashne, *Scientific American*, January 1976.

"A Genetic Switch in a Bacterial Virus" by Mark Ptashne, Alexander Johnson, and Carl Pabo, *Scientific American*, November 1982.

Scientific Temperaments: Three Lives in Contemporary Science by Philip Hilts, Simon & Schuster, New York, 1982.

Chapter 20.

Albert Einstein was born on March 14, 1879, in the town of Ulm an der Donau, Germany. He studied at the Technische Hochschule in Zurich and later at the University of Zurich, receiving his degree in 1905. He worked as a technical assistant in the Swiss patent office, as a private tutor, and then as professor of physics at a succession of universities: Zurich (1909), Prague (1911), Zurich again (1912), Leyden (1912), until settling at the University of Berlin in 1914. He lectured widely around the world in the 1920s. In 1933, he renounced his German citizenship and moved to the United States, taking up an appointment for life at the Institute for Advanced Study in Princeton, New Jersey. He became a naturalized American citizen in 1940. After the Second World War, he played a leading role in the movement for a world government. He was offered and declined the presidency of Israel. He died in Princeton on April 18, 1955.

Albert Einstein, the Human Side: New Glimpses from His Archives, ed. by Helen Dukas and Banesh Hoffman, Princeton University Press, Princeton, NJ, 1979.

Einstein on Peace by Albert Einstein, Schocken Books Inc., New York, 1968.

Quest: An Autobiography by Leopold Infeld, 2nd ed., Chelsea, New York, 1979.

INDEX